ABBA

THE BOOK

ABBA

THE BOOK

Jean-Marie Potiez

AURUM PRESS

For Stig Anderson – in tribute to his work with ABBA

First published 2000 by Aurum Press Ltd
25 Bedford Avenue, London WC1B 3AT

Copyright © Jean-Marie Potiez 2000
Translation copyright © Colin Collier 2000

A catalogue record for this book is available from the British Library.

ISBN 1 85410 698 8

1 3 5 7 9 10 8 6 4 2
2000 2002 2004 2003 2001

Design by TWO:design London
Additional illustration by Paul Wright
Printed and bound in Italy by L.E.G.O. S.p.A.

contents **Introduction**   *7*

'THE INTERESTING ASPECT OF THE ABBA SOUND WAS CREATED BY OUR DIFFERENCES.' AGNETHA

'I THINK ALL THE DREAMS I COULD POSSIBLY HAVE WITHIN A POP GROUP HAVE BEEN REALIZED WITH ABBA. NOW I CAN'T THINK OF ANYTHING ELSE!' BJÖRN

'I WOULD STILL LIKE TO KNOW WHY WE HAD THE SUCCESS WE DID WITH ABBA. BUT I HAVE NO IDEA. I MEAN, WE WROTE GOOD SONGS, WE MADE GOOD RECORDINGS, THE GIRLS ARE GREAT SINGERS … THAT'S NOT THE REASON FOR IT. THERE IS SOMETHING ELSE WHICH CAN'T BE DEFINED WHICH HAS NOTHING TO DO WITH US IN A WAY.' BENNY

'THE ABBA YEARS GAVE ME SO MUCH. I'M GLAD AND PROUD OF WHAT WE DID. IT'S NOT A CHAPTER I WANT TO FORGET.' ANNI-FRID

introduction   Abba: The Book could have started with the words 'Once upon a time', as the
ABBA story has an almost fairy-tale quality about it. Even if the gods did
smile upon Agnetha, Björn, Benny and Anni-Frid at birth, one must not
underestimate how hard they worked, nor overlook the fact that their
success was due in large part to the alchemy of talent, hard work, charisma,
and that indefinable something extra that all great stars possess. And
behind ABBA there was Stig Anderson, the man who made it all possible.
Without him, the group would certainly not have existed.

When I prepared my documentary Thank You Abba, I met and interviewed
Stig at his home in Stockholm. Contrary to what I had been told about him,
I found him charming, passionate and generous. He became very emotional
as he recalled the career of ABBA and talked of all the things he could have
done had the group not broken up. Stig loved France and understood my
passion for ABBA. His help, both with the documentary and the preparation
of this book, was invaluable. He opened his personal photographic archive to
me and recounted at great length the rise of ABBA to international stardom.

This book takes a new approach to the ABBA story. For the first time, the
career of each member of the group prior to the formation of ABBA is pieced
together. Access to numerous archives has enabled me to retrace their steps,
detailing all their activities and tours before and after they came together as
ABBA the group, and following the success of ABBA in Scandinavia, the UK
and the rest of Europe, Australia and the United States. As a result of
exhaustive research, Abba: The Book is the most complete and factually
accurate history of ABBA to date. The book is illustrated with many rare and
previously unpublished photographs, as well as a number of interesting
documents such as record sleeves, advertisements, tickets, newspaper
cuttings and magazine covers.

I want this book to be a gift for all the loyal ABBA fans and for all those who
want to know more about the musical and personal development of these
four extraordinary Swedes. The original fans will be able to explore the
complete history of their favourite group in detail, including much previously
unpublished information. Others can follow ABBA's fabulous success story
day by day, putting in context the numerous dramatic events of their career.

What gives me most pleasure is that each of you, on reading this book, is
going to discover – or rediscover – the story and the magic of ABBA.

Happy reading!

Jean-Marie Potiez
Paris, 2000

Agnetha

Agnetha Åse Fältskog, known as Anna in some countries, was born in Jönköping, a town on the shores of Lake Vättern in the south of Sweden, on 5 April 1950. The young girl grew up in a very musical and artistic environment. Her father, Ingvar, had a passion for shows, and regularly put on amateur reviews, sometimes even performing his own sketches on stage. Her mother, Birgit, would often sing at home, but always refused to display her talents in public.

Agnetha was just five years old when she discovered a piano belonging to a neighbour, who was a musician with the town's brass band. The black and white notes fascinated her and the sounds she could make with them captured her imagination. Every day, the little girl would tap away on the keyboard. She dreamed of having a piano of her very own. Two years later, her parents gave her the instrument she so desperately wanted. At the same time, Agnetha made her début on stage. Her father asked her to sing at a Christmas party, and in front of an audience consisting mainly of elderly people, she sang 'Billy Boy'. Her trousers fell down in the middle of the song, causing a great deal of hilarity, but this didn't diminish her passion for the stage.

The family grew: Mrs Fältskog gave birth to a girl, who was named Mona. During her spare time, Agnetha looked after her sister and took piano lessons, supported by her father, who was very proud of his talented daughter. Despite having some difficulties co-ordinating both hands on the keyboard, Agnetha very soon developed a particular gift for composition. She gave her first little song the title 'Två Små Troll' (Two Little Trolls).

As time passed, Agnetha filled numerous exercise books with her own lyrics and melodies. In the classroom, she had no interest at all in mathematics, physics or chemistry. On the other hand, she was very gifted where languages and music were concerned. With her two best friends, Elisabeth and Lena, she formed a vocal trio called the Cambers. The encouragement given to the group at local shows prompted them to send a cassette to Swedish Radio. They received a brutal response: 'No thank you!' Agnetha abandoned the Cambers and continued her stage apprenticeship in her father's shows. Alone in her room, she spent hours listening to and studying the songs of her idol, Connie Francis.

'CONNIE FRANCIS WAS MY GREAT IDOL. SHE WAS EASY TO IMITATE, IN SONGS SUCH AS "WHO'S SORRY NOW?" AND "MY HAPPINESS", IN FRONT OF THE LITTLE MIRROR IN MY ROOM. I'D LISTEN FOR HOURS ON END, ETCHING THE WORDS, MUSIC AND TIMBRE INTO MY MIND. I TAUGHT MYSELF THE PHRASING, AND TO BREATHE IN EXACTLY THE SAME MANNER AS CONNIE.'
AGNETHA

At the age of fifteen, after passing an audition, she was taken on by Bernt Enghardt's dance band, a group from the Huskvarna region of Sweden. This was where the fairy tale really began. The group's popularity grew, and the musicians were soon required to perform on week nights as well as Saturdays and Sundays. Agnetha had left school several months beforehand and was working during the day as a switchboard operator. She found it more and more difficult to reconcile her two occupations. She would often return home at around 5 o'clock in the morning and have to be in the office by 8 a.m., and she soon began to suffer dizzy spells at work. Her mother told her that she had to choose between music and her job. Without hesitation, Agnetha opted for music.

A new life began for the young girl. Like her idol, Connie Francis, she chose a repertoire of ballads and romantic songs. Following the break-up with her boyfriend Björn Lilja, Agnetha sat down at the piano and almost instantly composed 'Jag Var Så Kär' (I Was So In Love). She dreamed of making a record. When she tried out her own compositions with the band, the audience was very enthusiastic, and Bernt Enghardt decided to send a cassette to Little Gerhard (real name Karl-Gerhard Lundkvist), a Swedish ex-rocker who had become a talent scout for the record company CBS-Cupol. Among the songs included was 'Jag Var Så Kär'.

The response didn't take long. Within a few days, Little Gerhard personally rang Agnetha at home. He wanted her to record some songs in a Stockholm studio. Agnetha thought at first that it was a joke being played on her by her fellow band members, and eventually Gerhard told her: 'Here's my telephone number – call me yourself!' The producer was quite clear: he was impressed with Agnetha's voice but not with the band. How could she get out of this situation? She had been singing for several years with Bernt and had learned her craft with him. However, when fortune comes your way, you can't let it pass you by …

In the train on the way to Stockholm, Agnetha was nervous: it seemed that her dream was going to become reality at last. Mr Fältskog was present at the first recording session. It took place in Philips studio on 16 October 1967. Four songs were recorded: 'Jag Var Så Kär', 'Följ Med Mej' (Follow Me), 'Utan Dej Mitt Liv Går Vidare' (Without You My Life Carries On) and 'Slutet Gott, Allting Gott' (All's Well That Ends Well). Agnetha has never forgotten that time: 'When I entered the studio, my heart was beating like mad. And when I heard the musicians playing my music, I was very moved. I felt like I was floating in the clouds. It was the most beautiful day of my life!' Sven-Olof Walldoff conducted the orchestra. (In 1974, dressed as Napoleon, he would be ABBA's conductor in Brighton.) His advice was very precious to the young débutante singer. Little Gerhard was very pleased with the results. At first, his enthusiasm for 'the little girl from the provinces' wasn't well received by his immediate superiors: 'It will be a waste of the company's time and money,' they declared. Everyone changed their minds when Gerhard played them the tapes. Agnetha's voice, her slight Småland accent (the region that she came from) and the young girl's looks immediately won the team over. At the age of seventeen, she signed a record contract guaranteeing her a monthly income over several years.

Only a few weeks after the recording, her first single was released. 'One morning, as the family sat round the breakfast table, I suddenly heard my own voice on the radio,' Agnetha later wrote. 'I took the radio in my arms and danced around with it. I'll never forget it! When I look back now, that was one of the happiest moments in my whole working life.' (As I Am, 1997.)

Agnetha made her first television appearance on 10 January 1968, in a programme called Studio 8. Interestingly, Anni-Frid Lyngstad also performed her first record on the same show.

'ONE DAY I WAS SO TIRED AT WORK THAT I FAINTED AND WAS SENT HOME. MY MOTHER REALIZED STRAIGHT AWAY THAT I WAS WORN OUT, AND TOLD ME, "NOW YOU'VE GOT TO CHOOSE! YOU CAN'T CARRY ON LIKE THIS." I, TOO, WAS WELL AWARE OF THAT, SO I GAVE IN MY NOTICE.' AGNETHA

On 28 January, 'Jag Var Så Kär' reached No. 3 on the Svensktoppen (the chart of the most popular Swedish songs). The public seemed to prefer this track to the A-side, 'Följ Med Mej'. In Sweden, Svensktoppen is an institution. Every Sunday morning, two million people listen to host Ulf Elfving presenting the top ten songs in the chart that week. It is unusual for an unknown artist to reach such a high position in the first week a single is released, and when the artist is a seventeen-year-old girl from the provinces who is also the author and the composer of the song, it is quite an event. This is why the press made so much of it, presenting the young girl as 'the new Swedish Connie Francis from Jönköping'.

Agnetha left her home town and moved to Stockholm, but her father continued to give her sound advice. 'Neta' (as she was nicknamed by her parents) needed to be guided in her new career. 'It's thanks to him that I've been able to overcome certain difficulties in this profession,' Agnetha says. 'His patience and his encouragement have given me the strength to carry on. I owe him so much. I'll never forget what he has done for me!'

Agnetha soon seduced the Swedish public. Blonde, sweet, smiling – her songs fitted her romantic appearance perfectly. To those people who

During 1968, several singles were released and then the first album, simply entitled *Agnetha Fältskog*. The Swedish record company, CBS-Cupol, decided to launch the singer in Germany, via the company Hansa Schallplatten, and this is where Agnetha met her future producer, the young composer Dieter Zimmerman. It was a case of mutual love at first sight, and they got engaged on 23 July. The couple's idyllic artistic collaboration gave rise to a number of songs in Swedish and German. Dieter persuaded Agnetha to sing in German; she remembers: 'I wasn't at all satisfied with the choice of German songs. I tried to persuade the record-company people to use my own songs, but they would hear nothing of it!' The couple eventually split up after a year. Between 1968 and 1972, Agnetha recorded eight singles, with titles such as 'Robinson Crusoe', 'Senor Gonzales' and 'Geh' Mitt Gott'.

In the summer of 1968, Agnetha rejoined Bernt Enghardt's musicians for her first tour of the Swedish parks. The *folkets parks* (folk parks) played an important role in the careers of the four musicians who later became ABBA.

In Sweden, the majority of towns have a *folkets park*. Originally, these big green open spaces, equipped with a stage or a platform, were used for union meetings as well as for public festivals, rallies, and all kinds of

'MY FATHER WAS ENTHUSIASTIC RIGHT FROM THE WORD GO, AND SAID THAT HE WOULD TRAVEL WITH ME TO STOCKHOLM. WE WOULD STAY AT MY AUNT'S. I COULD HARDLY SLEEP THE NIGHT BEFORE WE LEFT. I GOT UP EARLY, SHOWERED AND WASHED MY HAIR. "I'LL BE THE CLEANEST PERSON IN THE WORLD," I THOUGHT.' **AGNETHA**

accused her of only writing love songs, she replied: 'I can sing other songs, of course, but what's more beautiful than a poetic, tender song, full of feeling? Love is the most marvellous thing of all. I sit in front of the piano, light two candles and let myself be guided by my inspiration.'

What made Agnetha so appealing was that she was so natural. Teenagers could easily identify with her. Her romantic appearance set young girls dreaming and young boys fantasizing, while reassuring their mothers. Yet behind her fragile, reserved exterior was concealed an assertive personality. Little Gerhard says: 'Agnetha knew what she wanted to sing. She has always refused to sing material which doesn't suit her. She is very instinctive and can immediately tell a good song from a bad one.' However, despite her numerous qualities, Agnetha was timid and tactless, which sometimes caused problems. One of her friends remembers: 'When she arrived in Stockholm, she was a bit awkward. One evening when we were dining in a restaurant with some other people in the business, she surprised everyone by calling the waiter over and complaining loudly about the food. She certainly wasn't aware of the impact of her remarks due to her acute shyness. In private, she was quite the opposite of an arrogant, aggressive person. I think she just lacked confidence in herself. She has often been blamed for not being very talkative in interviews. I think that because she was afraid of being misunderstood, in the end Agnetha preferred to say as little as possible.'

Agnetha's career continued to develop. The public took her next songs – 'Utan Dej Mitt Liv Går Vidare' and 'En Sommar Med Dej' (A Summer With You), which was written by her father – straight to their hearts.

demonstrations. Over the decades, these parks have become a real springboard for launching the careers of many Scandinavian artists. The stage, which is nearly always in the open air, allows them to show the full extent of their talent. Even today, performing in the parks is still a necessary step for many artists.

On 19 August, Agnetha recorded the two tracks for her new single, a duet with singer Jörgen Edman: 'Sjung Denna Sång' (Sing This Song) and 'Någonting Händer Med Mig' (Something Happens to Me). This single was to reach No. 9 in the Svensktoppen.

In the middle of October, Agnetha parted from Bernt Enghardt's musicians for good. She set out on tour with some new partners: Sten and Stanley, Marianne Kock, Nilsmen and Benny Borg. When her schedule permitted, she would also appear in the schools of her native region. For these occasions, she added an unreleased song to her repertoire: 'Borsta Tandtrollen Bort' (Brush The Tooth Troll Away). Only a limited number of these records, which taught children the art of brushing their teeth, were released!

In an astonishingly short time, Agnetha had become the most popular singer in the country. In 1969, when the album *Agnetha Fältskog Volume 2* was released, it was an instant hit. Even if certain members of the press continued to criticize the sentimentality of the lyrics, the public continued to ask for more, and Agnetha's songs stayed in the charts.

However, despite having an angelic face and a romantic image, the young singer became the object of some serious attacks in the press. Her new single 'Zigernarvän' (Gypsy Friend) caused a scandal. The song, recalling the legend of the gypsies, found itself at the centre of a controversy which was dividing Sweden at the time. The Swedish government was debating the problems of integrating gypsies, and Agnetha became the target of racist remarks, to which she replied: 'I'm sorry that people think like that. I wrote the music to go with Bengt Haslum's lyrics. It's just the story of a young girl who falls in love with a gypsy!'

The following year, Danish musician Per Hviid accused the singer of having plagiarized one of his melodies in the song 'Om Tårar Vore Guld' (If Tears Were Made of Gold). The composer claimed that Agnetha would have heard his song when he was touring Sweden. He lost all credibility when it was discovered that the tour took place in 1950, the year of the singer's birth.

These attacks, commercial failure in Germany, and the break-up with her fiancé all began to take their toll on Agnetha, and she started to doubt herself. However, clearly her guardian angel was at hand, for at the beginning of May, a chance meeting was to completely transform her life and career.

' "JAG VAR SÅ KÄR" (I WAS SO IN LOVE) WAS MY FIRST SINGLE… I REMEMBER THAT IT BECAME No. 3 IN THE SVENSKTOPPEN AND No. 1 IN THE KVÄLLSTOPPEN IN 1968, JUST BEFORE THE BEATLES.' AGNETHA

Agnetha Fältskog

Agnetha
FÄLTSKOG

Cupol

ALLTING HAR FÖRÄNDRAT SEJ
DEN JAG VÄNTAT PÅ

FÖLJ MED MIG · JAG VAR SÅ KÄR

Cupol

agnetha fältskog
och jörgen edman

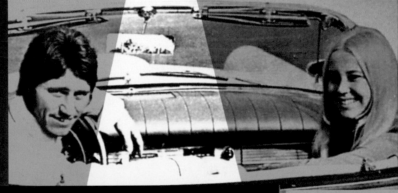

CS 213

AGNETHA
FÄLTSKOG

Marcus Österdahls orkester

EN
SOMMAR
MED DIG

FÖRSONADE

Cupol   STEREO
även spelbar i
MONO

AGNETHA
FÄLTSKOG

SNÖVIT
och de 7 dvärgarna

agnetha
FÄLTSKOG

SLUTET GOTT,
ALLTING GOTT

UTAN DEJ

Cupol

Björn

Björn Christian Ulvaeus was born on 25 April 1945 in Gothenburg, Sweden's second city, on the country's west coast. In 1951, the family moved to the small town of Västervik, on the east coast. His mother, Aina, and father, Gunnar, both loved music, and they gave Björn his first guitar on his eleventh birthday. He quickly got used to the instrument, learning some chords with his cousin, Jon Ulfsäter, and was soon beginning to try his hand at jazz and folk. Even though he was showing a great talent for music, the teenager continued his studies in law, following the advice of his parents.

At university, Björn and his friend Tony Rooth met two other musicians, Hansi Schwarz and Johan Karlberg, and soon the West Bay Singers were born. Encouraged by their music teacher, Lars Frosterud, the group put together a repertoire mainly inspired by the idols of the time – the Kingston Trio and the Brothers Four. The four students shared a passion for folk music and Dixieland jazz. The West Bay Singers became popular in the Västervik area, and after taking part in an amateur competition held in the neighbouring town of Gamleby, they decided to set off to conquer Europe.

In 1963, they borrowed an old Volvo, packed their instruments and left to launch an attack on the neighbouring countries. Even if their performances didn't leave much of a mark in the annals of rock history, the experience taught them a lot and the four boys managed to earn enough to pay for their food and lodging without any difficulty. The trip ended in Spain.

On their return to Sweden, a surprise awaited them. The West Bay Singers' number-one fan, Björn's mother, had entered her young protégés for a national talent show, *Plats På Scen* (Place On the Stage), organized by Swedish Radio during the autumn. 'I was stunned when my mother told me the news,' Björn recalls. 'I wanted to cancel our appearance straight away, because I thought that we weren't ready. And then finally, after some thought, I told myself that maybe we had a chance. Our name sounded good and fitted our repertoire perfectly.' The group were successful in the quarter- and semi-finals and then travelled to Norrköping for the final of the competition. There were seven finalists, and despite a good performance, the West Bay Singers were not among the prizewinners. (Interestingly, Anni-Frid Lyngstad also took part in the competition.)

Defeat was difficult to accept. However, fate intervened: Bengt Bernhag, a talent scout who had recently teamed up with publisher-composer-producer Stig Anderson, read an article about the competition and was instantly attracted by the name 'West Bay Singers'. Bengt and Stig were at that time looking for a group who would be able to sing folk music in Swedish. Discreet, polite and intuitive, Bengt had always had a flair for discovering new talent; he had successfully produced records for an ageing trumpet player who had lost his popularity, and had managed to push two female singers whom

'LENNON AND McCARTNEY WERE THE REASON WHY BENNY AND I STARTED WRITING. BEFORE THE BEATLES, NEITHER OF US HAD WRITTEN ANYTHING.' BJÖRN

'I LIKED BENNY INSTANTLY.
HE WAS OBVIOUSLY TALENTED
AND I FOUND HIM EASY TO
TALK TO. WE BOTH HAD THIS
LOVE OF MUSIC AND HAD
MUCH THE SAME TASTES.'
BJÖRN

everyone had described as 'untalented' up to the No. 1 spot in the charts. He had such good judgement that once he had mentioned the West Bay Singers to Stig, the latter didn't take much persuading. Bengt asked the group to send in a demo tape. 'We were certainly convincing,' Björn believes. 'Technically, the songs were perfect, since we'd recorded in a radio studio in Västervik. One of the songs was called "Ave Maria, No Morro". Bengt and Stig invited us for an audition in Stockholm. We were very excited to have the opportunity to sing in front of them. They immediately put us at ease. I think our performance was satisfactory.' Stig added: 'Bengt and myself sat down. What we heard was fantastic. The four of them made up a homogeneous group and their voices blended perfectly. I must confess that when I saw Björn singing and playing, I had a feeling that he had enormous potential. They were a good group, of course, but Björn stood out from the others. They were the first artists to be signed to our new Polar label. I set them two conditions: I wanted them to begin their career by singing in Swedish, and they had to change their name. "West Bay Singers" was old-fashioned. With a name like that I couldn't see them reaching No. 1 in the charts, even if [the name] was the English translation of their home town, Västervik.'

Stig thought it would be original to call the group 'The Hootenanny Singers', which loosely translated means 'meeting of folk singers'. With their name, their appearance and their repertoire, they seemed quite exotic in the Swedish Top 20. It was still rare for Swedish artists to sing in their mother tongue. Visually, they were also different from other groups: they had impeccable haircuts and always wore three-piece suits, both when they appeared on stage and on television. Although it ran contrary to fashion at that time, Stig and Bengt were right: the Hootenanny Singers' first single, 'Jag Väntar Vid Min Mila' (I'm Waiting By My Pile of Coal), beat other young talents to win a TV contest and went on to crush any competition in the Swedish charts. The song was a cover version of a very old Swedish ballad.

On 27 February 1964, the Hootenanny Singers gave their first concert at the Bromma high school, near Stockholm. The event was recorded by Swedish Radio. After releasing their first single, the group recorded an album of six songs in Swedish and six in English. They would always maintain this combination of songs in both languages, alternating cover versions and original compositions. Also, singing in English allowed them to attract a younger audience. Björn, influenced by the 'Liverpool Four', sometimes proposed songs in the style of the Beatles, but his three fellow band members always preferred a more traditional repertoire.

Björn, Tony, Johan and Hansi were not carried away by their new career; they continued with their studies and passed their exams in the spring of 1964.

The day after the exams, they were on the road. Their first summer tour started in Timmernabben park, near Oskarshamn. 'I haven't got good memories of those first concerts,' says Björn. 'The sound wasn't that good. We had brought our own instruments and we only had a small amplifier. To transport the equipment, one of us had borrowed a Volvo. The travelling was very tiring because we spent a lot of time on the road. All the weeks on tour taught us what to avoid for future shows.'

Between 1964 and 1966, the Hootenanny Singers went from strength to strength in Sweden. The summer months were dedicated to touring, while they spent the winter months in the recording studio or making television appearances. The group performed in Scandinavia and in Germany, and attempted a breakthrough in countries like England and the United States, using the name 'The Northern Lights'. In 1965, the single 'No Time' appeared in the South African charts. Even if their fame didn't reach beyond the borders of Scandinavia, the Hootenanny Singers were certainly a valuable commodity in Sweden. With their album *Evert Taube På Vårt Sätt* (Evert Taube – Our Way), dedicated to the Swedish poet Evert Taube, they really hit the big time.

The Hootenanny Singers seemed quite exotic in the Swedish Top 20

'THE FIRST YEARS IN THE PARKS WERE USEFUL IN THEIR WAY. I KNOW TODAY EXACTLY THE CONDITIONS IN WHICH ONE SHOULD NOT WORK. EVERYTHING WAS WRONG. THERE WAS NO POSSIBILITY OF GIVING THE AUDIENCE THE KIND OF SOUND THEY HAVE A RIGHT TO EXPECT.' BJÖRN

In 1966, the singles 'Björkens Visa' (Song of the Birch Tree), 'Baby Those Are the Rules' and the album *Många Ansikten* (Many Faces) also sold well. However, pessimists predicted the end of the group when, after managing to postpone it for several years, Björn, Johan and Tony announced that they would be doing their national service. However, the Hootenanny Singers were able to continue with their career during their military service, often appearing on stage and recording new songs.

On 5 June 1966, a fortunate coincidence occurred: the bus carrying Benny's group, the Hep Stars, and the one belonging to the Hootenanny Singers met at a crossroads in the countryside. The Hootenanny Singers were going to Linköping to appear at a party. Björn invited the Hep Stars to join them after the concert, and late that night, the two groups met up. Björn and Benny got on instantly, and it wasn't long before they started strumming their guitars, playing Beatles songs together.

Several weeks later, another meeting would seal their friendship: the paths of the two groups crossed again at a concert in Västervik, Björn's home town. At the end of their performances, Benny and Björn met up in the motel bar. Over a few beers, they joked, exchanged stories and industry gossip and finally fell into a serious discussion about their real passion: music. 'We had the same musical tastes,' says Björn. 'When Benny started speaking, our ideas were so similar that it was like I was listening to myself. We both thought that from now on it would be good to write all the material for our respective groups. Playing other people's material wasn't enough for us. We even started to write a song that very night!' Björn took Benny home to work in the basement of his parents' house, but their collaboration was soon interrupted by Björn's father. Woken by the noise, he came down to suggest they continue playing their music at his paper mill!

By daybreak, 'Isn't It Easy To Say', the first Ulvaeus/Andersson song had been written, and a new songwriting team was born. The song was recorded during the autumn of 1966 by the Hep Stars (with Björn on guitar) and included on the album *Hep Stars*.

At the same time, the Hootenanny Singers hired Benny for sessions on the song 'Blomman' (The Flower), featured on the *Många Ansikten* (Many Faces) album. Björn even joined the Hep Stars on stage on 26 December at the Härnösand's *folkets park*, standing in at the last minute for guitarist Janne Frisck, who was held up in Spain.

The following year, the Hootenanny Singers had one of their biggest hits with a song called 'En Sång, En Gång För Längesen' (A Song, Once Upon a Time, a Long Time Ago), the Swedish version of Tom Jones's hit 'Green Green Grass of Home'.

During the autumn of 1967, Björn went through a period of uncertainty about his future, and he returned to his studies in law and economics at the University of Stockholm. Hansi prepared a thesis at the University of Lund, Johan worked in Vimmerby, his birthplace, and Tony, who had just married, studied psychology at Lund.

Fortunately, this period of hesitation was short-lived. Björn had always had a flair for studying, but this time he found he had lost his passion for his college course. Lately, he had been working with Stig and Bengt in their music-publishing company. This side of the business really interested him more than anything else, and he made his mind up to learn the trade. However, he hadn't realized how determined Bengt and Stig could be. Both of them knew from the start that Björn's future lay on stage, not behind a desk; Stig was certain that one day Björn would have an international music career. After long discussions, the two men managed to convince him to carry on with composing and recording. He eventually left university when Benny phoned to ask if he could again stand in for guitarist Janne Frisck.

In February 1968, the Hootenanny Singers were in Saalbach, Austria, where they put the finishing touches to the songs for the new album, *Bellman På Vårt Sätt* (Bellman – Our Way). During breaks, the members of the group were able to go skiing. While waiting in the queue for the ski-lift, Björn exchanged glances with Marianne Åkerman, a pretty young Swede on holiday. The attraction was mutual, and Björn said later to the magazine *Bild Journalen*: 'Don't write that we are engaged. For the moment, we are very happy together. We go to restaurants and to the cinema, but there is nothing more between us.'

In April 1968, Björn recorded his first solo single called 'Raring' (Darling). The song was the Swedish version of the American hit 'Honey', by Bobby Goldsboro. The lyrics were written by Stig Anderson. Three other singles sung by Björn were to follow: 'Fröken Fredriksson' (Miss Fredriksson) in the same year and, in 1969, 'Saknar Du Något Min Kära?' (Do You Regret Anything My Dear?) and 'Partaj-Aj-Aj'.

On 21 December, the Hootenanny Singers left Gothenburg for the Caribbean; they had been invited to perform during a month-long cruise. The musicians were accompanied by their wives; in Björn's case, by his sister.

Between 1966 and 1968, Björn and Benny were completely involved with touring and recording with their respective groups and had little time to write anything together, apart from a second song at the end of October 1968, 'A Flower In My Garden', produced by Bengt Palmers. Björn played guitar on this song, which featured as the B-side of the Hep Stars' 'Holiday For Clowns' single.

Björn met Marianne in Saalbach, Austria

Björn with his parents Gunnar & Aina

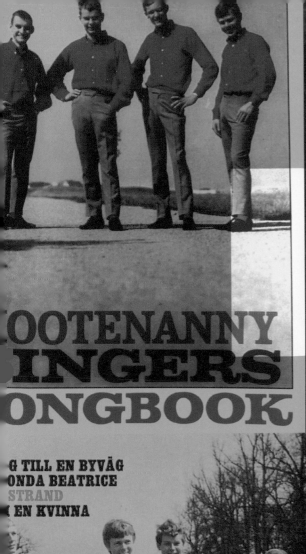

HOOTENANNY
SINGERS
SONGBOOK

TILL EN BYVÄG
ONDA BEATRICE
STRAND
EN KVINNA

HOOTENANNY
Singers

GABRIELLE * I LUM

(HONEY)
Raring

POLAR
MUSIC PRODUCTION

POS 1056

Björn Ulvaeus

FRÖKEN
FREDRIKSSON

POS 1062

Vår egen sång (Harper valley P.T.A.)

'I GREW UP ON ACCORDION MUSIC FROM THE AGE OF SIX AND THEN CAME ELVIS PRESLEY AND CATERINA VALENTE, THEN THERE WAS A LITTLE BIT OF MANTOVANI AND EDVARD GRIEG.' **BENNY**

Benny

Göran Bror Benny Andersson was born on 16 December 1946 in the Vasastaden district of Stockholm. The Andersson family moved to Vällingby, a town to the west of the Swedish capital, two years after his birth. It could be said that this child was born into music, as the Anderssons would often get together to sing and play.

Encouraged by his father, Gösta, and his grandfather, Efraim, young Benny advanced quickly. He was already playing the accordion at the age of six. The two men taught him not only musical technique, but also ancient Swedish folk songs. The first piece of music that the child learned to play by heart was called 'Där Näckrosen Blommar' (Where the Water Lilies Bloom). During the summer months, Benny would accompany his elders on the accordion at family celebrations. He was very talented and had soon completely mastered the instrument.

At the age of ten, Benny was given a piano. It was a revelation: 'Despite the fact that the first piano lessons I had at school were off-putting, I immediately felt that it was my instrument. Step by step, I developed my own way of playing. I never wanted to learn musical theory. As far as I'm concerned, the whole point of music is for it to be something you enjoy and not something you're forced to do. This passion has always been with me. Even today, whenever I see a piano, I can't help playing it!'

At fifteen, Benny left school. He wasn't really keen on studying, much preferring to listen to beautiful melodies and pop music. After having tried his hand at selling washing machines door to door for three weeks, he landed a job as a caretaker. In the evenings, he played in a club near where he lived, sometimes accompanied by a young singer called Christina Grönvall. The two teenagers became inseparable and fell in love. On 20 August 1963, Christina gave birth to a son, Peter.

At this time, Benny became the keyboard player with a local group, the Elverkets Spelmanslag, who regularly performed in the Vällingby area. It was here that things started to develop. The group got a contract to perform a long way from Stockholm and were forced to borrow a van from Svenne Hedlund, the singer with another local group, the Hep Stars. Svenne offered to take them to the venue at the *folkets park* in Virserum. He was present at the performance and noticed Benny's dexterity on the keyboards. Some months later, in October 1964, Hans Östlund, the Hep Stars' keyboard player, left the group, and Svenne offered the job to Benny, who accepted without hesitation. Svenne remembers: 'The funniest thing was that Benny stood out from the start. He had a perfect crew cut and wore a tie, while the

'I SOON REALIZED THAT THE PIANO WAS GOING TO BE MY INSTRUMENT. FATHER AND GRANDFATHER TAUGHT ME EVERYTHING. I HAVE VIRTUALLY NEVER TAKEN MUSIC LESSONS. I HAD TWO OR THREE PIANO LESSONS AT SCHOOL, BUT I THOUGHT THEY WERE DULL.' **BENNY**

The Hep Stars became national idols

' "SUNNY GIRL" IS A BALLAD. IT WAS No. 1 IN SWEDEN FOR SEVERAL WEEKS. I STILL THINK IT'S A GOOD MELODY, ALTHOUGH I'M LESS PROUD OF THE LYRICS. PURE SCHOOLBOOK ENGLISH.'
BENNY

rest of us looked a bit wild and had long hair, although he improved afterwards and became as much of a hippy as the rest of us!'

At that time, the Hep Stars were made up of Svenne Hedlund, Janne Frisck, Lennart Hegland and Christer Pettersson. After their first record went relatively unnoticed, they decided to record 'Cadillac', 'Farmer John' and 'Tribute To Buddy Holly', three songs inspired by the Beatles (it was no surprise that they were later nicknamed 'the Swedish Beatles'). Benny's arrival was beneficial to the group.

In January 1965, the group were invited to perform 'Cadillac' on Swedish Television. Their performance was a sensation: they climbed onto the loudspeakers, screamed and rolled around on the floor. Sweden's young people seemed to approve – within a few weeks, the five young men had become teen idols. Benny remembers: 'We were very influenced by the Beatles, but also by Elvis Presley, Chuck Berry and the Beach Boys. Yet our music was a mixture of country, rock and German rhythms. It's quite strange, but we thought we were really trendy. I think we arrived at the right time. People considered us to be Sweden's answer to other English-speaking groups, yet we sang in English.' On stage, the Hep Stars soon acquired a reputation for being manic. And the girls screamed for more, having eyes only for the singer Svenne, and for Benny, whose smile and carefree attitude drove them wild. An album called *Mashed Potatoes* strengthened the group's initial success. From now on they topped the charts. Benny wrote his first songs for the Hep Stars: 'No Response' and 'Wedding'.

But Benny was seeing less and less of Christina, now his fiancée. Despite the birth of a daughter, Helen, on 25 June 1965, he found family life incompatible with the demands of being a pop star, and in 1966, he left Christina. The young woman remained hurt for a long time after their separation, going so far as to reveal to the press in a scathing article: 'Benny never explained himself. He just phoned me and said that he was leaving! He never dared to admit that he had a fiancée and two children back at home. He was too afraid of risking his career and his image. He was scared of the jealousy of the fans. He couldn't put up with a woman with a pram around him. Once, when I followed the Hep Stars on tour, I was told to hide!' Benny was shocked by these revelations. He couldn't bear to see his private life in the newspapers.

In the same year, he wrote his first hit, 'Sunny Girl'. Although he admits to being satisfied with the melody, he regrets the weakness of the English lyrics, written with the aid of a dictionary.

Other hits followed, including 'It's Nice To Be Back' and 'Consolation', written by Benny. Yet, curiously, he was considered an outsider for a while by his colleagues in the Hep Stars, who teased him for not being around when the group was starting out. Always unflappable, he gave the impression of not having a care in the world, of never being affected by problems or quarrels within the group.

And there were indeed problems. Success had come too quickly. Without a manager, the musicians were caught up in a whirlwind of success for which they were unprepared. Problems with individual egos added to other pressures, and in the studio, they drove the sound engineers mad. They were incapable of arriving on time or agreeing on which pieces to record. While the other members of the group shouted and argued with each other, Benny tapped away on his piano or played his harmonica in the corner.

During the summer of 1966, Benny met up several times with Björn Ulvaeus, the singer and guitarist with the Hootenanny Singers. From this friendship there soon developed an intense and loyal collaboration. But for the time being, Benny teamed up with singer-composer Lasse Berghagen and together they wrote some songs for the Hep Stars and other artists.

In 1969, one of their compositions, 'Hej Clown' (Hello Clown), was performed by Jan Malmsjö in the Melodifestivalen (the selection of the song to represent Sweden at the Eurovision Song Contest), but it was not chosen to go forward to the final.

The incredible career of the Hep Stars continued. They became national idols. However, even if every record sold more than 100,000 copies (an enormous figure for a small country like Sweden), they still lacked a proper manager. In a joint decision, they decided to create their own publishing and production company, called Hep House, but musicians do not necessarily make good businessmen. Nothing was managed properly, and money was going out faster than it was coming in.

The Hep Stars launched headlong into filming a musical entitled *Habari-Safari*. The group went off to Africa for two weeks with a film crew. The director, Åke Borglund, and the manager of Hep House made the most of the trip and gave themselves an extra week's holiday at the expense of the group. Added to the already large bill were ten days of filming in Denmark, as well as the cost of hiring a private plane to take the group to London to record in a Soho studio.

On their return, it became clear that what had been shot was unuseable. They had neither a story nor a main theme. It was then that things suddenly began to fall apart. It emerged that nobody had ever declared any income to the taxman, and the amount outstanding was more than a million Swedish crowns. In December 1967, the newspapers exposed the 'Hep Stars scandal'. Faced with these debts, the musicians became disillusioned. In July 1968, Hep House Productions was declared bankrupt, and each member of the group had to pay back their share.

For Benny, this was a bitter pill, from now on he would have to work without ever seeing a penny of his earnings. In two years, his income dropped from 174,000 to 8,000 kronor. However, he managed to repay his debts fairly quickly. But the Hep Stars' troubles were by no means over: a further demand for 83,000 kronor arrived, relating to earnings for 1968. Things were no longer going well within the group. The creative atmosphere and the motivation had gone. Guitarist Janne Frisck left at the end of February 1969. He was temporarily replaced for the duration of a tour by Björn Ulvaeus.

'I DON'T HAVE A BROTHER BUT BJÖRN IS MY BROTHER. NOTHING WILL ALTER THE FACT THAT WE ARE TRUE FRIENDS. AS WITH A BROTHER, ANYTHING COULD HAPPEN AND HE WOULD STILL BE TO ME WHAT HE HAS ALWAYS BEEN.' BENNY

Anni-Frid

Ballangen is a small Norwegian village situated about 35 kilometres to the west of Narvik. In 1945, the country was still occupied by German troops, whose brutal methods aroused both fear and hatred among the Norwegians. However, nineteen-year-old Synni Lyngstad had befriended a non-commissioned officer, Alfred Haase, six years her senior. Gradually, the bond between them grew deeper and they fell in love. Synni didn't think of him as a uniformed enemy soldier. All she could see was a man far from home, forced to fulfil a duty he detested. Despite warnings from her friends and family, Synni continued to see Alfred in secret. However, their affair soon became common knowledge all over the village and fingers began to point.

Their happiness was short-lived, as the end of the war meant that the troops began to leave the country. Alfred had to return to Germany, but he promised Synni he would come back as soon as he could. The young woman didn't dare to tell him that she was pregnant, and Alfred didn't admit to her that he was married. His wife was waiting for him in Karlsruhe.

Alfred Haase

Synni Lyngstad

When Synni felt her first contractions on 15 November 1945, the midwife was sick and her replacement didn't arrive in time. The young woman, helped by her mother, Agny, and her sister, Olive, gave birth to a little girl, who she named Anni-Frid. The inhabitants of Ballangen gave her the nickname 'German child', and people would spit, shout insults at her or cross the street when they saw the young mother coming. Synni couldn't care less – her child was more important to her than anything else. She still believed that Alfred would return, and even if her letters remained unanswered, she could always live in hope. Her mother, her four sisters and her brother were there to look out for her, so she wasn't alone, but life was difficult for the young mother and her child. Eventually, Synni and her mother decided to leave town.

Synni found work in a hotel in the region of Hardanger, in the south, and left Anni-Frid in the care of her mother. Some time later, Agny and Anni-Frid crossed the Swedish border and stayed temporarily in Härjedalen before settling in Torshälla, a small town 7 kilometres from Eskilstuna. Agny rented a small two-room flat and worked as a dressmaker. When money was short at the end of the month, she would work washing dishes in a café.

Anni-Frid with her grandmother Agny

Far from her family and daughter, and still with no news from Alfred, Synni could stand it no longer. She left her job and Norway, and rejoined her family in Torshälla where she found a job as a waitress. Sadly, after several months, she became seriously ill. Before she died, she made her mother promise to take care of Anni-Frid. Synni died in hospital in Flen in September 1947. She was just twenty-one years old.

'MY MOTHER WAS ONLY TWENTY-ONE, SHE WAS REALLY PRETTY AND SHE HAD A BEAUTIFUL SINGING VOICE. THAT'S ALL I KNOW. WHEN I WAS YOUNGER, I OFTEN IMAGINED HOW MY PARENTS WERE.' FRIDA

The next few years were difficult for Anni-Frid's grandmother. Elsa Larsson, a neighbour and friend, would later say: 'Agny was a stern woman, but very courageous. She went to a lot of trouble. I often looked after Anni-Frid and we both had great fun. She was a good little girl, and was always singing!' Anni-Frid has fond memories of her childhood with her grandmother. 'I always called her "Mum". I remember long evenings sitting by the fireside. She taught me old Swedish and Norwegian songs. It was because of her that I became interested in singing. She always encouraged me whenever I was trying something new. Even if communication was difficult sometimes, because of the age difference, I owe everything to her.'

Anni-Frid spent the summers in Norway with her aunts and cousins – with Olive Lunde in Trondheim or Aase and Ingvald Olsen in their little chalet in Ballangen. Olive remembers: 'She was always singing. Music was her driving force. At the age of seven, she was already saying that she was going to become a singer!'

Anni-Frid made her first real stage début at the age of ten, at a gala organized by the Red Cross. She wore traditional Norwegian dress and sang 'Fjorton År Tror Jag Visst Att Jag Var' (I Believe I Was Fourteen Years Old). Anni-Frid devoted more and more time to singing. She joined the school choir and sang with a church group called the Good Companions. She also entered various amateur competitions, and soon developed a taste for the stage.

and Duke Ellington. Anni-Frid had also found love: she and the group's bass player, Ragnar Fredriksson soon became inseparable. On 26 January 1963, the young woman gave birth to a son, Hans. Ragnar and Anni-Frid married the following year and spent their honeymoon in the Canary Islands.

In 1963, everyone was going mad for the twist and rock music. Orchestras like Bengt Sandlund's weren't making money any more, and the group gave their very last concert the day before Easter. However, Ragnar and Anni-Frid didn't want to give up. While working as a carpet salesman, Ragnar found the time to put together a new group and the Anni-Frid Four was born. The quartet was made up of Anni-Frid (vocals), Ragnar (bass), Agne Andersson (keyboards and trumpet) and Conny Lindblom (drums). At the rate of four or five performances per week, the group soon became the main attraction of the Eskilstuna area. 'It was like a dream come true,' says Anni-Frid. 'We were singing for pleasure and we were being paid. Our repertoire pleased the audiences in the restaurants and nightclubs, as did the fact that we were always smiling and were so easy-going. We were natural and happy to be playing the music we loved. At that time, we were singing a lot of old ballads but also standards by Glenn Miller. I worked out my own technique by listening to songs by Ella Fitzgerald and Peggy Lee.'

This was a turning point in Anni-Frid's life. But this success did not fulfil her ambitions as a singer. She would soon be nineteen years old, and despite

'I WAS FOURTEEN. I WAS A VOCALIST IN A DANCE BAND, WORKING EVERY SATURDAY. I SANG THE CONTEMPORARY MUSIC OF THE TIME LIKE *SCHLAGERS*, POP MUSIC. AND THEN MY TASTE IN MUSIC CHANGED WITH THE YEARS.' FRIDA

At the age of thirteen, she was introduced to the musician Ewald Ek, who gave her an audition. He remembers: 'I immediately felt that she had something. I asked for special permission from her guardian because she wasn't fifteen yet, and the following Thursday, she became our lead singer.' The group, directed by Ewald, was made up of an accordion player, a clarinetist, a bass player, a drummer and a vibraphone player. The group travelled by van and performed in the Värmland and Sörmland regions of Sweden, their only equipment being a microphone (for Anni-Frid) and two 15-watt loudspeakers. 'She adapted well to all different styles of music,' recalls Ewald. 'She sang like no one else.'

Officially, Frida was too young to go into clubs and nightclubs. However, the teenager lied successfully about her age as, both physically and vocally, she seemed older. She was already a very good-looking young woman. 'I was pleased to leave school because I wanted to devote myself totally to music,' remembers Frida. 'I sang from 8 in the evening until 1 o'clock in the morning. My friends thought I was crazy. And even though I was having a really exciting time, between the ages of thirteen and fifteen, life wasn't always easy for me. I felt the absence of my parents very strongly and saw things through different eyes. I felt like an adult but I don't think that I really was.'

During the spring of 1961, Ewald Ek's group broke up, following the departure of three of its members. However, Bengt Sandlund was in the process of putting together a big orchestra, made up of about fifteen musicians, and he needed a singer. On Saturday 7 October, Anni-Frid started out with them on stage in Eskilstuna's folk park and pocketed 60 Swedish kronor. The following Saturday, her fee increased to 85 kronor for a concert in Rättvik park. She was happy because, with Bengt Sandlund, she could continue to cultivate her taste for jazz, as their repertoire centred around Glenn Miller, Count Basie

being a wife and mother, she more than ever felt the desire to move on, to express herself and to make it as an artist.

In September 1964, she took part in an amateur singing competition held in Västerås. Wearing a red dress, she performed the international hit 'Besame Mucho', which she had heard while on her honeymoon (one member of the audience applauded louder than everyone else – Ragnar was very proud of his wife). She won over the jury and the public and carried away the first prize ahead of fifteen-year-old Gudrun Rönsen. On the strength of this victory, she decided to take part in other radio competitions, while still carrying on with the shows she was doing with her husband and the Anni-Frid Four. Her son Hans was entrusted to his great-grandmother as Anni-Frid increased her appearances. In order to perfect her vocal technique, she was now taking lessons with opera singer Folke Andersson. She was also starting to feel restricted by the group and dreamed of a solo career which would give her more freedom. She wanted to work with more ambitious musicians, but to do so she would have to move to Stockholm.

1967 would be a key year for the young woman. On 25 February, she gave birth to a second child, a little girl who was named Lise-Lotte. A short time afterwards, she won the chance to take part in the famous national competition Nya Ansikten (New Faces) which took place on Sunday 3 September in Skansen park in Stockholm, as part of the celebrations for Barnens Dag (Children's Day).

Anni-Frid chose a song which proved to be lucky for her, 'En Ledig Dag' (A Day Off). She won first prize, and when the presenter Lasse Holmqvist asked her what she was going to do next, Anni-Frid naïvely replied: 'I'm going back to Eskilstuna to sleep.'

The amused presenter replied: 'Well, no you're not, because a car is waiting outside to take you straight to a television studio.' The singer was completely stunned and quickly had to pull herself together. Anni-Frid knew that a record contract was on offer to the winner but didn't know that EMI – who were sponsoring the competition – had arranged for the winner to perform that evening in front of the cameras on the programme *Hylands Hörna* (Hyland's Corner), presented by celebrity Lennart Hyland.

Backstage at the TV studio, Anni-Frid was nervous. During a short rehearsal, pianist Leif Asp reassured her: 'Relax, you'll soon be famous!' When her name was announced, she stepped out in front of the cameras and Swedish viewers saw an elegant young woman who, despite her nerves, expressed herself with ease. Lennart Hyland introduced her and asked her a few questions. Anni-Frid, who would soon be twenty-two years old, was forthright in her answers. When he asked her what she did for a living, she replied 'I am married and have two children – this is my job!'

Right from the very first notes of 'En Ledig Dag', Anni-Frid captivated the television audience. With her magical voice and her graceful movements, Anni-Frid had successfully made her début in the world of showbusiness.

It didn't take long before offers of recording contracts came in. Her future producer, Olle Bergman, travelled to Eskilstuna in person on 4 September so that he could be the first to get her to sign – for the EMI label. He would later declare: 'We were very enthusiastic about her. I knew she had all the assets required to make a great career.' The first recording session took place in the Europa Films studio on 11 September. Anni-Frid recorded four songs: 'En Ledig Dag', 'Peter, Kom Tillbaka' (Peter, Come Back), 'Du Är Så Underbart Rar' (You Are Wonderfully Kind), and a song which wouldn't be

released, 'Du Är Lyckan, Du Är Glädjen Inom Mig' (You're My Happiness, You're My Joy).

Anni-Frid's first single, featuring 'En Ledig Dag' and 'Peter, Kom Tillbaka', was released on 18 September. Despite some promotion and frequent radio airplay, the record did little more than get good reviews from the critics.

On 11 November, the Folkparkernas Artist Forum took place in Halmstad, on Sweden's west coast. This annual event brings together all the managers of the folk parks as well as various other event organizers. Many artists new to the business, as well as established ones, perform at this gathering. Among them was Anni-Frid, who gave a performance which resulted in her being signed up for her first folk-park tour the following summer, together with singer Lars Lönndahl.

On 15 December, EMI released another single, 'Din' (Yours), but it was the B-side, 'Du Är Så Underbart Rar', which would capture the public's attention. The song, which was played a lot on the radio and in clubs, is a cover version of the Andy Williams hit 'Can't Take My Eyes Off You'. This second single would sell more than the first but didn't do any better than being *Toppentipset* (Tip For the Top) in the Swedish charts.

On 10 January 1968, Anni-Frid was invited to sing 'En Ledig Dag' on the television show *Studio 8*. Among the other six guests in the Malmö studios was another new talent, Agnetha Fältskog, who performed her first hit, 'Jag Var Så Kär' (I Was So In Love).

On 22 May, Anni-Frid and Lars Lönndahl gave their first concert of the folk-park tour at the Central School of Tranemo Theatre, in front of an audience of

600 people. The tour would take them to about forty towns. On stage, they were accompanied by Bengt Hallberg (piano) and his musicians: Rune Gustafsson (guitar), Ronnie Pettersson (bass) and Rune Carlsson (drums). Lars Lönndahl remembers: 'I really enjoyed working with Frida. She was just starting out in the business but was already very professional. She had lots of charisma. She always has had, in fact. She had this natural grace and elegance which wasn't affected. You knew that she was going to be someone. Do you know that at that time she still made her own stage clothes?'

Anni-Frid seems to have enjoyed this first tour: 'Despite long days on the road, I've always enjoyed doing shows. It was hard work but I learned a lot from it. At the time, I was living like those were the best days of my life. It has to be said that Sweden is a beautiful country, especially in the summer. What I missed most of all was my children. I was far away from them and I rarely saw them. Their father was very important during that period. I was lucky to have such an understanding husband. He considered my career to be important and never blamed me for anything.' The tour concluded on 30 June.

Anni-Frid still hadn't had a record in the charts. Was it because her songs were a bit too 'jazzy' and not 'poppy' enough? She was held in high esteem by a lot of people in the music industry, but critics said that she had a limited audience. Yet the young woman was a big hit whenever she appeared on stage and was considered one of the best singers in the country.

It was now 1969, and Frida was spending a lot of time away from her family. Despite missing her children, the young woman decided to move to Bro, north-west of Stockholm, so that she could devote more time to her musical activities. 'I was violently criticized at the time. I was accused of abandoning my family just because I wanted to see my name up in lights. I had considered bringing my children with me to live in Stockholm, but my flat was too tiny and I would have been constantly absent. I really made the right choice. Hans and Lise-Lotte were better off with their father, in our house in Eskilstuna, rather than in my tiny home in the capital. People were very cruel; no one could have imagined how much this decision broke my heart. The worst thing was that when I was on my own at home, I would spend all my time thinking about them. In public, I always tried to hide my pain. My smile concealed a deep sadness.'

Anni-Frid went back to Eskilstuna whenever her timetable permitted. 'It was a real joy to see my children again. On the other hand, Ragnar and myself didn't have anything to say to each other any more. The spark had gone. So, we decided on an amicable divorce. In retrospect, I think we got married when we were too young, without really realizing what life as a couple was all about. The children stayed with him, which was better for everyone.'

Lasse Lönndahl & Anni-Frid on tour, 1968

The Anni-Frid Four was born

Anni-Frid & Agnetha on the Studio 8 TV show

'En Ledig Dag', Skansen park, 3 September 1967

ANNI-FRID
LYNGSTAD

En ledig dag

Peter, kom tillbaka

XPRESSEN

EMI SVENSKA AB
Box 1289, 171 25 Solna

ANNI-FRID LYNGSTAD

EMI SVENSKA AB
Box 1289, 171 25 Solna

EMI SVENSKA AB
Box 1289, 171 25 Solna

ANNI-FRID LYNGSTAD

'HE WAS ONE OF THE FIRST MUSIC PUBLISHERS TO DEVELOP WORLDWIDE. HE WAS ALSO KIND-HEARTED – A HUMANIST IN THE FULL SENSE OF THE WORD.' QUINCY JONES

Stig

Stig Erik Leopold Anderson was born in the Mariestad maternity hospital on 25 January 1931. His mother, Ester, lived alone in the village of Hova, halfway between Laxå and Mariestad, in the Västergötland region of Sweden. It was difficult being a single mother in those days, and Ester was often the subject of spiteful gossip, but she was a strong woman and wasn't afraid of hard work. She was a hairdresser during the day and made ends meet by taking in people's washing and ironing. Every Friday, she would cycle the 20 kilometres to Finnerödja, where she worked in a sweet shop. 'I used to sit on the basket on the bike,' remembered Stig. 'I was really scared crossing the huge dark forest at night. The reflection from the light used to dart about on the stony road and I used to look up at the sky to make myself feel better. You used to hear terrible stories about the robbers who were around!'

Stig never knew his father. He learned at a very early age that you had to work hard to succeed in life. 'At the age of eleven, I used to get up an hour before my classmates to light the coal stove at our school. I would earn 5 kronor for doing that. Sometimes there was a lot of smoke and I had to clear the air before the other school kids arrived.'

Stig left school when he was thirteen and started work as a delivery boy for Källéns Diversehandel, a grocery store. 'I used to earn 5 kronor a week,' he said. 'It was more of an encouragement than a salary, but it wasn't enough for me.' Stig then got himself a job with the Hova Sports Association in Movallen, where he was responsible for all the equipment. 'I used to wash the players' kits, tidy the changing rooms and paint the lines on the pitch. Every Sunday I would run the sweets and drinks kiosk during the match. Källéns Diversehandel used to give me special prices on what I sold. Sometimes I could earn up to 30 kronor on some matches.'

'STIG IS ONE OF THE BEST PEOPLE I KNOW. ONE HUNDRED PER CENT HONEST. HE IS VERY INTELLIGENT AND ALWAYS KNOWS HOW THINGS SHOULD BE. I GET MAD WHEN THEY TREAT HIM UNFAIRLY ON TV. THEY PAINT HIM THAT WAY JUST BECAUSE THEY WANT HIM THAT WAY.' FRIDA IN 1977

'STIG WAS VERY IMPORTANT. HE WAS THE ONE WHO FIRST BELIEVED IN BENNY AND ME AS SONGWRITERS. AT THE BEGINNING OF THE SEVENTIES, HE TOLD US: "ONE DAY, YOU'LL HAVE A WORLDWIDE HIT!" WE WORKED CLOSELY TOGETHER AND HE HAD AN ENORMOUS INFLUENCE.' BJÖRN

Börje Crona & Stig in 1954

Stig worked hard during the week and dreamed of one day becoming a musician. 'I grew up on porridge and music. I must have been five years old when my mother brought home a record player and six second-hand records. The ones I listened to the most were *Zeppelinarvalsen* and *Axel Öhman*. One of them had a big scratch at the beginning so I had to go straight into the chorus without ever hearing the verse.'

Music became a passion for him the day that his mother bought him a guitar. 'It cost 15 kronor, complete with cover. My first attempts at playing it were terrible. Then I took some lessons and started playing with some local musicians.' At the age of sixteen, Stig left home and found a place to live near the village square. He was becoming more and more interested in jazz music, and he perfected his style of playing at the Sven Stiberg-Folke Eriksberg guitar school. He joined an orchestra in the neighbouring town of Lyrestad. In 1947, he joined Bobby's Orkester in Töreboda, a professional group which toured the region. He wrote his first song after being rejected by a young girl he'd fallen in love with.

Stig wrote more and more music. Helped by his friend, pianist Sigvard Augustsson, who would write scores for him, he decided to send some of his work to the specialist magazine *Orkester-Journalen*. 'Once I saw my name in print, I never looked back. I told myself that ultimately there could be a place for Stig Anderson in the world of music.' Inspired by this first experience, he sent some songs to his idol, Ulf Peder Olrog, who sent him an encouraging letter back which ended: 'Keep in touch!'

In July 1948, Ulf Peder Olrog was performing at Adolfsberg park in Örebro. As soon as Stig read about it in the newspaper, he immediately bought two tickets for Örebro. 'It's now or never!' he told Sigvard Augustsson. Stig remembered: 'Ulf Peder was very kind to us and offered us strawberries and cream. This was a decisive meeting for me.' Ulf Peder thought that Stig's songs were promising but suggested to the young composer that he should carry on with his studies in order to increase his knowledge of harmony and poetry.

'I wanted to study music at the Ingesund high school,' Stig explained. 'But I was too young to go there. Meanwhile, I worked at the Arvika co-operative which was where I met Bengt Bernhag.' His circle of friends began to grow when he enrolled at Ingesund a year later, where he met Börje Crona, and his future wife, Gudrun Rystedt. Together with Bengt and Börje, Stig formed a musical trio called 'Stig Anderson och hans Mosiga Gräddklickar' (Stig Anderson and his Cabbages in Cream). Together, they put on a show of sketches and songs entitled 'Grädde På Moset' (Cherry on the Cake) and performed in the district of Arvika, in the Värmland region. The local press weren't very keen on them. 'You could say that we were ahead of our time, or maybe that the people who lived in Arvika weren't mature enough for our style …' Stig explained.

At the beginning of 1950, the trio were fortunate enough to be invited to perform the song 'Grädde På Moset' on the very popular Swedish Radio show *Frukostklubben*. 'I then went straight to Stockholm with Börje Crona to meet music publisher Georg Eliasson,' Stig recalls. 'All we had in our luggage were some songs, including "Tivedshambo" and "Grädde På Moset".' Georg Eliasson agreed to publish the second song, and he had it recorded by singer Harry Brandelius. The record came out in November, but Stig wasn't pleased with the interpretation. Fortunately, a few weeks later, Rolf Bengtsson, a friend of Börje Crona, recorded 'Tivedshambo' and 'Valsen Om Frans-Oskar' (Frans-Oskar's Waltz) for the company Metronome. The record was released at the beginning of 1951, and Rolf was given a good response every time he sang it on stage at the Harlem (Nalen) nightclub in Stockholm.

In the spring of 1951, Stig left Ingesund to go to the Karlstad higher teacher-training college. He continued his studies in Stockholm after a break to do his national service. Music still played a large part in his life. While on leave, he joined his friends Bengt and Börje back in Stockholm and recorded 'Dom

Finns På Landet' (They Are Found In the Country) and 'Tivedens Ros' (Tiveden's Rose), with Stig Holm's orchestra.

In 1953, at the end of his military service, Stig moved to Stockholm with Gudrun, now his fiancée. The couple bought a tiny studio flat on Bondegatan, in the Södermalm district of Stockholm. At the same time as studying to become a teacher, the young man continued with his musical activities. 'Working in Stockholm was an excuse to be near the entertainment world which Bengt had described to me so well. Recording with Philips was one of the most important things for me. We were now ready for what would happen next.'

The following year, Stig put together a show and played in the Swedish parks with Börje Crona as his partner. The pair recorded numerous songs including 'Det Blir Inget Bröllop På Lördag' (There Won't Be Any Wedding On Saturday) and 'Tro Lilla Hjärta, Tro' (Believe Little Heart, Believe). Börje would subsequently be replaced by other artists such as Rolf Bengtsson, Minimal Åström and Akke Carlsson.

In 1955, Stig married Gudrun and got a teaching post at a school in Aspudden, near Stockholm. The couple moved from Södermalm to a villa in Lännersta, east of the capital. 'Stikkan was a good teacher,' says Gudrun. 'His students often called him at home. He would sometimes try his new songs out on them in class.' This led to him being nicknamed 'the singing teacher'.

One day, he received a letter from Robert Bosmans, of Belgian publishers Editions Charles Bens. 'He proposed starting up a company together for the countries of Scandinavia. It would also give me the opportunity to make contact with the Benelux countries as well as Germany, Austria, Switzerland and maybe even France and Italy. I made the most of the school holidays to go and meet him in Brussels. I didn't hide the fact from him that I didn't know anything about how music-publishing companies were run. He told me: "I'll teach you. We can do it all by post, it's the easiest thing to do!" From that day on, there was a strong collaboration between the two men. Robert Bosmans sent foreign songs to Stig, who, for his part, would write Swedish lyrics for them, find an artist and arrange recording and promotion for the songs.

In the autumn of 1960, Stig gave up his job at Aspudden school. Gudrun says: 'I told Stikkan it would be best to devote all his time to music, to give up his job as a teacher and work in the kitchen during the daytime instead of at night.' The first six months were hard, as he didn't receive any royalties for his first hit by Lill-Babs until the following year. Stig later said in an interview: '1961 was a terrible year. Business wasn't going well and we had the house to pay for, as well as the car and two children. Fortunately, Gudrun had found a second job in the evenings. I wouldn't want to live through that time again.'

Fate smiled on him again when Ivan Mogull, an American partner of Robert Bosmans, called to offer him a deal. 'He wanted to buy the rights to "Klas-

'STIG WAS VERY EFFICIENT AND VERY MUCH INTO WORK. MAYBE TOO MUCH, I DON'T KNOW.' FRIDA

'I'VE LEARNED EVERYTHING FROM STIG; HE WAS INCREDIBLY GENEROUS.' GÖREL HANSER

Although Stig liked his job, he dreamed of being able to make a living from his real passion. Every evening he would sit at the kitchen table and tirelessly write new songs, with the help of a rhyming dictionary. In 1957, his hard work paid off when he had a sizeable hit with 'Vi Hänger Me' (We Are Still Here), which was adopted as the theme tune of the Nacka-Skoglund football team. At around the same time, Gudrun gave birth to a daughter, Marie. Stig hadn't abandoned the stage either, and every weekend he would perform at parties and parks with his latest partner, Akke Carlsson.

In 1959, Stig had his first real hit with 'Är Du Kär I Mig Ännu, Klas-Göran? (Are You Still In Love With Me, Klas-Göran?), a song he had written for magazine Vecko-Revyn's Flugan musical tour. When Bengt Bernhag played the song for his boss at Karusell, Simon Brehm, he immediately thought it would be suitable for his new protégée, singer Lill-Babs. 'Är Du Kär I Mig …' became a hit and drew the public's attention to both singer and composer. 'That was when I realized that it was essential that I create my own company, so that I could keep my royalties,' Stig explained. 'So I created Sweden Music, a name which sounded great from the start.'

Without wasting any time, Stig borrowed 500 kronor from a colleague at school so that he could print his score. At the end of class, he would dash off in his old Opel to visit his friend Gnesta-Knalle and his wife Kerstin, who were publishers and distributors, so that his songs could be sent to all four corners of Scandinavia and also to Holland, where the song would be adapted in Dutch. The song also became a hit in Denmark, sung by Grethe Sönck and in Norway ('Er Du Gla I Meg Ennu, Karl Johan?') by Nora Brockstedt. Stig still had a lot to learn about the industry. He said: 'Thanks to Gnesta-Knalle and Kerstin, I learned a lot and managed to avoid falling into any traps with contracts. Their help was very precious to me.'

Göran" and asked if I'd like to translate and adapt "You Can Have Her". We met in Copenhagen and finalized the deal. When I got back to Stockholm, I called Curre Pettersson at Philips. He was looking for material for Anita Lindblom and suggested that I write three songs for her forthcoming EP. Among the songs was "Sånt Är Livet" (Such Is Life).' This was the first time that Stig had written lyrics for a foreign song. Hundreds of others would follow, and he would sometimes write under the pseudonym of Stig Rossner.

Stig's finances improved from 1963 onwards. During the summer, he received 60,000 kronor from STIM (the Swedish Society for Artists) in respect of royalties received from Charles Bens. He decided to create Polar Music with his friend Bengt Bernhag, with each of them owning 50 per cent of the company. 'I realized that the future was in records. It was hard to just work as a publisher because it didn't earn enough.' The first artists to be signed to the Polar Music label were four young men who had been discovered by Bengt Bernhag during the autumn of 1963, the Hootenanny Singers; the most important member was of course Björn Ulvaeus. After several singles and two albums, they quickly became idols in Sweden. Thanks to their enormous success, Polar Music was now one of the most important record companies in the country. It was a very small team, since Gudrun was the only one helping her husband in the office, doing administrative and financial work.

His work as a producer and music publisher didn't stop Stig from writing songs for a multitude of artists, and he wrote many lyrics for Lill-Babs, Ann-Louise Hanson, Östen Warnerbring, Siw Malmkvist, Anita Lindblom, and Lars Lönndahl, to name the most famous. His songs were constantly at the top of the charts.

Stig, Gudrun & their children, Marie & Lars

In 1967, Stig produced the single 'Jag Tror På Sommaren' (I Believe In Summer), sung by Mats Olin, which became the big hit of the summer. At one point, he had six songs in the Svensktoppen Top 10 at the same time. Some said that everything he touched turned to gold. 'Obviously I worked hard,' says Stig. 'During the day, I took care of the day-to-day business in the office, and during the evening, I wrote lyrics to my songs. At night, I kept in contact with my foreign correspondents. That's how I worked, without a secretary, for eight years.'

The secretary who would help Stig and Gudrun with administration was Görel Johnsen. She began working for Sweden Music on 8 September 1969. Görel came from Skultorp, near Skövde, in the west of Sweden, and replied to an advert which read: 'Music-publishing company seeks secretary with a good knowledge of English. Call Gudrun Anderson or Ove Hansson.' The young lady, whose dream was to teach either languages or history, knew nothing about show-business and had never heard of Stig Anderson. Nevertheless, she was given an interview by Gudrun, as Stig was in the United States. 'When I met Gudrun, I immediately felt relaxed,' says Görel. 'She was calm, reassuring, and had a kind look about her. She was used to young people. I was a student and a country girl and Stig would never have given me the job if he had interviewed me!'

'BENNY AND I DIDN'T HAVE MUCH TROUBLE WORKING WITH HIM. BUT THEN, WE SORT OF GREW APART BECAUSE HIS TIME WAS MORE AND MORE OCCUPIED BY BUSINESS.' BJÖRN

Stig bought two small properties, including a ground-floor flat at 18 Jungfrugatan for the new offices of Polar Music/Sweden Music. The company now had seven staff: Stig, Gudrun, Görel, Bengt Bernhag, Ove Hansson, Leif Karlsson and Rolf Lönberg. It was around this time that Björn Ulvaeus and his friend Benny Andersson began writing songs for the other Polar Music artists. Stig recalls the day that Björn introduced him to Benny: 'When the two of them arrived at the office, I really couldn't see what they could have in common because they had such different personalities. Björn tried to convince me to take him on. I said why not, because it wouldn't cost anything to try it out. As soon as I heard the first demos they'd made, I realized that there was a real magic in some parts of their songs. That was only the start, but you could immediately feel that the two of them worked incredibly well together. There was a feeling of ease and lightness in their work.'

With the first musical successes of the Björn Ulvaeus/Benny Andersson partnership, Stig realized he had found a promising team. He said: 'I very quickly made a promise to Björn and Benny that with my help, they would be able to carve out an important place for themselves internationally.' And that is exactly what happened.

Starting from nothing, Stig slowly built up the Polar Music empire through sheer courage, hard work and talent. But if Stig was an emperor, he was far from being a dictator as, apart from a few exceptions, he always made important decisions together with Björn and Benny. Stig also knew how to surround himself with an efficient team. The team that worked around him and ABBA were more like a family unit than employees – even his daughter Marie would later join the team.

To sum up the man and his philosophy of life, here are the four principles he always gave when asked the secret of his success:

• Always work hard

• Give your best

• Don't ever forget anything

• Don't take life too seriously

Björn, Gudrun & Stig

'I'M A GOOD ORGANIZER, I'VE GOT A FEELING FOR MARKETING AND I CAN HEAR IF A SONG IS A GOOD ONE OR A BAD ONE. BUT I ALSO HAVE BUSINESS SENSE.' **STIG**

'MOST OF THE TIME, I DON'T WRITE THE SWEDISH LYRICS MYSELF, BECAUSE I HAVE THE FEELING THAT THEY ARE NOT RIGHT. BUT WHEN I WRITE A SONG, I ALWAYS WRITE ORIGINAL LYRICS IN ENGLISH. THE SWEDISH VERSION IS OFTEN ITS TRANSLATION.'
AGNETHA

1969

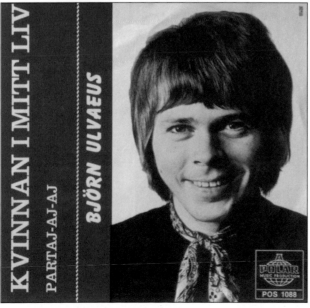

At the beginning of 1969, Johan Karlberg left the Hootenanny Singers to devote all his time to the family firm. Johan said: 'I don't want to be performing on stage at folk parks all my life. I have other ambitions. At the beginning, the popularity was fun. In recent years, it has become a burden!'

This demotivated the group somewhat, and their career seemed to slow down as a result. Björn, for his part, could now get more involved with working with Benny and also concentrate on his solo career. He was single again: his relationship with Marianne Åkerman had just ended.

6 January   Agnetha was one of twenty-two artists and groups to perform at the Apollonia in Stockholm before an audience consisting mainly of concert organizers. Agnetha also sponsored a new talent, the young singer Hans Smedberg.

8 January   Anni-Frid Lyngstad was on stage at the Valand club in Gothenburg, together with Charlie Norman and his musicians. *The Charlie Norman Show* played there until the end of the month.

Benny meets Anni-Frid
On 1 February 1969, the Hep Stars began their tour of Sweden's biggest clubs at the Hamburger Börs in Stockholm. At the end of the month, however, guitarist Janne Frisck left the group for good to run a restaurant in Torremolinos. Björn Ulvaeus replaced him for ten days or so. The tour brought them to the Arkaden club in Malmö from 4 to 6 March.

After a concert, Benny went to the Kocksa Krogen bar for a drink and happened to bump into Anni-Frid. The singer was appearing at the Ambassadeur club with Charlie Norman. 'Our meeting wasn't really memorable,' Anni-Frid remembers. 'We talked about our work and about life on the road, but it wasn't a very interesting conversation. We had a drink together and went our separate ways without imagining for a second that we would see each other again a few weeks later.'

Fate would bring them together again on 31 March in Stockholm for the recording of the radio programme *Midnight Hour*; Anni-Frid and Benny were both members of a jury called Flip Eller Flop. At the end of the programme, Benny asked the singer to join him at a restaurant. 'We found that we had a lot of things in common,' says Anni-Frid. 'Benny was going through a difficult time like myself. That's what brought us together. We talked for hours. We had very different, but complimentary, personalities. He came into my life at the right time, I think, because I was really beginning to doubt everything. I was all alone and depressed in my flat and far away from my children. So much so that I sometimes wondered if my work was really worth all these sacrifices. Benny brought me the comfort that I needed. From that moment on, we were always together.'

1 March   Anni-Frid took part in the Melodifestivalen, organized by Swedish Television at the Cirkus in Stockholm. In Sweden, the Melodifestivalen is a real institution and one of the most important television events of the year, watched by more than half the population of Sweden. Pekka Langer presented the ten candidates competing to represent Sweden at the Eurovision Song Contest. Anni-Frid Lyngstad sang 'Härlig Är Vår Jord' (Our World Is Wonderful), wearing a yellow tunic with a black trim.

'THE BEST THING THAT EVER HAPPENED TO ME WAS BENNY, NOT ABBA.' FRIDA

Anni-Frid & Benny were officially engaged in August 1969

'WHEN WE STARTED WRITING, I'D SAY BRIAN WILSON WAS MY BIGGEST SOURCE OF INSPIRATION, BECAUSE HE HAS DONE EXACTLY WHAT I THINK WE'RE TRYING TO DO – DOING IT ALL.' BENNY

Lennie Norman & Anni-Frid on stage in *The Charlie Norman Show*

Anni-Frid with Sacha Distel

Her song was well received by the audience. However, the jury chose Tommy Körberg, with his song 'Judy, Min Vän' (Judy, My Friend). Anni-Frid received only 8 points and finished in joint-fourth position with singer Ann-Louise Hanson. Göran Sellgren wrote in the newspaper *Dagens Nyheter*: 'A beautiful young woman with a beautiful song. Anni-Frid's performance was rare in this kind of competition. Her song – a bossa-nova number – was lovely and wasn't at all lacking in personality. Unfortunately, the song isn't memorable, even though the arrangement was very good.' Thanks to 'Härlig Är Vår Jord', Anni-Frid entered the Svensktoppen for the first time on 27 April and reached No. 8.

5 March Swedish singer Brita Borg recorded 'Ljuva Sextital' (Sweet Sixties), one of Björn and Benny's compositions. The lyrics for this song, which spent several weeks on the Swedish charts, were written by Stig Anderson.

13 March Anni-Frid went to Germany for several days of promotion. Her producer, Olle Bergman, was keen to conquer the German market with the new single 'Härlig Är Vår Jord'. Unfortunately, this attempt ended in failure.

21 March The Hep Stars recorded two Benny and Björn songs: 'Speleman' (The Musician) and 'Precis Som Alla Andra' (Just Like All the Others).

1 April – 3 May The company of *The Charlie Norman Show* (Charlie Norman and his musicians, Anni-Frid Lyngstad and Hasse Burman) were at the Hamburger Börs in Stockholm. Among the songs and sketches included in the show was one in which Anni-Frid, Charlie Norman and Hasse Burman did a parody of the Supremes singing 'Bebbi-Läv'.

The day after the show's premiere, Göran Sellgren wrote in the daily newspaper *Dagens Nyheter*: 'Having become a real institution, this new show is quite entertaining. Its success owes a lot to the presence of Lennie Norman [Charlie's son] and Anni-Frid Lyngstad. Both of them have injected a new youthfulness into the show. Anni-Frid, who is just starting out as an artist, is pretty to look at and nice to listen to. However, the show would be perfect if Hasse Burman didn't pull so many faces and if Anni-Frid were to find a new dressmaker!'

Björn meets Agnetha

On 4 May 1969, Swedish Television recorded a documentary in Gothenburg and in Malmö paying homage to the Swedish composer Jules Sylvain. Among the guests were Agnetha Munther, Ingalill Nilsson, Sten Nilsson, Agnetha Fältskog and Björn Ulvaeus. Björn was on his own, performing the songs 'Tangokavaljeren' (The Tango Dancer) and 'Titta In I Min Lilla Kajuta' (Look In My Little Cabin). Long before the cameras started rolling, the two young singers had already become acquainted. Agnetha, who had admired the Hootenanny Singers' vocalist for a long time, went up to Björn and began, 'Hello, Björn, I've wanted to meet you for a long time. I really admire you!' Björn remembers the moment well: 'I recognized Agnetha immediately, as I'd seen her many times on television. I must admit that even if I didn't like the style of her songs, I found her seductive as a performer. I like her crystal-clear voice. We talked a lot, and I had the impression that we had known each other for a long time.' After the show, Björn and Agnetha began to see more of each other, and in August, they moved into a small studio flat in the Kungsholmen district of Stockholm, overlooking the Karlberg canal.

For the time being, the two young singers had to honour their respective professional engagements. Björn went on the road with the Hootenanny Singers and their new bassist, Lars Christian. Agnetha, for her part, began a summer tour with the singer Hans Smedberg and the eccentric Bertil Bertilsson. She does not have good memories of the summer of 1969: 'I was really fed up with shows. I couldn't stand being apart from Björn. Obviously, we phoned each other often, but that didn't make up for not having him with me.'

The couple tried to keep their relationship secret for as long as possible, but the news soon broke: the headline of one newspaper read 'Agnetha and Björn – the pop romance of the year', forcing the two young lovebirds to make their relationship public. Agnetha announced: 'I don't deny it – we are living together and we're very happy. My only regret is that we couldn't have kept our relationship hidden for longer.' Björn was more reserved with his announcement: 'We've been together for some time and we're in love. For the moment we don't want to make any plans. We are getting to know each other. Time will take care of the rest.' During the autumn, Björn and Agnetha left their tiny Kungsholmen studio flat for a three-roomed flat on Lilla Essingen island, close to the centre of Stockholm.

During the month of May, the Hep Stars decided to split up. Three of the musicians (the new guitarist Gus Horn, Lennart Hegland and Christer Pettersson) carried on under the name of the Rubber Band, with a more rock-style repertoire. Benny, together with singer Svenne Hedlund and his partner Charlotte Walker (better known as Lotta), would carry on with their cabaret tour. Before splitting up for good, the Hep Stars honoured their contract and toured the Swedish parks throughout the summer (this time without Björn, who was on tour with the Hootennany Singers).

Anni-Frid's life took a new turn. Supported by Benny, she now felt stronger and started building on her career, despite numerous criticisms in the press. Between 18 and 29 August, she was appearing again at the Hamburger Börs in Stockholm with *The Charlie Norman Show*. Anni-Frid and Benny were officially engaged on the opening night. This decision was savagely criticized by the daily newspaper *Aftonbladet*, who published a photo of Anni-Frid with Ragnar and their two children, declaring that the singer had intentionally destroyed her marriage to live a dream-like existence with Benny. The journalist added various details about the singer leaving for Stockholm, leaving her family behind, and so on. In response, Anni-Frid didn't mince her words: 'This is all complete fabrication. My divorce had been decided long before I met Benny. Ragnar and myself spent a long time talking before we decided to separate. In view of our situation, there was no other solution.'

31 August   The Hep Stars gave a farewell concert at Kungsträdgården in Stockholm in front of 25,000 people.

3 September   Agnetha appeared at the Aladdin club in Stockholm for one night only, together with her musicians and Bertil Bertilsson.

10 September   Anni-Frid recorded a new single: 'Peter Pan' and 'Du Betonar Kärlek Lite Fel' (You Pronounce the Word Love Badly). Benny produced the two songs and played piano on the tracks. 'Peter Pan' was written by Benny Andersson and Björn Ulvaeus. This was the first time that three future members of ABBA had worked on the same project.

12 September   Benny and Björn produced two songs for the Swedish singer Anna-Lena Löfgren.

25 September   Agnetha and Björn took part in the Grammisgalan 69 (Sweden's music-awards ceremony). Stig Anderson received the Best Songwriter Grammis for his song 'Gröna Små Äpplen' (Little Green Apples), recorded by Swedish jazz singer Monica Zetterlund.

2 October – 29 November   Charlie Norman, Anni-Frid, Hasse Burman and the rest of the company appeared at the Lisebergsteatern in Gothenburg. Maria Salomon wrote in the daily newspaper *Expressen*: 'Yes, Anni-Frid Lyngstad knows how to sing but she doesn't yet have a real stage presence.'

During October, Agnetha and Björn's work brought them together when the couple took part in a nightclub and discotheque tour called TOPP 69, intended to promote new talent from the Swedish charts. Also on the bill were Ola Håkansson, Nilsmen, Nina Lizell and Barbro Skinnar.

The month of November was quite busy for Björn and Benny. They were working on a new project: the writing and recording of music for a Swedish film called *Inga* II. Among the songs was 'Någonting Är På Väg' (Something's On Its Way), which would later feature on their *Lycka* (Happiness) album, and also the song 'She's My Kind of Girl'. Some of the recording sessions were carried over into December. The two musicians, along with Svenne Hedlund and his wife Lotta, were also signed up for a four-month tour of Sweden's main nightclubs, together with their musicians and the Danish comedian Finn Albert. For the whole of December, they performed at Valand in Gothenburg. The reviews were excellent. Göran Sellgren wrote in *Dagens Nyheter*: 'The artists work well as a group. Björn and Benny have got humour, personality and charm. The whole thing is fun, fresh and modern. I would have liked to have heard a bit more of Svenne and Lotta. But in view of the show's qualities, it's certain that there'll be a follow-up.'

From 3 December onwards, Anni-Frid appeared with the rest of the company of *The Charlie Norman Show* at the Berns music hall in Stockholm. Thorleif Hellbom wrote in *Dagens Nyheter*: 'The singers Anni-Frid Lyngstad and Laila Dahlin are not on their best form. This doesn't really work. Maybe it will during the course of the coming performances!' Despite the critics giving Anni-Frid and some other singers a rough ride, the show was a definite success. It stayed at this venue until the end of January before going on tour.

During this period, Stig Anderson and his partner Bengt Bernhag invited Björn and Benny to go into partnership with them to create the music-publishing company Union Songs AB. The Benny Andersson/Björn Ulvaeus partnership could now function on a full-time basis. After having had serious financial problems dogging him for many years due to the Hep Stars' debts, Benny felt the end was in sight. 'All my royalties went straight to the taxman,' he says. 'It took me four years to put right the errors of the past.'

Björn remembers: 'When I introduced Benny to Stig, he didn't think much of our future collaboration. He was finally convinced when he heard the first pieces that we had written together. From the start, we adopted quite an effective way of working. Benny would sit at the piano and I would pick up my guitar. Since we haven't ever been able to write or even read a single note of music, we would record our ideas on tape or play them to Stig in his office straight away.' The three men soon became a very prolific team. Once a melody had been decided upon, Stig would write the lyrics and get his two associates to record the song. By writing the words in English, he promised Björn and Benny an international career.

'BJÖRN WAS WARM AND TENDER. I LOOKED UP TO HIM. HE WAS WELL READ AND INTELLIGENT, VERY WELL INFORMED AND AT HOME WITH MOST THINGS. I WASN'T … HE HAD A CHARMING VOICE AND WAS AN ARTIST, LIKE ME. I FELT THAT WE WERE MARITALLY COMPATIBLE, WHICH IS QUITE APPARENT IN SOME OF THE PICTURES FROM THAT TIME!'
AGNETHA

1970

Björn and Benny's nightclub tour with Svenne and Lotta was due to continue until March, and between 2 and 31 January, the four artists were appearing at the Hamburger Börs in Stockholm as well. They would then appear at the Arkaden in Malmö and tour several other towns. Björn and Benny were also working in the studio on new compositions and preparing demos for other artists, including two tracks for the Swedish singer Billy G-son.

21 January Agnetha recorded two new songs, 'Litet Solskensbarn' (Little Child of the Sun) and 'Om Tårar Vore Guld' (If Tears Were Made of Gold). The second song would be a massive hit in Sweden.

27 February Björn and Benny were in the studio with singer Billy G-son. They wrote and produced two songs for him: 'There's a Little Man' (Agnetha sang in the chorus) and 'I Saw It In the Mirror' (a later version of this track would feature on ABBA's *Ring Ring* album).

March saw the release of Björn and Benny's first single, 'She's My Kind of Girl' and 'Inga Theme'. The two songs were taken from the soundtrack to the film *Inga* II, which wouldn't be released until 30 October 1971.

6 March Anni-Frid recorded two new tracks at EMI studios: 'Där Du Går Lämnar Kärleken Spår' (Love Leaves Its Mark Wherever You Go) and 'Du Var Främling Här Igår' (You Were a Stranger Here Yesterday). Her previous recordings hadn't been as successful as expected, so her record company hesitated before allowing her to record an album. This would eventually take place in the autumn, with Benny producing. But for the time being, Anni-Frid carried on with her performances with *The Charlie Norman Show*, finally leaving the company at the end of June. As far as her single was concerned, *Helsingborgs Dagblad* wrote: 'With her tiny voice, Anni-Frid shares "Där Du Går Lämnar Kärleken Spår" with us, a song better known in English as "Love Grows". Anni-Frid sings a lovely Swedish version which ought to have as much success in this language as the English version. "Du Var Främling Här Igår" is a beautiful ballad which gives us a break from the torrid atmosphere of the A-side. These are two well-chosen songs.'

8 March Anni-Frid took part in a live television transmission lasting the entire evening entitled *Malmö – Stand By*, the proceeds of which would be given to charity for research into multiple sclerosis.

1 April Benny and Anni-Frid moved into a furnished studio flat in Vasastan in Stockholm. The first-floor flat was dark and so cramped that Benny couldn't move his piano in. He smiles when he remembers those days: 'We didn't have any choice, it was either the bed or the piano. For the first time since I was a child, I was living in a house without a piano. I was forced to practise at friends' houses or before concerts. I even played in a church, on a monumental organ. To pass the time, I listened to records a lot, but I really missed my keyboard. Nevertheless, despite these disadvantages, Frida and myself were very happy to be living together.'

A week later, Agnetha, Björn, Benny and Anni-Frid left Sweden for a few days' rest and sunshine in Cyprus. This trip marked the starting point of their future collaboration. 'We took along our guitars,' remembers Björn. 'And for the first time we realized that the girls' voices sounded perfect together. We immediately decided to include Agnetha and Frida in the recording of a future album, *Lycka* [Happiness].'

30 April Björn and Benny went back on tour with Svenne and Lotta, but this time they performed mainly in the country's *folkets parks*. They were accompanied by two Swiss musicians, bassist Gus Horn and drummer John Counz. The show mixed Swedish and English songs. Björn spoke to the audience and cracked jokes between songs. Anders Björkman wrote in

Lotta, Svenne, Benny & Björn on their nightclub tour

Agnetha Fältskog

"Om tårar vore guld"

Veckans komet på Svensktoppen. Direkt in på 5:e plats!

Best.nr. CS 264

CBS-Cupol AB

Expressen: 'This is a good family show. More spontaneous than last winter's tour. As soon as Björn begins a pot-pourri of his hits, you can hear all the young girls sighing. The jokes between the songs are amusing. To tell the truth, the whole show is straightforward and varied. Svenne, Lotta, Björn and Benny have clearly made progress!'

As for Anni-Frid, she was back on tour with Charlie Norman and his company. On 10 May, the singer made a significant return to the Svensktoppen when her single 'Där Du Går Lämnar Kärleken Spår' stayed at No. 8 for two weeks. A touch disillusioned, Anni-Frid declared in *Expressen*: 'The charts and me, that's a long story! I think I must hold the record for the greatest number of songs which have never made the charts … In three years, I've made eight records. Two of them have made the charts. The first one, "Härlig Är Vår Jord" spent a week in the hit parade. No longer than that.' Concerning the new song, Anni-Frid said: 'It won't stay in the charts for long. The public prefer songs with more melody. My style is too independent for the charts. But I like my records. And I think there's a quality about my songs.' Regarding her work with Charlie Norman, she said: 'We stay with him because we feel good with his company. But to tell the truth, I don't feel at ease on stage. I'm not sure of myself and I have stage fright. As a result, I become too static. I'll find a remedy for that in the future.'

16 May Agnetha gave the first concert of her summer tour in Karlshamn, in front of an audience of about 1000 people. She was accompanied on stage by singer-comedian Bert-Åke Varg and Rolf Carvenius's orchestra: Tommy Wåhlberg (guitar), Hans Johnsson (keyboard), Per-Arne Eklund (bass) and Birgitta Nordgren (drums). Among the songs that were best received by the audience were her new single 'Om Tårar Vore Guld' and a duet with Bert-Åke entitled 'Blommor Och Bin' (The Flowers and the Bees). Agnetha said of her partner: 'It's great to work with Bert-Åke, he's a real comedian. He knows how to work the audience.'

At the beginning of June, Björn and Benny began the studio recordings for *Lycka*. For several months, they had been preparing numerous demos. Not having found any musicians to perform them, they decided, in agreement with Stig, to work on an entire album on which they would sing together. Agnetha helped to write the song 'Liselott' and sang backing vocals with Anni-Frid on several songs. The ABBA musical 'family' gradually formed around the four young people, along with Sven-Olof Walldoff (conductor and arranger) and especially Michael B. Tretow, who would become Björn and Benny's sound engineer. Despite earlier professional concerns, Agnetha's optimism returned during her summer tour. Every time she started to sing her hit 'Om Tårar Vore Guld', the audience went wild. She told a journalist from *Aftonbladet*: 'It's fantastic, as soon as they play the first notes of the song, I can see people kissing each other in the audience.'

21–25 June Agnetha took a break from her tour. A recording session was arranged in a Parisian studio (probably for the French version of 'Om Tårar Vore Guld'), but curiously the session was cancelled at the last moment, and was replaced by a German-language recording session in Berlin.

'WE ASKED THE GIRLS TO HELP OUT WITH THE BACKING VOCALS FOR ONE OF THE RECORDS AND THAT WAS THE BIRTH OF THE WHOLE THING. PURE COINCIDENCE; I MEAN, WE COULD HAVE MET WITH TWO OFFICE GIRLS WHO COULDN'T SING AT ALL AND THEN THERE WOULDN'T HAVE BEEN ANY ABBA, I'M SURE.' BJÖRN

7 July Björn joined his friends Tony and Hansi (from the Hootenanny Singers) for a single concert given as part of the Västervik Song Festival, held in the ruins of Stegeholm Castle. Agnetha went along to support him.

25 July Agnetha and her company were singing in Gamleby. A few days later, Anders Björkman wrote in *Expressen*: 'The Agnetha Fältskog show is really going well, better than her show last year. However, there is one problem. When Agnetha and Bert-Åke Varg sing their duets "Blommor Och Bin" and "Inge Och Sten", everything goes perfectly. However when they perform their numerous solo numbers, it doesn't go so well. Why don't they stay together on stage for those numbers?'

29 August Agnetha ended her summer tour in Västerfärnebo, after forty-two concerts.

30 August Björn and Benny gave their last concerts with Svenne and Lotta in Bollnäs and Hudiksvall.

4 September On her return to Stockholm, Agnetha went into the studio to complete her third album, *Som Jag Är* (As I Am). Björn co-produced the record with Karl 'Little Gerhard' Lundkvist and performed a superb duet with Agnetha entitled 'Så Här Börjär Kärlek' (That's How Love Begins). The song very nearly didn't appear on the album because Stig Anderson usually refused to let any Polar Music artist feature on a rival label's record. He was against the release of the song as a single and Björn wasn't credited on the sleeve of Agnetha's album.

8 September Benny began producing Anni-Frid's first album at EMI studios. Among the songs recorded were several cover versions: 'Lycka' (by Björn and Benny), 'En Ton Av Tystnad' ('Sound of Silence' by Simon & Garfunkel) and 'En Lång Och Ödslig Väg' ('The Long and Winding Road' by the Beatles). 'At that time,' Frida says, 'you had to have several hit singles to your credit before you were able to record an entire album. That wasn't the case for me. In addition, my record company considered that I still hadn't found my style. They categorized me too much as a "jazz singer" and thought that I wasn't commercial enough. Benny let me tackle a repertoire which was more pop-based.'

Björn and Benny put the finishing touches to their *Lycka* album, due for release in the autumn. Although it received a lukewarm reception from the critics, the first single, 'Hej Gamle Man' (Hello Old Man), seemed to be popular with the radio programmers and the public. With Agnetha and Frida on backing vocals, 'Hej Gamle Man' can be considered to be the first song recorded by the future quartet.

29 September The two couples took part in the radio show *Våra Favoriter*. Agnetha sang 'Som Ett Eko' and Anni-Frid performed 'Barnen Sover', accompanied by Björn and Benny. The quartet also performed their new hit, 'Hej Gamle Man' and talked about the show they would be doing at the Trägårn nightclub in Gothenburg. Rehearsals would begin at the beginning of October.

4 October Anni-Frid, Benny and Stig attended Charlie Norman's fiftieth birthday party at his house in Bro.

Agnetha's third album, *Som Jag Är*, was released in October. It was accompanied by a single, 'Som Ett Eko' (Like an Echo). Göran Sellgren wrote in *Dagens Nyheter*: 'Agnetha Fältskog isn't too fussy as far as the choice of her singles is concerned – "Zigenarvän" proved that. And her new album *Som Jag Är* doesn't show any improvement. However, she doesn't sing too badly and the record is well arranged by Sven-Olof Walldoff.'

'I MUST HAVE SOME SORT OF RECORD IN FAILING TO GET INTO THE CHARTS.' FRIDA

'HOW CAN YOU CRITICIZE TWO COUPLES WHO HAD FALLEN IN LOVE AND WERE SINGING TOGETHER? THAT'S WHAT WE DID! IT WAS NOT A CONTROLLED IMAGE, IT WAS ABSOLUTELY NATURAL!' BJÖRN

'WE REALLY STARTED WORKING TOGETHER A LOT IN 1970 AND THE GIRLS BECAME INVOLVED AS WELL. I THINK BJÖRN AND I DECIDED THAT IT WAS STUPID FOR US TO SING WHEN WE HAD TWO SUCH GREAT SINGERS CLOSE TO US.' **BENNY**

Björn & Benny with Finn Alberth on TV in Sweden

21 October Swedish Television screened the first in a series of four music programmes entitled *När Stenkakan Slog*. Each programme featured current artists singing old Swedish hits from 1915–55. Anni-Frid was one of the celebrities invited (with Svenne, Lotta and Björn Skifs). Among other songs, she sang 'Ole Lukköje, Vad Gör Det Att Vi Skiljs För I Afton?' (What Does It Matter That We're Breaking Up Tonight?), 'Att Älska I Vårens Tid' (To Love In the Springtime), 'Min Soldat' (My Soldier), 'Söderhavets Sång' (Song of the Southern Sea), 'I Min Blommiga Blå Krinolin' (In My Flowered Blue Crinoline).

The media was becoming more and more interested in the four Swedes and their record 'Hej Gamle Man'. On Saturday 31 October, they appeared together on television for the first time on a programme called I *Stället För Tarzan* (Instead of Tarzan).

1 November A very important date: Björn, Benny, Agnetha and Anni-Frid gave their first concert together at the Trägårn in Gothenburg. Performing at this club has become a traditional route to the top for the majority of Swedish artists. They called their show *Festfolket* (a play on words which loosely translates as 'engaged couples'). The show consisted of several songs sung by the four of them together and various cover versions, interspersed with sketches. With the exception of some strong numbers like 'Hej Gamle Man' and Frida's song 'Tre Kvart Från Nu' (Three Quarters of an Hour From Now), the show was not a success. The reception they received from the critics was lukewarm, and for the first few evenings, there weren't many people in the audience. Björn has never been proud of this performance: 'The results weren't too good. It was one of the worst times we ever had. Fortunately, we repaired the damage afterwards, when we sang at the Strand club in Stockholm. The problem, we realized, was in the material and not in us. This experience proved that if we wanted to carry on together, it would be better to perform our own songs.'

Sonya Hedenbratt was quite positive in *Expressen*: 'It's a show for everyone – it makes you laugh a lot but also gives you something to think about. "Lycka" is a song which stays in my mind. I was pleasantly surprised by Agnetha who I'd never seen on stage before. Anni-Frid, for her part, seems to have matured since the last time. Finally, it can be said that the four young people provide a varied and rhythmic musical show, with lyrics that do not lack bite. The *Festfolket* works just as well on stage as in town!' And Viveca Sundvall wrote in *Aftonbladet*: 'For the first time, Benny, Björn and their fiancées Anni-Frid and Agnetha, appear live. Agnetha Fältskog, who doesn't quite have an ear for music, as shocking as it may seem, sang her way through a sentimental classic. The two engaged couples are really cute and that's how they want to be seen.'

After a series of concerts at the Strand club in Stockholm (1–20 December), they all returned to their previous activities. Anni-Frid continued with the recording of her new album, while Agnetha promoted her new single 'En Sång Och En Saga' (A Song and a Story). The song is a cover version of 'La Première Etoile' by Mireille Mathieu; the Swedish lyrics were written by Stig Anderson.

The year finished well for them all, with 'Hej Gamle Man' staying at No. 1 in the Swedish charts for five consecutive weeks. Björn and Benny received a letter of congratulation from the Salvation Army. Björn announced in an interview: 'We've been invited to sing soon at a Salvation Army gala in Gothenburg. The lyrics of our song have got nothing to do with religion. It simply asks the question: how does a Salvation Army soldier always manage to keep his smile?'

1971

7–8 January Björn and Benny (accompanied by Agnetha and Anni-Frid) recorded 'Hej Musikant', the German-language version of 'Hej Gamle Man'. For the B-side, they chose 'Livet Går Sin Gång' (Life Goes At Its Own Pace), which became 'Was die Liebe Sagt' in German. The German lyrics were written by producer Hans Bradtke. The single was only released in Germany. The two musicians discovered that their song 'The Language of Love' (in Swedish, 'Livet Går Sin Gång') would soon be recorded by Françoise Hardy in both French and English.

In the middle of January, Anni-Frid and Benny completed the studio recordings for the album *Frida*. Prior to its launch, the record company EMI released a first single from the album, featuring the tracks 'Tre Kvart Från Nu' and 'En Liten Sång Om Kärlek' (A Little Song About Love). During this time, Agnetha and Björn spent two weeks on holiday in The Gambia.

26 January The two couples were among 225 guests at a massive party organized by Stig Anderson at his villa in Nacka, near Stockholm, for his birthday. Among the numerous gifts the producer received was a 10-metre-high flagpole!

20 February Björn and Benny celebrated an encouraging success overseas, when the English-language version of 'Livet Går Sin Gång' (The Language of Love) came sixth in the Malaga Song Festival. American singer Donna Hightower won first prize.

14 March Agnetha, Björn, Benny and Anni-Frid gave a concert in Hammarby, Stockholm, to mark the opening of the OK Biva-Huset service station.

31 March Frida's first album was released. The cover, designed by Ola Lager, had a gatefold sleeve. Although the photos inside the sleeve were excellent, the cover photo of Anni-Frid didn't do her justice. The album was praised by the critics. Hans Fridlund wrote in *Expressen*: 'I really don't know why Anni-Frid's records aren't more successful. She is one of our best singers, superior to all the other women in the charts. At least with Miss Lyngstad, she has personality and an unusual style.' *Dagens Nyheter*'s view was: 'It's time to take Anni-Frid Lyngstad seriously. It's a strong, perfect first album, gentle but still with lots of personality, humour, tenderness and even anger. When she sings, you realize that she's got something between her ears. Her style, which is quite simple, is unusually intelligent.' In *Folket*, Tommy Eriksson wrote: 'The *Frida* album is the perfect exclamation mark. A completely professional product with surprising precision. Not only does she have a voice full of great feeling but she is also sensual and expressive. She sings "Telegram För Fullmånen" so well that she really warms our hearts. It has everything: emotion, warmth and tenderness, which all adds up to make Anni-Frid a rare and intelligent artist.'

23 April Björn and Benny recorded a new single, 'Det Kan Ingen Doktor Hjälpa' (No Doctor Can Help That) and 'På Bröllop' (At the Wedding). Agnetha and Frida sang backing vocals.

30 April Agnetha, Björn and Benny began a tour of the parks which would last for several months (the first concerts were in Alingsås and Lidköping). The shows usually took place at the end of the week, leaving the three artists time to work on other projects. During a half-hour set, they performed about a dozen songs – their hits, of course, but also a cover of Graham Nash's 'Teach Your Children' and two comic sketches: 'Arga Unga Män' (Angry Young Men) by Bosse Carlgren and 'Koskenkorva' (the brand name of a Finnish vodka) by Lars Berghagen. They were accompanied on stage by Göran Lagerberg on bass and Kjell Jeppson on drums.

Hans Fridlund wrote in *Expressen*: 'It's a charming show from the trio Agnetha, Björn and Benny. They are good on stage and Björn and Agnetha seem very

loving as a couple. In total, there are ten songs which are very chart-oriented, although some of the songs are quite weak. Most memorable is a superb version of Graham Nash's "Teach Your Children" and two amusing sketches. Björn Ulvaeus still sings with a little nasal sound which is characteristic of him, whilst Miss Fältskog is still limited vocally. I'm sure that will change over the years . . .'. Bengt Melin, in *Aftonbladet*, wrote: 'The show is sincere, simple and very "hit parade". Agnetha Fältskog has more stage presence and sings more in tune now. Björn Ulvaeus got lots of applause for "Hej Gamle Man" and for his duets. As for Benny Andersson, he's a real stage animal these days. But it looks like they've gone for the easy option. It's a shame they don't put more into different songs. Benny is one of our rare real composers.'

13 May   Agnetha went back into the Metronome studios to begin recording her fourth album *När En Vacker Tanke Blir En Sång* (When a Beautiful Idea Becomes a Song). Björn helped to write some of the songs and produced the entire record.

25 May   The two couples were together again in the Europa Film studios for the recording of Lill-Babs's single 'Välkommen Till Världen' (Welcome To the World). The song, composed by Björn and Benny, had been rejected by the Swedish Eurovision-selection jury. The two musicians produced the record, provided some of the musical parts and, together with Agnetha and Frida, sang backing vocals.

At the beginning of June, Anni-Frid went to Malta with singer Lars (Lasse) Berghagen to rehearse for their summer tour of the Swedish parks. Lars and Frida recorded two duets which were released as a single on the Polydor label, 'En Kväll Om Sommaren' (A Summer's Evening) and 'Vi Vet Allt Men Nästan Inget' (We Know Everything But Almost Nothing).

15 June   Agnetha, Björn and Benny sang on the television programme *Midsommardans Från Solliden* on Sweden's TV2. This programme, recorded at Skansen park in Stockholm, brought together a host of stars including Lill-Babs, Brita Borg and the conductor Sven-Olof Walldoff. Among other songs, Agnetha sang the two tracks from her new single, 'Kungens Vaktparad' (The Parade of the Royal Guard) and 'Jag Vill Att Du Ska Bli Lycklig' (I Want You To Be Happy).

6 July   Björn and Agnetha were married in the little church of Verum, a parish of Skåne in southern Sweden. The couple tried to keep the ceremony secret, but more than 3000 people invaded the village to witness the wedding of the year. Agnetha arrived in a horse-drawn carriage, and when she made her entrance into church, Mendelssohn's 'Wedding March' rang out, followed by 'Wedding', an old Hep Stars song, played on the organ by Benny. Björn recalls: 'When I contacted the minister Uno Wardener, he asked me what our profession was and he thought I said "atheist" instead of "artist". Shocked, he replied that he wouldn't be able to carry out the service!'

Anni-Frid with Lars Berghagen & his musicians, Bo Dahlman, Lasse Svensson & Lukas Lindholm

When they came out of the church, the crowd surged forward. The couple fought their way through to the waiting carriage and Agnetha had her foot trodden on by one of the horses. The ceremony was followed by a dinner at the Wittsjö inn for thirty-nine guests and Ada, the newlyweds' black bulldog. On the menu were smoked eel, tournedos and Arctic berry ice-cream.

'Björn and I found this church when we were on tour,' remembers Agnetha. 'I'd always dreamed of getting married in a little white church. I must say that I was overjoyed, the ceremony was definitely one of the best days of my life. After the service, part of the crowd followed us to the inn shouting "We want to see the newlyweds!" Björn and myself were forced to appear on the first-floor balcony. We were treated like a royal couple.' There was to be no honeymoon, as Agnetha and Björn were due back on tour four days later.

'WE WANTED A FAMILY AND PLANNED CHILDREN FROM THE START, BUT NO BABY CAME ALONG. I BEGAN TO GO FOR TESTS. EVERY MONTH I WAS DISAPPOINTED WHEN NOTHING HAPPENED. WE EVEN THOUGHT ABOUT ADOPTION … WHEN I EVENTUALLY BECAME PREGNANT, I COULD HARDLY BELIEVE IT… I RANG BJÖRN AND YELLED DOWN THE PHONE, "WE'RE GOING TO HAVE A BABY!" HE WAS OVERJOYED AND CAME STRAIGHT HOME WITH A BOTTLE OF CHAMPAGNE.' **AGNETHA**

Linköping Folkets Park

The day after the ceremony, Stig received a telephone call from Stockholm informing him of the suicide of his friend and associate Bengt Bernhag, who had been one of the founders of Polar Music. Bengt had discovered the Hootenanny Singers and had personally taken care of their career. He had suffered serious health problems during the past year and had turned down the invitation to the wedding of his protégé, thinking that he was too physically run-down. Björn, who had thought of him as a second father, was profoundly affected by his death. 'I owe him so much,' he explained. 'He taught me the ropes of this profession. Still shocked by this terrible news, Stig asked me to go out with him for a boat trip on the lake next to the inn. He wanted to ask me discreetly to take over from Bengt at Polar Music. I accepted on the sole condition that Benny would also be part of our collaboration. Stig accepted but offered just one salary between us.'

12 July Anni-Frid recorded two new songs for her next single, 'Min Egen Stad' (My Home Town) and 'En Gång Är Ingen Gång' (Once Is Not At All).

15 July Benny and Björn recorded some new demos with a view to making a second album as a duo. A single was released the following month, including 'Tänk Om Jorden Vore Ung' (Just Think If the World Was Young), with Agnetha and Frida on backing vocals, from the *Lycka* album and a new song, 'Träskofolket' (People In Clogs). This song was inspired by 'Utvandrarna' (The Emigrants), a classic book by Swedish writer Vilhelm Moberg in which he relates that in the nineteenth century, Americans nicknamed the Swedes who had emigrated to the United States 'the people in clogs'. Despite the fact that some other songs were completed during the following months, for some reason, Björn and Benny's second album would never see the light of day.

From now on, the two men would be full-time producers at the heart of Polar Music. Their first production was a compilation album for the Hootenanny Singers entitled *Våra Vackraste Visor* (Our Most Beautiful Songs). They then produced an album entitled *Lena* for Swedish singer Lena Andersson, and the first record for Polar Music's promising new artist, Ted Gärdestad. Stig remembered: 'We auditioned Ted and his brother Kenneth two years previously. They had a lot of talent but were too young to start a singing career.

When Ted came back to see us again, Björn and Benny immediately wanted to work with him. His first album worked really well and he was even the subject of a TV documentary.'

8 August   Anni-Frid and Lars Berghagen reached No. 8 in the Svensktoppen with 'En Kväll Om Sommaren'. Their tour of the Swedish parks ended on 28 August. Hans Fridlund wrote in *Expressen*: 'It's saying a lot to describe it as a real show. The ensemble enter the stage from the left and go off in the same direction 35 minutes later. In that time they give us eight songs and two very bad monologues, written by Lena Hansson … But thanks go to Miss Lyngstad, who is an exceptional singer!'

28 August   Agnetha, Björn and Benny ended their summer tour with two concerts in Eskilstuna and Köping.

During the month of September, Björn and Benny dedicated their time to writing and recording new songs for Lena Andersson and Ted Gärdestad. Agnetha and Anni-Frid sang backing vocals on a number of the songs.

22 October   Anni-Frid made her début at the Folkan Theatre, Stockholm, in a variety show called *Mina Favoriter*. The show, devised by entertainer Kar de Mumma, was produced by Hasse Ekman. He brought together a host of stars including Siw Malmkvist, Siv Ericks, Lars Berghagen, Stig Järrel and Rolf

Bengtson. Anni-Frid performed three songs in the show, including a duet with Lars Berghagen, 'Vem Släcker Månen' (Who Turns Out the Moon) and another with singer Siv Ericks. *Mina Favoriter* ran for seven months.

Anni-Frid's single 'Min Egen Stad' went straight into the Svensktoppen at No. 3. The song, which stayed in the charts for six weeks, reached No. 1 on 7 November. It was her first real hit, and EMI decided to issue a new pressing of the *Frida* album featuring 'Min Egen Stad'.

During the autumn, Benny, Björn and Anni-Frid finished the recording of Agnetha's fourth album, *När En Vacker Tanke Blir En Sång*. Its release was planned for the end of November.

30 October The film *Någon Att Älska* (Someone To Love) – formerly titled *Inga* II – was released, with music by Björn Ulvaeus and Benny Andersson. Filmed in Sweden by the American director Joseph W. Sarno, with Tommy Blom in the main role, the full-length feature lacked a plot and was a resounding flop.

3 December Polar Music released the Hootenanny Singers compilation album. To mark the occasion, Swedish Television screened a 35-minute programme entitled *Visunderhållning* (Entertainment By Song). The Hootenanny Singers, accompanied by Benny on accordion, were interviewed and performed six new songs.

1972

10 January Anni-Frid recorded her last single for the EMI label. The A-side, 'Vi Är Alla Bara Barn I Början' (We Are All Just Children In the Beginning), was written by Benny and Björn and featured backing vocals by Agnetha. The B-side was called 'Kom Och Sjung En Sång' (Come and Sing a Song). In France, the singer Sheila recorded the song under the title 'Plus De Chansons Tristes'.

During January, Benny and Frida left their flat in Stockholm to move into a house that they had bought in Vallentuna, in the north of the capital.

24 January Björn accompanied Agnetha to Gothenburg, where the singer was to audition for the role of Mary Magdalene in the Swedish production of the musical *Jesus Christ Superstar*. The production team were very impressed with Agnetha's voice, and at the end of the auditions, producer Lars Schmidt announced: 'This is the singer we've been looking for.' The rest of the cast of forty and the musicians would be chosen over the next few days.

25 January Some of the Swedish cast (including those chosen for the leading roles, Agnetha Fältskog, Titti Sjöblom and Funny Holmqvist) went to see the Danish production of *Jesus Christ Superstar*, playing in Copenhagen, and met Peter Winsnes, who was going to play the part of Jesus in Sweden. On their return to Gothenburg, rehearsals began immediately, as the premiere was scheduled for 18 February. Conductor Peter Kragerup declared in *Expressen*: 'If we want to be ready in time, we need to rehearse 12 hours a day!'

29 January Björn and Benny were in London with Lena Andersson to record 'Säg Det Med En Sång' (Say It With a Song) and 'Cecilia' (a song which was intended for inclusion on Björn and Benny's second album). Lena would perform 'Säg Det Med En Sång' at the forthcoming Melodifestivalen. Assisted by Wayne Bickerton and Tony Waddington (the future producers of the Rubettes), they also recorded 'Better To Have Loved', the English-language version of 'Säg Det Med En Sång'. Even though the jury didn't choose the song to represent Sweden at the Eurovision Song Contest (it came third), it became a hit in Scandinavia anyway, entering the Swedish charts at No. 1 on 9 April.

4 February Agnetha was in the Metronome studios recording two songs from *Jesus Christ Superstar*: 'Vart Ska Min Kärlek Föra' ('I Don't Know How To Love Him') and 'Nu Ska Du Bli Stilla' ('Everything's Alright'), which were produced by Björn. A double album from the show would be recorded the following month.

14 February The photographer Roger Thuresson organized a session of promotional photographs of Björn and Benny in the snow in Skansen park.

19 February The day after the premiere of *Jesus Christ Superstar* at the Scandinavium in Gothenburg, the show was slated by the critics and also by a preacher, Ingemar Simonsson, who declared to the press: 'This is forgery and a commercial exploitation of the Bible. Jesus is portrayed as an insipid, tasteless character. The show is misleading!' Journalist Alf Thoor wrote in *Expressen*: 'The Gothenburg version is worse than the one in Copenhagen: weaker, more abstract and without any character of its own. The show was professional in Denmark. In Gothenburg the performance verges on amateurism. Perhaps there is enthusiasm and good intentions, but no knowledge of theatrical techniques. Peter Winsnes doesn't really seem to be in his role as Jesus. Agnetha Fältskog, as Mary Magdalene, is a sweet young girl and she knows how to sing, but no more than that. The same applies to the rest of the cast, who just sing their songs and mime their roles. And the sound system was a real catastrophe too!'

'I REMEMBER THAT
NEWSPAPERS
ASKED IF I REALLY
WAS A RELIGIOUS
PERSON. I AM
NOT RELIGIOUS,
ALTHOUGH I NEED
TO BELIEVE IN
SOMETHING,
LIKE MANY PEOPLE.
SO IN A WAY YOU
CAN SAY THAT
I AM A RELIGIOUS
PERSON. I THOUGHT
IT WAS TREMENDOUS
TO GET A ROLE,
TO ACT AND SING
AT THE SAME TIME.'
AGNETHA
ON *JESUS
CHRIST SUPERSTAR*

Benny, Anni-Frid, Titti Sjöblom & Bruno Wintzell at Expressen's annual Spring Party

At the beginning of March, the song 'She's My Kind of Girl', which had been released two years earlier in Sweden, became a hit in Japan. A Japanese publisher had heard the song by chance while visiting Paris and arranged to distribute the record in his own country. Only Björn and Benny were credited on the sleeve.

After about a dozen performances at the Scandinavium in Gothenburg, the *Jesus Christ Superstar* company went on tour. Agnetha, completely absorbed with rehearsals for her new solo show, left the company. The role of Mary Magdalene was taken over by Titti Sjöblom.

26 March   Agnetha went straight into the Svensktoppen at No. 2 with 'Vart Ska Min Kärlek Föra'. She announced to the press: 'I had no doubt that the song would be a success but I didn't think that it would happen so quickly. It's a real surprise!' The singer had just come back from Frankfurt, where she had recorded some songs in German, and was now getting ready to face the audiences in the Swedish parks. 'Even if I'm no longer playing the role of Mary Magdalene,' she explained, 'I'm going to sing the song in my new show. On stage I'll be accompanied by four musicians and four dancers.'

During March and April, Björn, Benny, Agnetha and Anni-Frid were in the studio putting the finishing touches to some new songs. Among the new tracks was 'People Need Love', which is thought to be the first song to feature

the ABBA sound. Björn explains: 'We wanted this record to sound like the mixed groups who were in fashion at that time, in the style of Middle Of The Road or Blue Mink. The idea of yodelling at the end of the song came from Agnetha and Frida.'

10 April   Björn, Benny and Anni-Frid were present at the traditional Spring Party organized by *Expressen* at the Operakällaren restaurant. Among the four hundred guests were members of the cast of *Jesus Christ Superstar*, now playing in Stockholm: Titti Sjöblom and Bruno Wintzell, and also Tim Rice, the show's original lyricist.

29 April   The Hootenanny Singers stepped back into the spotlight in Sweden. This time the group was made up of Björn, Benny, Hansi Schwarz, Tony Rooth, Kjell Jeppson, Hans Bergkvist and Rutger Gunnarsson, who replaced bassist Johan Karlberg. For Rutger, it was the beginning of a long and fruitful collaboration with Björn and Benny. The tour lasted the whole summer, but the group performed only at weekends.

30 April   It was Agnetha's turn to begin her tour of the Swedish parks in Kisa and Gamleby. Inger Marie Opperud wrote in *Expressen*: 'This summer, Agnetha offers a show which is a bit more complicated than usual. Instead of just standing on stage and performing her own songs, she gives us another repertoire. Among the songs she performs is one by singer Git Gay. Agnetha

Agnetha's Git Gay parody

is also joined by the four dancers of the Cocco ballet. Agnetha sings with lots of self-confidence. Contrary to what we might think, she is more than just a recording artist. She is worth listening to on stage, without all the techniques of the recording studio.'

At the end of May, Lena Andersson was invited to compete in the Tokyo Song Festival with 'Better To Have Loved'. This song, composed by Björn, Benny and Stig, received an ovation from the audience. It was announced that the song had won the prizes for Best Song and Best Lyrics. Stig and Lena went on stage to receive the awards, but the next day something astonishing took place. Stig recalled: 'During the prizegiving, Lena and I each received a cup. The next day, the festival organizers called to tell me that Lena had not received the prize for Best Song. The real winner would be the French musician Frank Pourcel. I must admit that I didn't understand! However, we were not disappointed, because Lena achieved great success in Japan. We had a lot of interest from television, radio and the press.'

During June, the single 'People Need Love' was released in Sweden, under the name of 'Björn, Benny, Agnetha and Anni-Frid'. It reached No. 17 on Kvällstoppen (the evening chart which included songs sung in other languages as well as Swedish). Agnetha and Anni-Frid were still under contract to their respective record companies and a credit saying 'by courtesy of …' was included on the sleeve. For the B-side, Björn and Benny chose an English adaptation of their song 'En Karusell', which became 'Merry-Go-Round'. In Japan, the record company curiously chose this track for the A-side, but with a different mix. This first record as a group marked a new stage in the careers of the four young Swedes. 'From that time on, we were convinced that we could work together as a quartet and contemplate doing more things,' says Björn. 'But we weren't in a rush, since Agnetha was still under contract to CBS-Cupol.'

'IT GOT TO THE POINT WHERE THE GIRLS WERE DOING MORE OF THE UPFRONT SINGING THAN WE WERE OURSELVES. SO WE SAID "WHY DON'T WE MAKE A REGULAR GROUP OF IT ALL?"' BENNY

At this time, Björn and Agnetha announced to the press that they were expecting their first child.

1 July Agnetha participated in the television programme *Gammeldans*, transmitted live from Mollagården in Östarp. It consisted of a mix of popular artists and folk-dance groups. The other guests were Sten Nilsson, Annika Risberg and Arne Bertini.

2 July Agnetha performed on stage at Kungsträdgården in Stockholm as part of the *Sommar i Centrum* gala presented by Hagge Geigert. She was accompanied by her musicians and the ballet company Cocco.

After the success of 'People Need Love' in Scandinavia, Stig decided to test the song in the United States. The record was released on the Playboy Records label, under the name of Björn and Benny with Svenska Flicka. Unfortunately, as the result of distribution problems, the single went unnoticed in America.

During various recording sessions, Björn and Benny got to know new musicians. Bonds were formed and little by little their musical family grew. Drummer Ola Brunkert, guitarist Janne Schaffer and bassists Mike Watson and Rutger Gunnarsson were regularly in the studio and on stage with them.

At that time, Anni-Frid was touring the Swedish parks with Roffe Berg. Her contract with EMI having expired, she naturally signed to the Polar Music label, for whom she recorded two new songs, 'Man Vill Ju Leva Lite Dessemellan' (You Still Want To Live a Bit In Between) and 'Ska Man Skratta Eller Gråta' (Should We Laugh Or Cry). The single was produced by Björn and Benny, who also sang on the backing vocals together with Agnetha.

26 August Agnetha's summer tour ended with two concerts in Örebro and Vretstorp.

The Japanese record company were looking for a follow-up to the hit 'She's My Kind of Girl'. There was even talk of a special album for the Japanese market. Nevertheless, Björn and Benny had some difficulties with their Japanese representatives, who thought their lyrics were not commercial enough. After 'Santa Rosa' was rejected, the song 'Love Has Its Ways', written by Koichi Morita, was submitted to the two musicians. After some negotiation, the single was released with a new track entitled 'Rock 'n' Roll Band' on the B-side.

With December approaching, Stig was planning to release a record of the most popular Christmas tunes in Sweden. He asked Björn and Benny to produce *När Juldagsmorgon Glimmar* (When Christmas Morning Is Shining), an album bringing together all of Polar Music's artists (including Lena Andersson, Svenne Hedlund and Arne Lamberth). Agnetha was not available, due to her contract with CBS-Cupol. Frida chose to sing her two favourite songs, 'När Det Lider Mot Jul' (When Christmas Is Coming) and 'Gläns Över Sjö Och Strand' (It's Shining Over the Lake and the Shore). Two tracks by the Hootenanny Singers were also featured on the album: 'Nu Tändas Tusen Juleljus' (A Thousand Christmas Candles Are Being Lit) and 'Gå Sion, Din Konung Att Möta' (Go Sion, To Meet Your King).

Then, for the second time in her career, Anni-Frid hit No. 1 on the Swedish hit parade. This time, it was the song 'Man Vill Ju Leva Lite Dessemellan' which had taken her to the top of the charts. The song, which entered the Swedish charts on 17 September, was a cover version of the Italian song 'Chia Salta Il Fosso'.

18 September Agnetha recorded a new single which was produced by Björn, 'Tio Mil Kvar Till Korpilombolo' (Ten Miles More To Korpilombolo) and 'Så Glad Som Dina Ögon' (As Happy As Your Eyes). The record entered the Swedish charts on 10 December and reached No. 5.

8 October EMI, hoping to benefit from Anni-Frid's recent success, released a compilation album featuring a selection of her best Swedish songs from the period 1967–71.

10 October The single 'People Need Love' was released in France and Belgium on the Vogue label, thanks to Alain Boublil, one of the first to sign a contract with Stig Anderson. Alain recounts: 'I had created Baboo, my own music production and publishing company. One day Stig, who was a very good friend, brought me 'People Need Love'. That's how it all started. We signed the contract and the disc was distributed by Vogue.'

21 October Björn and Benny were working again with Ted Gärdestad, who was recording his second album, *Ted*, in the Metronome studios. By now, the project for Björn and Benny's second album as a duo had definitely been abandoned. After the success of 'People Need Love', Stig reckoned that from now on the quartet could envisage a career beyond Scandinavia. He persuaded the four of them to do an album in English, with Agnetha and Anni-Frid doing most of the singing. Among the first tracks to be recorded were 'Nina, Pretty Ballerina' and 'He Is Your Brother'.

In the middle of November, Björn, Benny, Agnetha and Frida flew to Japan, where their single 'She's My Kind of Girl' had sold more than 500,000 copies. The two couples were welcomed as superstars. CBS Japan took advantage of the visit to release the single 'Love Has Its Ways'.

At the same time, Polar Music released the quartet's second single in Scandinavia, featuring 'He Is Your Brother', with 'Santa Rosa' on the B-side.

On their return to Stockholm, as the group were busy preparing the new album, some good news arrived from the National Television Society. The quartet were invited to put forward a song for selection for the Eurovision Song Contest. Stig, Benny and Björn saw it as an excellent opportunity to reach a larger public. The three men quickly set to work, deciding to compose the song in the calm environment of the island of Viggsö, in the Swedish archipelago, where Björn and Agnetha, Benny and Frida, and Stig and Gudrun all owned chalets. Benny said: 'Out there, you can really get stuck into things. No unwanted telephone calls, no recording studios, nothing. We just write and eat and down the odd beer – or something a bit stronger.' Stig added: 'We usually write a great deal at Christmas and New Year. And once we really get started, it doesn't matter what time of the day or night it is. If we've been working all night, we can sleep all day instead. Nobody comes to disturb us.'

Agnetha's pregnancy was closely documented by the women's press. At the beginning of December, *Vecko-Revyn* magazine chose to put the group on the front of their Christmas issue. The two couples were photographed in a Christmas Eve dinner setting, in Agnetha and Björn's flat. The coverline was: 'At home with Björn Ulvaeus and Agnetha Fältskog: their last Christmas without a child.'

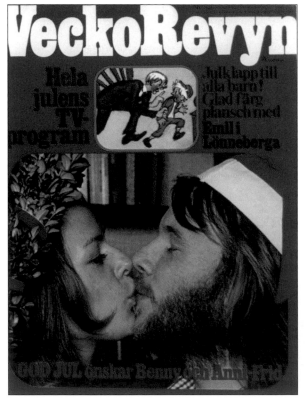

Frida & Agnetha during the *Vecko-Revyn* Christmas photo session

'WE HAVE TO CONFESS THAT IT WAS A BIT OF A GIMMICK TO HAVE SOMEONE AS WELL KNOWN AS NEIL SEDAKA WRITING "RING RING". WE THOUGHT THAT MIGHT CREATE AN INTEREST IN THE SONG.' BJÖRN

1973

On their return from Viggsö, the whole team began planning their work schedule for the next few months. From now on, Björn, Benny, Agnetha and Anni-Frid would be working together full-time as a group and Stig intended to ensure that his four protégés would be successful beyond the borders of Scandinavia. Stig knew the Eurovision Song Contest was an opportunity not to be missed. He had every confidence in Björn and Benny, who had already written several songs for the event. 'From the start we knew that we had to present a pop song, as opposed to the usual sugary-sweet songs which are in the contest,' remembers Björn. 'As for the lyrics, Stig searched for a short title. This is how "Ring Ring" came out. At the time, it was definitely our best song.'

9 January Björn and Benny went to Michael B. Tretow's home to prepare themselves for the following day's recording session at the Metronome studios. The two musicians played Michael the test recordings they had made on Viggsö and discussed how the song would be put together. 'Michael played a key role from that moment on,' Björn emphasizes. 'One of the first bright ideas he had was to slightly change the speed of some of the tracks, giving more depth to the recorded sound. This technique subsequently became one of the ingredients of the "ABBA sound".'

10 January The Swedish version of 'Ring Ring' was recorded, as well as the demo for an English version. Stig, wanting to check that the English lyrics were correct, asked Neil Sedaka and Phil Cody to put the finishing touches to a definitive version which would be recorded and mixed at a later date.

22 January Björn took part in the TV programme *Får Vi Lämna Några Blommor?* (Should We Leave Some Flowers?). The guests on this programme were invited to sing popular Swedish songs, both old and new. Björn sang with Hansi Schwarz and Tony Rooth (from the Hootenanny Singers) and performed a duet with Lena Andersson.

25 January Björn and Benny recorded 'Me And Bobby And Bobby's Brother', a new track for the *Ring Ring* album. Anni-Frid put the finishing touches to two demos, 'Love Is Always Young' and a track she would sing at the Caracas Song Festival, 'Feel'. (*The Complete Recording Sessions*, 1994.)

10 February On the night of the Melodifestivalen, the four members of the group were unsure right up until the last minute whether they would be able to perform, as Agnetha's baby was due at any moment. But all went well, and their Swedish version of 'Ring Ring' was well received by the audience. According to the forecasts, they were sure to win, but that was without taking into consideration the jury of 'experts' (critics, musicians and showbusiness professionals). Everyone was astounded when the presenter Alicia Lundberg announced that the winner was 'Sommaren Som Aldrig Säger Nej' (The Summer That Never Says No) by the duo Malta, and even more so when 'Ring Ring' was placed third. Björn recalls: 'It was as if the sky had come crashing down around us. We were really sickened by the result because we had gone to such great lengths to win the competition. We really were the best!'

It was not only the choice of song but also the existence of the jury which was criticized by the public. Some people suggested that Sweden had never won the competition because of this professional jury. One of the main Swedish daily newspapers even went as far as to set up a telephone poll the day after the competition to ascertain the public's choice. The results of the survey proved that once again, the jury had been mistaken: the readers chose 'Ring Ring'. Malta went on to finish fifth at the Luxembourg final.

14 February Polar Music released the Swedish version of 'Ring Ring' as a single, backed by 'Åh Vilka Tider' (Oh, the Good Old Days), a track which had been recorded eight months earlier. Five days later, the English version was released, with 'She's My Kind of Girl' on the B-side. 'Ring Ring' entered the Swedish charts on 27 February and stayed at No. 1 for eight weeks.

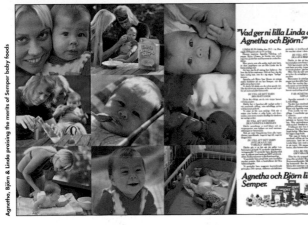

Agnetha, Björn & Linda praising the merits of Semper baby foods

23 February Agnetha gave birth to a baby girl, who was named Linda Elin. A few days later, Björn allowed journalists and photographers into the Danderyd hospital room for a press conference with mother and baby at his side. Both were in excellent health, with the baby weighing 3.1 kilograms and measuring 51 centimetres. Agnetha returned home on 29 February.

Stig Anderson, encouraged by the success of 'Ring Ring', was eager to promote the record outside the borders of Scandinavia. The foreign release of the single would be supported by a promotional tour of several northern European countries. Polar Music announced to the press that the album would be released at the end of March. In the middle of March, the group recorded the last three tracks: 'Disillusion', 'Love Isn't Easy (But It Sure Is Hard Enough)' and 'I Saw It In the Mirror'. 'Disillusion' had originally been a Swedish track entitled 'Mina Ögon' (My Eyes), composed by Agnetha and later appearing on her solo album.

18 March 'Ring Ring' set a record in the history of the Swedish charts: at the same time as the Swedish version was at No. 1 in the Svensktoppen (the chart for songs sung in Swedish), the English-language version went straight in at No. 1 in the Tio I Topp (Top 10) and also in the Kvällstoppen evening chart.

20 March At Stig's request, the group set out on a promotional tour of Germany, Austria, Holland and Belgium, accompanied by their manager. It gave the group an opportunity to meet their agents and foreign partners. Agnetha didn't take part in the trip, as she was looking after the baby; one of Anni-Frid's friends, Inger Brundin, stood in for her. The trip ended in Brussels, where Björn, Benny, Anni-Frid and Inger performed 'People Need Love' and 'Ring Ring' for Belgian TV. Bob Navez from Vogue Belgium has an amusing tale to tell: 'On their first visit, we went to a restaurant for a meal. At the end of the dinner, they signed a Swedish 100-kronor note for me. They joked that if they became famous one day, it would be worth much more. I've taken good care of that note!'

26 March The long-awaited first album was released. Sales were impressive for a country with only eight million inhabitants: 250,000 copies of the single and 100,000 copies of the album, which reached No. 2 in the Swedish charts.

Hans Fridlund wrote of the album in *Expressen*: 'Björn, Benny, Agnetha and Frida, occasionally with the help of Stig Anderson, have quite naturally emerged as the most prolific pop group in Sweden. And this record promises to be another hit for Messrs Ulvaeus and Andersson. Even so, if you wanted to be difficult, you would be justified in saying that a large number of their songs seem to be quite superficial. There are many people who are growing tired of the repetition of "People Need Love". There are, however, more good songs here than bad ones: "He Is Your Brother" is a bit like the little brother of a New Seekers song. While "I Saw It In the Mirror" isn't mature enough to be exported, "Love Isn't Easy" has international class. "Ring Ring" isn't bad and "I Am Just a Girl" has a soft melody and is sung well. All in all, the record is good.'

9 April Agnetha, Björn, Benny and Anni-Frid attended the Spring Party organized by *Expressen* at the Operakällaren restaurant.

11 May Vogue released 'Ring Ring', the second single by the four Swedes, in France and Belgium. Perhaps as a result of a typing error, the girls became 'Anna' and 'Frieda' on the sleeve. On the B-side was 'Rock 'n' Roll Band'. The record company didn't think it would be worthwhile releasing the album, since the group were still relatively unknown. In Belgium, success came quickly: 'Ring Ring' spent eleven weeks on the charts, reaching No. 2 on 7 July. In both Holland and Germany, the record reached No. 5.

In May and June, the Hootenanny Singers (Björn Ulvaeus, Tony Rooth and Hansi Schwarz) went back into the studio to record a new album entitled *Dan Andersson På Vårt Sätt* (Dan Andersson – Our Way). This record, paying homage to the Swedish poet Andersson, would be released in the middle of August throughout Scandinavia.

In Sweden, there were offers coming in from all sides. Stig released 'Love Isn't Easy' as a single and began to plan a tour of the country's main *folkets parks* from 15 June to 7 September. The first concert took place in Gothenburg's Liseberg park.

23 July The group were back in the studio. Björn, Benny, Agnetha and Anni-Frid recorded the German versions of 'Ring Ring' (with lyrics by Peter Lach) and 'Another Town, Another Train', which became 'Wer Im Wartesaal Der Liebe Steht' (lyrics by Fred Jay). The single was released in Germany on 10 August. A Spanish version of 'Ring Ring' (lyrics by Doris Band) was recorded soon afterwards, but it never saw the light of day.

Benny, Björn, Frida with Inger Brundin on a promotional tour in the Benelux countries

'IN ONE WAY IT WAS QUITE AN ADVANTAGE HAVING TO WAIT ANOTHER YEAR BEFORE WINNING, BECAUSE IN THE MEANTIME WE LEARNED QUITE A LOT ABOUT HOW THINGS WORKED IN OTHER COUNTRIES. LATER ON, WHEN WE WON THE CONTEST WITH "WATERLOO", THE ORGANIZATIONAL SIDE OF THINGS WORKED EXTREMELY WELL. WE WERE PREPARED IN A COMPLETELY DIFFERENT WAY.' BJÖRN ON EUROVISION

For some time, the two couples had been faced with numerous problems concerning the name of the group. Obviously Björn, Benny, Agnetha and Anni-Frid was too long, too difficult to pronounce and too hard to remember. 'In private,' explained Stig, 'I'd got into the habit of calling them ABBA, because of their initials. I liked the name, but to be honest, we hadn't gone to any great lengths to try to find another name. With the assistance of the newspaper *Göteborgs-Tidningen*, we ran a competition to find a name for our group. The results were surprising and we had suggestions as varied as Flower Power, Black Devils, Golden Diamonds, Baba, and strange as it may seem, 80 per cent of people chose ABBA. How could we reject a name which we liked and which was short, international and easy to remember? The only problem was that Abba is the name of the largest brand of canned herring in Sweden. Nevertheless, I was determined to keep this name, even though we were left open to all kinds of jokes. I made a point of phoning Anders Ekström, managing director of the company which produces this famous Swedish product, and he very kindly allowed us to use the name "Abba" on one condition: that the group wouldn't discredit his company. He confessed that he couldn't have dreamed of better publicity for his product!'

At the beginning of August, ABBA went to Oslo to perform 'Ring Ring' on the TV show *Momarkedet*. All the profits from this famous Norwegian programme went to the Red Cross.

13 August A big night for Polar Music. Stig had invited numerous people to celebrate several different events: the tenth anniversary of the record company, the tenth anniversary of the Hootenanny Singers, and also to present awards to the artists on the label. Agnetha, Björn, Benny and Anni-Frid were presented with a gold disc for sales of the Swedish and English versions of the 'Ring Ring' single, as well as a diamond disc for the 'Ring Ring' album. Members of the Hootenanny Singers received gold discs for sales of their albums *Våra Vackraste Visor 2* and *Dan Andersson På Vårt Sätt*, and Ted Gärdestad received a gold disc for his album *Ted*. To mark the event, Polar Music released a retrospective album commemorating ten years of the record company.

The defeat of 'Ring Ring' in the Melodifestivalen was in many ways a beneficial experience for Björn, Benny and Stig. The next year, the jury of experts would be replaced by a panel made up of a cross-section of people from different regions of Sweden. The three men were determined to go all out to win the 1974 Eurovision Song Contest, and with Stig's professionalism, it was clear that not even the tiniest detail would be overlooked.

From September until the end of the year, the three men composed, wrote and recorded at the Metronome studios, working on the tracks which would feature on the group's second album, scheduled for release in the spring of 1974. The first songs were 'Dance (While the Music Still Goes On)', which is reminiscent of Phil Spector, 'Suzy-Hang-Around', one of the few songs sung by Benny, 'My Mama Said', 'Honey Honey' (of which a Swedish-language version would later be recorded), 'What About Livingstone', 'King Kong Song' and the excellent ballad 'Gonna Sing You My Lovesong', sung by Frida.

11 October Vogue released the single 'Nina, Pretty Ballerina', with 'He Is Your Brother' on the B-side. The 'Ring Ring' single had flopped in France; Alain Boublil's team had underestimated the song's potential.

12 October 'Ring Ring' was released in Britain, much later than in other countries. Stig had had the single refused by three record companies (EMI, Decca and PYE), and it was only after long negotiations that he finally managed to sign a contract with Epic/CBS. Due to the lack of promotion, the single wasn't a hit. However, Irish group the Others managed to get into the Top 20 with their version of the song.

18 November The Hootenanny Singers' song 'Omkring Tiggaren Från Luossa' (Around the Beggar From Luossa) broke a Svensktoppen record, having been in the chart for fifty-two weeks. At the same time, the Polar Music team learned that 'I Am Just a Girl' had entered the Japanese charts.

'I THINK THE REASON THAT BJÖRN AND I WORK SO WELL TOGETHER IS THAT WE COMPLEMENT EACH OTHER'
BENNY

Completely absorbed by the group's activities and especially by her daughter Linda, Agnetha was now recording less and less as a solo artist. During the autumn, CBS-Cupol released a compilation album, *Bästa* (Best of), and a single from it, 'En Sång Om Sorg Och Glädje' (A Song About Sorrow and Joy). This was the first track produced by Agnetha. It climbed to the top of the Svensktoppen chart over six consecutive weeks. The lyrics were written by Stig Anderson.

After having officially announced ABBA's participation in the forthcoming Melodifestivalen, Stig brought his team together to present the results of his recent enquiries, having sounded out the opinions of numerous European showbusiness professionals as to what kind of song ABBA should select for the contest. It seemed that a rhythmic song which was more pop-oriented would be successful with the Eurovision jury. The public were tired of sugary-sweet ballads. Stig was convinced that they had to present a short, catchy song which could be understood in every language. During the course of this meeting, he also told the group about his ideas regarding their conquest of the European market.

Björn and Benny had never been so prolific as they were towards the end of 1973, putting the finishing touches to all the songs for the forthcoming album and completing even more songs than necessary. Among these demos, Stig found two tracks which interested him. He made the most of a trip to the Canary Islands – away from the telephone and professional obligations – to take the tapes away and set to work. 'I was very inspired by these melodies,' he explained. 'My first idea was a name I'd found in a cookery book, "Honey Pie", but I had trouble developing lyrics around this title. Finally, after searching through an encyclopedia, I found "Waterloo". As for the second track, while I was on holiday in Las Palmas, I often heard people say "*Hasta mañana*" on the radio and in the street. I liked this expression and thought it fitted the music perfectly. The text came together very quickly.'

17 December The whole team were in the Metronome studios for the recording of 'Waterloo' and another track, 'Watch Out'. The following day, they recorded 'Sitting In the Palmtree' and 'Hasta Mañana'.

It was now time to choose the song which ABBA would take to the Melodifestivalen the following February. After having played the songs for the group's entourage, 'Waterloo' was finally chosen. There were several reasons for this decision, but the most important factor was that the song was sung by the whole group, whereas 'Hasta Mañana' has only one vocalist, Agnetha. The rhythm and energy of 'Waterloo' were also deciding factors. 'I remember that they asked me which song I thought they should choose,' says guitarist Janne Schaffer, 'and I told them that they were fools if they didn't go for "Waterloo".' (*The Complete Recording Sessions*, 1994.)

☆ ☆ ☆ ☆

Agnetha, Björn, Benny and Anni-Frid toured the Swedish parks from 15 June (Gothenburg) until 9 September (Malmö). In order that the tour should not interfere with their studio work or Björn and Agnetha's family life, the group chose to perform only at weekends. Accompanied by three musicians, the two couples gave their audiences a 30-minute show. The star attraction was a song sung by Benny, accompanying himself on the ukulele.

The show received mixed reviews. Anders Björkman wrote in *Expressen*: 'This monotonous show follows on from their chart successes. The girls dance and the boys play their instruments. Only Benny manages to lift the show from the depths of lethargy with his song. The rest of the show is mechanical.' On the other hand, the *Göteborgs-Posten* wrote: 'Throughout the entire show, you can see how pleased the group are to be giving their audience a show of quality. They work well together, with a fast tempo and an interesting style.'

Anni-Frid explains: 'There are happy memories of this tour, but it was time for it to come to an end because we were all exhausted. I lost 7 kilos. When you realize that sometimes we even did three shows on the same day, it was madness!'

JUNE

Friday	15	Gothenburg (Liseberg Park)	
Saturday	16	Rättvik	21.00
Saturday	16	Avesta	24.00
Sunday	17	Högsjö	16.00
Sunday	17	Årjäng	21.00
Sunday	17	Åmotfors	23.00
Friday	22	Lappvattnet	22.00
Friday	22	Lycksele	01.00
Saturday	23	Överkalix	21.30
Saturday	23	Tärendö	24.00
Saturday	30	Östervåla	22.00
Saturday	30	Gävle	24.00

JULY

Sunday	01	Söderbykarl	17.00
Sunday	01	Stockholm (Kungsträdgården)	19.30
Wednesday	04	Gamleby	
Thursday	05	Simonstorp	22.00
Friday	06	Oskarshamn	23.00
Saturday	07	Södertälje	22.00
Saturday	07	Mariefred	23.30
Sunday	08	Grängesberg	19.30
Sunday	08	Dala-Floda	22.00
Friday	13	Köping	
Saturday	14	Säter	21.30
Saturday	14	Borlänge	23.30
Sunday	15	Mora	23.00
Friday	20	Sunnemo	23.00
Saturday	21	Lysvik	21.30
Saturday	21	Sysslebäck	24.00
Sunday	22	Kungsbacka	18.00
Sunday	22	Vegby	21.00
Friday	27	Viskan	
Friday	27	Hammarstrand	
Saturday	28	Noraström	21.30
Sunday	29	Svenstavik	

AUGUST

Friday	03	Alstermo	21.00
Friday	03	Kalmar	23.30
Saturday	04	Mariestad	21.15
Saturday	04	Falköping	23.30
Sunday	05	Lerdala	16.30
Sunday	05	Trädet	19.00
Saturday	11	Kiruna	
Sunday	12	Skellefteå	
Tuesday	14	Söderhamn	21.00
Wednesday	15	Östersund: Jamtli	19.30
Friday	17	Nykroppa	22.30
Saturday	18	Hofors	
Monday	20	Stockholm (Malmen Club)	24.00
Friday	24	Österbybruk	22.30
Saturday	25	Örebro	21.30
Saturday	25	Kristinehamn	24.00
Sunday	26	Karlstad	15.00
Friday	31	Mysen (Norway)	

SEPTEMBER

Saturday	01	Karlskoga	21.00
Saturday	01	Vretstorp	23.00
Sunday	02	Göteborg (LOBO restaurant)	
Friday	07	Sölvesborg	20.30
Saturday	08	Kristianstad	21.00
Sunday	09	Malmö	20.00

'MOST OF THE SONGS IN THE CONTEST WERE BOOMPA-BOOMPA. WE DECIDED TO WRITE SOMETHING THAT WAS MORE OF A POP SONG AND WHICH WOULD CHANGE THE EUROVISION SONG CONTEST SITUATION.' STIG

1974

The new year began with the recording of the Swedish-language version of 'Honey Honey' at the Metronome Studios and some extra sessions to finish off the recording of 'Waterloo'.

9 February As in previous years, Swedish Television would screen the Melodifestivalen live. Agnetha, Björn, Benny and Anni-Frid were confident. Their performance of 'Waterloo' in Swedish was excellent and their conductor Sven-Olof Walldoff caused a sensation in his Napoleon costume. When presenter Johan Sandström announced the winners who would be going on to compete in Brighton, the result surpassed all expectations: ABBA had come first, with an overwhelming victory of 302 points against 211 points for Lars Berghagen and his song 'Min Kärleksång Till Dig' (My Love Song To You). *Aftonbladet* announced: 'The voice of the people – the best song has won at last!'

The evening came to a close with a massive party organized by Stig at his villa in Nacka. Surrounded by all their friends and colleagues, the four group members relived the events of the evening with a video borrowed from Swedish Television. For fun, Stig also offered his guests some *Napoleon bakelse* (Napoleon cake).

10 February Prior to the Eurovision Song Contest, Stig had put together a promotional strategy to ensure that whether or not they were victorious in Brighton, the single would be released simultaneously in every European country. Over five days, he had visited the record companies and music publishers of Copenhagen, Hamburg, Vienna, Amsterdam, London, Brussels and Paris. In his briefcase was an English-language version of 'Waterloo', a press release and a biography of the group in four languages. 'By doing this I was reinforcing our presence in the contest,' explained Stig. 'I didn't want to miss even the tiniest detail because this event is a superb springboard for singers who want to reach an audience outside their own country. It also gives you the opportunity to compete with international artists. In the United States, I even paid for advertising pages in the monthly publications *Billboard* and *Cashbox* to promote the song.'

21 February Benny began work on *Frida Ensam*, Anni-Frid's second solo album.

With the recording of the *Waterloo* album complete, photographer Ola Lager organized a photo shoot to illustrate the sleeve. This took place in the magnificent setting of Gripsholm Castle, near Mariefred, about 50 kilometres west of Stockholm. It was bassist Mike Watson who wore the Napoleon uniform in the photos.

During March, Björn and Benny finished recording Ted Gärdestad's *Upptåg* (Practical Joke) album. Agnetha and Frida sang backing vocals on some of the tracks.

4 March Polar Music released the *Waterloo* album in Sweden, and the singles of the same title in Swedish and English. After just four weeks, the group had sold 125,000 copies of the album and 85,000 copies of the singles.

Hans Fridlund, always harsh, wrote in *Expressen*: 'It's obvious that this album is going to achieve monstrous sales. The Swedes, in voting for ABBA and their song "Waterloo", made the right decision. Björn and Benny have analysed current pop trends well but also remember the sounds of the past. "Honey Honey" and "Suzy-Hang-Around" are a bit reminiscent of the Beach Boys (although ABBA don't sing quite as well).

Stig's party at his villa in Nacka after the Melodifestivalen

Abbas Waterloo i Napoleonsås
Ingredienser: ABBA, Sweet, Elvis, Dr Hook, Slade Poster, Rocket, Osmonds, Alice, David

'WE WERE YOUNG, EXTREMELY AMBITIOUS AND SELF-CONFIDENT AT THE SAME TIME. AND ALL THAT PLAYED A PART. THAT'S THE SORT OF THING THAT YOU ONLY DO ONCE IN YOUR LIFETIME.'
BJÖRN

'While "Watch Out" is a clumsy attempt at soul, "Gonna Sing You My Lovesong" is a bluesy ballad in the Leon Russel gospel style. "Sitting In the Palmtree" has Caribbean-reggae influences and "Hasta Mañana" leans towards the German *schlager* sound. One shouldn't complain about these changes. And all those who previously thought of ABBA as a sugary-sweet band will find quite a few songs here which really move because of Janne Schaffer's guitar. But do Björn and Benny really have to mix all these different styles on the same record? They're obviously clever. But as far as I'm concerned, I much prefer it when I can feel the real personality of the musicians rather than listening to this outpouring of abilities. I would also like Benny Andersson to use less piano-moog on the musical backing.'

7 March   The 'Waterloo' single had a quiet release on the Vogue label in France and Belgium. After the Brighton victory, a new edition would be released with the caption '*1er Grand Prix Eurovision 1974*'.

15 March   The group recorded the German-language version of 'Waterloo', written by Gerd Müller-Schwanke. Polydor Germany released the single on 5 April.

27 March   Frida returned to the KMH studio to record two new songs, 'Chapel of Love' and 'That's When the Music Takes Me'. Unfortunately, neither of these tracks was included on the *Frida Ensam* album.

28 March   Agnetha recorded a new solo single, featuring 'Golliwog' and 'Came For Your Love'. The first track would feature on her forthcoming album, but in a Swedish-language version entitled 'Gulleplutt'.

1 April   ABBA, their musicians, Stig and the whole entourage left for London. In the British capital, the group met journalists at a press conference organized by music-publishing company United Artists. It was a chance for Agnetha, Björn, Benny and Anni-Frid to test the water before the Eurovision Song Contest. The response was quite warm, with comments such as 'You've got a good song!'. Two days later, ABBA left London and travelled to Brighton.

5 April   Epic released the 'Waterloo' single in Britain. The following evening saw the famous victory (see the next chapter, 'Brighton Fever').

8 April   The group left Brighton for London. E*n route*, Agnetha, Björn, Benny and Anni-Frid had the opportunity to bask in their victory when they heard 'Waterloo' on the radio. A second surprise was the announcement by the DJ that 15,000 copies had been sold within two hours that morning.

A champagne reception awaited them at the Grosvenor House hotel. During their stay in London, the two couples tried to give themselves some time to do a little shopping, despite their hectic timetable of press conferences, radio interviews, photo sessions in Hyde Park and at Waterloo station (for the *Daily Express*) and a reception with the Swedish ambassador to Britain, Ole Jödahl, who congratulated them on their performance. Agnetha, who was suffering from acute tonsillitis and a temperature, only managed to keep going due to medication.

10 April   ABBA performed on *Top of the Pops*, Britain's most popular TV pop-music programme, watched by 14 million viewers. The impact of their performance was so great that a week afterwards, 'Waterloo' went from No. 17 to No. 2 in the charts.

11 April   The members of the group flew to Hamburg and recorded an Easter show for German television, surrounded by rabbits and chicks. Just before midnight, they landed back at Stockholm's Arlanda airport. 'Our arrival was very quiet because we weren't expected until the following day,'

Performing 'Waterloo' on the TV show *Domino*, Paris

remembers Benny. 'We couldn't wait to get back home. After all the stress and strain we needed to rest. Anni-Frid and myself went straight back home to Vallentuna, a suburb of Stockholm. At last we could have some peace and quiet. We opened a bottle of champagne and reminisced about our trip to England.'

During the Easter weekend, Agnetha, Björn, Benny and Anni-Frid, together with their close friends, went to the island of Viggsö to relax before launching into promoting 'Waterloo'. 'When we were in Brighton, surrounded by journalists, we often dreamed of this moment,' said Benny. 'For the first time in ages we were free again. It was also the chance to review things with Stig and to think about future engagements. It was in fact at this moment that we made the decision for cancel the summer tour of the Swedish parks.'

16 April Stig sent an apologetic letter to the directors of the thirty parks where the group had planned to perform. The press reacted with headlines such as: 'ABBA no longer need Sweden because they are now going to conquer the whole world.' Stig and Björn responded with a statement: 'We are very proud to represent Sweden overseas. From now on, we have to guarantee that the group is promoted in all four corners of the world. Refusing to do television in New York or Madrid would be a big mistake. In addition, we are preparing ABBA's next album and have to spend time producing other artists at Polar Music, for instance Ted Gärdestad and Lena Andersson. If we go on tour, we have to allow a month for preparation and rehearsals as well as a month on the road. We don't want to exhaust ourselves! Nevertheless, we are planning a tour of Europe and Sweden at the end of the year. No contract had been signed with the parks, it was only a verbal agreement.'

17 April After this short break in Sweden, Agnetha, Björn, Benny and Anni-Frid flew to Paris. Unfortunately, they had little time to explore the capital, as their schedule was so tight. In three days, they took part in the radio programme RTL N*on Stop* (presented by Jacques Martin), and the TV shows *Midi-Première* (presented by Danièle Gilbert) and Guy Lux's *Domino*. Photo

shoots and even a recording session at the Vogue studio for the French-language version of 'Waterloo' took place. The track was produced by Claude-Michel Schönberg and Alain Boublil (who wrote the French text); this was the partnership that went on to write the musical *Les Misérables*. The single was released on 10 May in limited quantities. For the B-side, Vogue chose 'Gonna Sing You My Lovesong'.

22 April The group returned to Stockholm to attend the annual *Expressen* party at the Operakällaren restaurant. Every major artist and media personality was invited.

24 April ABBA recorded T*he Eddy Becker Show* for Dutch television. In England, their success was so great and demand for them so high that the BBC decided to buy and televise the Dutch recording. ABBA continued promotion with a visit to Germany where they appeared on T*he Peter Frankenfeld Show*.

On the same day, *Expressen* printed the first details of ABBA's chart successes in Europe. Two weeks after the Brighton victory, 'Waterloo' was already No. 2 in England (it would reach No. 1 on 4 May), No. 3 in Austria, No. 1 in Germany, No. 1 in Belgium, No. 3 in Holland, No. 13 in France, No. 23 in Italy, No. 1 in Norway, No. 1 in Sweden and No. 3 in Denmark.

2 May Vogue released the *Waterloo* album in France and Belgium. In France, the single made great progress (No. 3 on the RTL chart), but this did not help to boost sales of the album, which were still quite weak.

3 May Anni-Frid and Benny made the most of a short stay in Stockholm to record two new tracks for the forthcoming F*rida Ensam* album. Five days later, Björn and Benny went back into the studio to finish a new version of 'Ring Ring', made especially for the English market. The original orchestration was enriched by a saxophone and extra guitars. In England, the *Waterloo* album was released on 17 May. It climbed no higher than No. 28.

13–16 May ABBA were in Germany. After Hamburg, the group travelled to Frankfurt to appear on the TV show *Drehscheibe* which was recorded in a town park. The following day they went to Saarbrucke, where ABBA took part in a live transmission of *Star Parade*.

17–18 May ABBA were in Brussels. In Belgium, ABBA's success was almost instant. 'Waterloo' went straight to No. 1 in the charts. However, sales of the album began slowly. The group's visit was good for promotion. On the first day, the two couples took part in the monthly RTB programme entitled *Chansons à la Carte* (presented by André Torrent), in which they performed 'Ring Ring' and 'Waterloo'. They were then invited to the Cinéma (a Belgian discotheque on the avenue des Celtes) by a group of young people wearing Napoleonic soldiers' uniforms. After having performed their winning song, the four members of the group were presented with a replica of the hat worn by Napoleon as well as a bottle of The Waterloo (a special vintage of mandarin-flavoured Napoleon brandy). There was another surprise for ABBA the following morning: the mayor of Waterloo had arranged for them to visit his town. However, the reception had to be brief because ABBA were expected in Paris that afternoon to sing on the TV show *La Une Est à Vous* (presented by Bernard Golay). To speed up their journey, the group's car was given a motorcycle escort as far as the French border.

20–22 May The group made a promotional visit to Madrid. 'Waterloo' was already No. 1 in Spain, and the song would be in the charts for a total of fifteen weeks. As well as the usual promotion, record company Carnaby organized a recording session for a Spanish version of the song which was later cancelled. The climax of their visit was the recording of a TV show called *Señoras y Señores*, on which ABBA performed 'Ring Ring', 'Honey Honey', 'Hasta Mañana' and 'Waterloo'. The TV station had prepared well for the show. Each song was staged and accompanied by a ballet. Björn, who had always been gifted with languages, addressed the audience in Spanish. After Madrid, the group went to Lisbon and then returned to Stockholm.

20 June Polydor Germany released 'Honey Honey'. It was an immediate hit and reached No. 2 in the charts just two weeks after its release. On top of that, the record stayed in the German charts for a total of five months. At the end of June, the group appeared on James Last's *Star Parade*, where they performed 'Waterloo' and 'Honey Honey'.

In France, Vogue decided not to release 'Honey Honey' as a single. In Belgium the song would reach No. 19 in the charts. In the United States, the Atlantic label released the record during August and it did very well to reach No. 27 in the Top 200. In Spain, during six weeks of chart success, the song would reach its highest position at No. 5.

In England, record company Epic did not believe in the potential of 'Honey Honey' at all and decided not to release it. This may have been a strategic error, since a version of the song by duo Sweet Dreams would reach No. 6 in the Top 10. Epic chose instead to release the new version of 'Ring Ring' on 21 June. The group were scheduled to appear on the inevitable *Top of the Pops*, but unfortunately a major BBC technicians' strike halted the recording of the programme. ABBA did sing the song on The *Tommy Cooper Hour*. However, 'Ring Ring' rose no higher than No. 32 in the English charts.

RTL Non Stop radio programme, Paris

The members of ABBA stayed in Sweden throughout the summer. Benny and Björn made the most of this break to compose and finish off some new tracks. Since their Brighton victory, Agnetha, Björn, Benny and Anni-Frid had received television offers from all over Europe. Half the offers had to be turned down due to time constraints. Stig and his team called on film producer Lasse Hallström to record some short promotional videos for each song, beginning with 'Waterloo' and 'Ring Ring' which were filmed in a Stockholm studio at the beginning of July. From now on, these video clips, in 16mm format, would be systematically sent to television companies worldwide.

11 July Anni-Frid recorded two songs for her forthcoming *Frida Ensam* album: 'Som En Sparv' (Like a Sparrow) and 'Syrtaki'.

22 July The boys were in the Metronome studios to finish off the Hootenanny Singers' final album, *Evert Taube På Vårt Sätt* (Evert Taube – Our Way), a tribute to the Swedish composer and poet.

For her part, Agnetha began the first recordings for her fifth album, *Elva Kvinnor I Ett Hus* (Eleven Women In a House) at Glen studios. The singer, backed by Bosse Carlgren, produced the entire album and wrote all the music with the exception of the song 'S.O.S.'. Agnetha remained under contract to CBS-Cupol until the end of 1975.

22–23 August Björn and Benny began to record ABBA's new album. The recording would last until March of the following year. During these sessions, sound engineer Michael B. Tretow – always on the lookout for new sounds – would keep on surprising everyone with his discoveries. After 'Ring Ring', his creativity and innovative genius proved invaluable. Benny and Björn would keep one of the songs being prepared, 'Crazy World', under wraps until 1976.

25 August Phonogram released the *Waterloo* album in Japan. The single of the same title, released in June, was already a big hit, reaching No. 6 in the charts.

29 September ABBA set out on their first promotional trip to the United States, where 'Waterloo' was selling well. The song was No. 6 on *Billboard's* Hot 100. During their three-day visit, the group met Canadian and American journalists, and the Swedish consul to New York (Gunnar Lonaeus) organized a press conference. Before leaving America, the group made a detour to Philadelphia to sing on the very popular *Mike Douglas Show*. A few weeks later, journalist Ken Barnes wrote in *Rolling Stone*: 'The arrival of ABBA in the charts has been the most comforting musical event of the past few months. Just when the Top 40 had begun to rapidly go unhealthily downhill, "Waterloo" arrived. The production is bursting with modernity. It immediately makes you want to turn up the car stereo.'

During the autumn, Agnetha, Björn, Benny and Anni-Frid went to Holland to sing 'Honey Honey' on *The Eddy Becker Show*.

6–15 November ABBA were rehearsing at the amphitheatre of the Rudbeck school in Stockholm. During these ten days, they perfected the songs for their new tour. This would be divided into two parts: northern Europe from 17 to 30 November and Scandinavia from 10 to 22 January.

'WE WANTED TO DO VIDEOS WHERE THE FANS COULD ACTUALLY SEE US A LOT. AT THAT TIME, THERE WERE MANY VIDEOS THAT WERE VERY, VERY OBSCURE, VERY ARTISTIC AND WHERE YOU ACTUALLY COULDN'T SEE THE GROUP AT ALL AND WE WANTED TO TAKE THE OTHER ROUTE. I CAN REMEMBER THAT DISTINCTLY.' BJÖRN

'WE LISTEN TO OTHER PEOPLE'S MUSIC A LOT. THAT'S BY FAR THE GREATEST INSPIRATION WHILE WE'RE WRITING. WE WRITE VERY REGULARLY – MORE OR LESS OFFICE HOURS. AS FOR EQUIPMENT, WE'RE PRETTY FLEXIBLE. WE CAN WRITE WITH AN OLD GUITAR WITH OLD STRINGS, AND A BATTERED PIANO THAT'S OUT OF TUNE. BUT USUALLY WE TRY TO SET UP A FEW AMPS." **BJÖRN**

18 November Polar Music released the single 'So Long'. The Swedish public didn't take to this particular track immediately. The single did not enter the charts until 29 January 1975, eventually reaching No. 7. Benny says: 'It's not a good song at all. At this point, we wanted "Rock Me" as a single, but we were advised that with Björn singing, it would be difficult for people to identify it as an ABBA record.' (*The Complete Recording Sessions*, 1994.)

26 November Polydor released 'So Long' in Germany. The public's reaction was favourable: the record stayed in the charts for sixteen weeks and climbed to No. 11. From 'Ring Ring' onwards, ABBA would occupy a special place in the hearts of the German public. Radio Luxembourg named them Most Popular Group of the Year. During December, the four members of ABBA went to East Germany to record a TV show on which they would sing 'Waterloo', 'Honey Honey' and 'So Long'.

29 November 'So Long' was released in England, Belgium and France. ABBA travelled to Paris early the next year to promote the track. In Spain, the song reached No. 24. Unfortunately, ABBA were not able to make a promotional film for 'So Long' – the group were too busy touring at that time – as it would have been seen worldwide on television.

☆ ☆ ☆ ☆

The Polar Music empire was growing. Stig Anderson had just bought an exclusive hotel in the embassy district of Stockholm for a reputed 2.3 million Swedish kronor. The building, built in 1906, had belonged to Paul U. Bergström, the man behind the PUB department store. Stig wanted to turn this building into ABBA's headquarters. He had planned numerous alterations. The work would be supervised by his wife Gudrun. The total cost for the renovation and refitting was 1.5 million kronor.

☆ ☆ ☆ ☆

4 December ABBA were in London to record *Top of the Pops*. Despite a brilliant performance and several promotional pushes, 'So Long' didn't do very well in the British charts.

At the end of December, the group took a break on the island of Viggsö where Björn and Benny worked on new compositions such as 'I Do, I Do, I Do, I Do, I Do' and 'Tropical Loveland'.

The end-of-year accounts couldn't have been better. In France, the 'Waterloo' single was awarded a gold disc for sales exceeding 500,000 copies. In Belgium, it reached gold-disc status three months after its release. 'Waterloo' charted in fourteen countries, notably reaching No. 1 in the UK and No. 6 on the American *Billboard* chart – the United States having a reputation for being difficult to crack as far as pop music is concerned. Total global sales of the single were six million copies (of which 800,000 were in the United States). For its part, the album sold more than 3.5 million copies.

In the UK, the flop of 'Ring Ring' and the lukewarm reception given to 'Honey Honey' seemed to confirm the views of the British critics. From the start, they had said things like: 'ABBA won't survive Eurovision. They won the contest but they'll never be able to return to the top of the charts with another strong song. Nobody has ever made a career from it.' Stig took a different view: 'Even if we hadn't won, ABBA would still have had an international breakthrough. Things would have taken longer to have fallen into place, but we would still have made the charts. Don't forget that in the United States, Japan and Australia, nobody knows the Eurovision Song Contest!'

In Australia, the record company released two singles at the same time, 'So Long'/'Hasta Mañana' and 'I've Been Waiting For You'/'King Kong Song'. Stig commented: 'From "Ring Ring" onwards, the Australians appreciated ABBA. This year, "Waterloo" reached No. 4 and "Honey Honey" No. 30. The RCA representatives have told us that they'd like to meet the group.'

'I REMEMBER THE VOTES WERE COMING IN AND IT WAS OBVIOUS NO ONE COULD BEAT US. FROM THAT MOMENT WE ALL KNEW THAT IT HAD HAPPENED, WE WERE ABOUT TO ACHIEVE WHAT WE HAD BEEN WORKING FOR.' **BENNY**

BRIGHTON FEVER 1974

All over town, posters on walls and buses announced: 'Brighton welcomes Eurovision'.

Following a series of recent attacks carried out by the IRA in England, the Eurovision Song Contest had become a potential target, putting the army and the police under great pressure. Each participant in the contest had been issued with a name badge and everyone was being searched frequently. These constraints didn't stop Agnetha, Björn, Benny and Anni-Frid from making the most of their trip. By either fate or coincidence, the four Swedes were staying in the Napoleon Suite of the Grand Hotel. They were a bit tense, but as they were not considered the favourites to win this year's contest, they were free to explore the town without being followed by a horde of photographers, unlike Olivia Newton-John, representing the United Kingdom, and Dutch duo Mouth and McNeal.

None of the journalists – except the Swedish ones – believed ABBA could win the contest. But Stig had motivated the whole team: 'From the very start, I knew we were going to win. Nothing could discourage me. And even without the first prize, the Eurovision Song Contest gave us the status of international artists. In 2 minutes and 50 seconds the whole of Europe would get to see ABBA. No one could dream of better publicity than that!'

The pressure was mounting each day. Rehearsals hadn't yet begun but the artists still had to play their part: interviews, photo sessions, TV appearances, cocktail parties and meetings with potential distributors. Some contracts were even being signed before the day of the contest. The ABBA members entered into all this very amicably and professionally. To reassure herself, Agnetha had tucked away in her luggage a furry toy donkey, her lucky mascot, and Anni-Frid wouldn't go anywhere without her black hat.

When the participants were finally invited into the hall of the Dome for rehearsals, the two couples were overcome with emotion. The tension increased as a technical problem disrupted ABBA's first performances. The BBC technicians persisted in playing the group's backing track at a very low volume, killing the song's dynamic effect. 'I couldn't believe that technicians of this quality could blame the age of the equipment,' said Björn.

'AT THAT TIME, THE EUROVISION SONG CONTEST WAS THE ONE AND ONLY VEHICLE TO REACH OUTSIDE SWEDEN. BECAUSE THERE WAS NO WAY ANYONE IN ENGLAND OR AMERICA WOULD LISTEN TO ANYTHING COMING OUT OF THIS OBSCURE COUNTRY. YOU COULD SEND YOUR TAPES, KNOWING THEY WOULD THROW THEM AWAY IMMEDIATELY. SO THE ONLY CHANCE WAS TO ENTER THE EUROVISION.' BJÖRN

'WHEN YOU ARE IN A SITUATION LIKE THAT, YOU HAVE TO CHANGE A LOT IN YOUR LIFE TO BE ABLE TO TAKE ADVANTAGE OF WHAT'S HAPPENING TO YOU IN THE RIGHT WAY.' FRIDA

'Stig, Benny and myself turned the volume up and we were promised that everything would be sorted out. I wasn't convinced because we didn't have complete control. Right up to the last minute, I was afraid that the same thing would happen again. Even so, on the Friday night, we were all quite relaxed after having drunk some champagne and celebrated Agnetha's birthday in our hotel room.'

On the Saturday morning, everyone was suffering from nerves. The group went back to the hall to run through the last-minute details of the day's programme. Eddy Becker, the producer and presenter for Dutch television, was very impressed with ABBA during rehearsals, and he invited them to come and sing on his show. As Eddy had no contract with him, he simply handed over his business card with the date of the show and offered them five free return plane tickets between Stockholm and Amsterdam.

The dress rehearsal began at 2 p.m. The technicians had now managed to resolve the sound problems. ABBA's performance was superb and they began to feel slightly more relaxed.

They returned to the Dome at about 8.45 p.m. Outside the dressing room, space was limited. All the artists had been put in the same room and they were watching each other nervously. At 9.30 p.m., tension began to grow as the theme music began and presenter Katie Boyle stepped out on stage. Seventeen countries would be battling to win the contest. Sweden were eighth in the running order of the show. The last artists to appear would have a long wait. To try to calm their nerves, the members of ABBA went into a corridor linking the dressing rooms and watched the evening's show on a TV monitor.

'IF WE HAD HAD TO SING IN SWEDISH IN BRIGHTON, IT WOULD NEVER HAVE HAPPENED FOR SURE!' BJÖRN

ABBA leaving the Brighton Dome after rehearsals

After the seventh country (Yugoslavia), the Swedish entry was introduced. Björn, Benny, bassist Rutger Gunnarsson and drummer Ola Brunkert were invited on stage while a film clip introduced ABBA on screen. Conductor Sven-Olof Walldoff arrived in his Napoleon costume, causing applause and laughter. As the first notes of 'Waterloo' were played, Agnetha and Frida ran out on stage: 'My, my, at Waterloo, Napoleon did surrender ...'. The sound was powerful, the music was dynamic and the girls' voices soared. The visual effect was very glam rock: lamé platform boots, and satin costumes covered in glitter and sequins. Björn had had a guitar made in the shape of a star especially for the occasion. This had never been seen before in the history of the Eurovision Song Contest. On top of everything else, ABBA gave off such infectious energy. 'I remember that I immediately thought about the 500 million viewers,' remembers Benny. 'And then everything just mixed up in my head and I felt the stress disappear. The fact that there were four of us helped a lot since we kept giving each other encouraging looks from time to time.' As soon as the song was over, ABBA received an ovation. The group went backstage and the suspense set in. 'The wait was unbearable,' remembers Frida. 'After we had given our all on stage, I then felt deflated like a balloon. And then having to wait in this tiny room made us feel ten times more uncomfortable.' As for Björn, he was so nervous that he paced up and down the corridor.

The last votes confirmed that ABBA had won by 24 points, ahead of Gigliola Cinquetti for Italy with 18 points and Mouth and MacNeal for Holland with 15 points. It was the first time that Sweden had won the Eurovision Song Contest and also the first time that a group had won.

'MY COSTUME WAS SO TIGHT THAT I COULDN'T SIT DOWN IN IT.
IT WAS TERRIBLE AND I CURSED MYSELF FOR NOT SLIMMING A BIT
BEFORE [WEARING] THAT THING. AND AFTERWARDS, OF COURSE,
I WENT ON THE STRICTEST DIET YOU CAN IMAGINE.' BJÖRN

Stig went out on stage to receive the trophy from Sir Charles Curran, director-general of the BBC and thanked the audience in five languages. It suddenly became clear that there had been some misunderstanding, as Björn and Benny weren't with him. Forty-five endless seconds ticked by, which Stig tried to fill by announcing that Björn and Benny were 'shocked by their victory'. It was later revealed that a security guard had refused to let them go on stage, claiming that the prize was for the composers of the song and not the artists. Eventually, everything was put right and the whole group were able to perform 'Waterloo' once again as the finale to the evening. As soon as the BBC cameras stopped rolling, Agnetha, Björn, Benny and Anni-Frid were besieged by all the photographers and journalists who climbed onto the stage. Everybody wanted to have a few words with the winners. 'We lost all contact with reality,' said Frida. 'It was like we were in a bubble. I don't have any recollection of the questions or the answers we gave that night.' This wasn't the case for Stig, who had bad memories of Swedish journalist Ulf Gudmundsson trying to unsettle him: 'Don't you think it's provocative to sing about "Waterloo", the scene of a battle where 40,000 men were killed?' Stig never forgot that: 'I was so shocked that I couldn't respond. Why do journalists always have to make everything seem so political? Couldn't he have just have congratulated us instead of trying to knock us down?'

At about midnight, the group got back to their hotel, took a shower and changed their clothes. 'As for me,' says Björn, 'I was glad to get my costume off. The trousers were so tight, I couldn't sit down the whole evening.' The whirlwind was far from being over. At 2 o'clock in the morning, Polydor Germany threw a party and the champagne flowed. The mayor of Brighton offered ABBA a week's holiday in the best hotel in Brighton. The stream of congratulations and questions continued until 4 o'clock. On their return to the hotel, the two couples savoured the calm after the storm. 'Although we were exhausted, we couldn't get to sleep nor believe what had happened,' Björn recalls. 'It took us a few days to come back down to earth.'

'AFTER THE CONTEST THERE WAS AN OFFICIAL PARTY AND AFTER THAT
WE DID OUR OWN CELEBRATING. IT WAS CHAMPAGNE ALL THE WAY,
INCLUDING WITH OUR CORNFLAKES. SUNDAY WAS OUT OF THIS
WORLD – NO ONE SAID A SERIOUS WORD.' BENNY

'EUROVISION REALLY JUST MADE THINGS HAPPEN FASTER FOR ABBA. IT WOULD HAVE HAPPENED REGARDLESS OF IT. AFTER ALL, AMERICA AND AUSTRALIA AREN'T INTERESTED IN THE EUROVISION.'
STIG

CBS/EPIC · THE MUSIC PEO

'THERE WAS A FEELING THAT SOMETHING REALLY BIG HAD HAPPENED AND THE WORLD LAY AT OUR FEET. WE HAD SUCH CONFIDENCE IN THE GROUP THAT [WE THOUGHT] SOMETHING BIG WAS GOING TO HAPPEN FROM NOW ON.' BJÖRN

On the Sunday morning, at 9.30 a.m., the group were invited to a champagne breakfast organized by the British record company, Epic-CBS. Another interview was followed by a long photo session on Brighton beach. Everyone then went back to their hotel rooms for several hours' rest. During the evening, Stig, ABBA and some of their close associates met up to put together a new plan for the group. They also had to sort through the numerous offers which had come in from television and radio companies. Eddy Becker, who had made an offer the day before, was concerned that there was now great competition between all the television producers. He recalls: 'Everyone wanted exclusive rights to have the winners on their programme. I was worried that my offer had only been verbal. Thomas Johansson and Stig reassured me, they had agreed and they wouldn't change their minds. I have to say that during my whole career I have rarely seen such integrity from artists and their manager.'

Agnetha, Björn, Benny and Anni-Frid made the most of the peace and quiet to read and comment on the 236 congratulatory messages they had received. Benny says: 'We were very proud to have received a telegram from the Swedish Navy and from the local borough of our district Vallentuna, near Stockholm.'

E AT EUROVISION:1974

Epic

CBS/Epic artists at Eurovision: Ireen Sheer, ABBA and Gigliola Cinquetti

There were also numerous articles in the press. Claudine Gherardi wrote in the Belgian daily newspaper *Le Soir*: 'Here is a well-constructed song combined with some intelligently written music. The group give a feeling of togetherness and force.' Roger Briano commented in *Le Parisien*: 'Contrary to previous years, this nineteenth Eurovision Song Contest marks the powerful return of a quality song. "Waterloo" was really well performed by ABBA.' As for the Swedish press, *Expressen* said: '"Waterloo" and ABBA are now worth millions.' And the *Daily Telegraph* wrote: 'The Andersson formula proved a winner, and this was certainly helped by the highly professional performance of the ABBA group.' Björn added: 'The fact that the Eurovision Song Contest took place in Brighton gave us the opportunity to reach the British press and media directly. We were immediately invited to take part in the famous show *Top of the Pops*.'

1974-75 TOUR

For the first time ever, ABBA were to tour outside Scandinavia. The tour took place during the winter, in two separate sessions, each lasting two weeks. This arrangement pleased Agnetha, who no longer wanted to be away from her daughter Linda for long periods.

Thomas Johansson (EMA-Telstar) was entrusted with organizing the tour, assisted by Hansi Schwarz (ex-Hootenanny Singers). Nothing was left to chance. Björn and Benny now had to reproduce on stage the same perfect sound they had created in the studio – ABBA's reputation depended on it.

The 4 tons of sound and lighting equipment was transported in several trucks. The sound system was on loan from the Swedish company Hagström, who were also sponsoring the tour. Twenty-one people travelled with the group. Behind the mixing desk was Michael B.Tretow, assisted by Clabbe af Geijerstam. ABBA were joined on stage by the Swedish group the Beatmakers (Boris Lindqvist, Torsten Dannenberg, Caj Högberg, Peter Kott, Wojciech Ernest and Zbigniew Ryta), who were also the support act.

As usual with ABBA, the visual part of the show had been well prepared. The group presented a complete glam-rock show with special lighting effects, soap bubbles, costume changes and a firework display at the end. Agnetha and Frida had rehearsed the choreography with the American choreographer Graham Tainton. Owe Sandström and Lars Wigenius created a new set of stage clothes which were more extravagant than ever, and even rather outrageous in Björn's case. There were ostrich feathers, sequins, glitter and a green-satin cape with a white skintight suit for Agnetha, and feathers, glitter, white-satin cape, bustier and sparkly antique-style skirt for Frida. There were also tight-fitting sequinned costumes for Björn and for Benny, who also sometimes wore a burgundy satin shirt and a leopardskin jacket.

Rehearsals took place between 6 and 15 November in the amphitheatre of the Rudbeck school in Sollentuna, near Stockholm. The show, which lasted about an hour, was made up of about twenty songs, including some new ones which would feature on the next album. On stage, the group performed with amazing energy. Frida was wilder than ever, even performing a solo dance routine on a podium. The rhythm was very strong and the orchestrations were more 'rocky' than the studio versions. Some songs had been modified, like 'Rock 'n' Roll Band', with Agnetha and Frida on lead vocals and Björn and Benny on backing.

'THERE WAS THIS GLITTER PERIOD IN EUROPE, MID-1970s GROUPS LIKE SWEET, MUD, GARY GLITTER. WE THOUGHT THAT WAS KIND OF FUN. I MEAN, WE WANTED TO TRY EVERYTHING. IN THE BEGINNING, THE MORE CRAZY IT WAS, THE BETTER IT WAS. HIGHLY UNSOPHISTICATED, I WOULD SAY TODAY. I AM ASHAMED WHEN I LOOK AT SOME OF THE COSTUMES, BUT THEN AGAIN WE HAD FUN.' BJÖRN

'WE THINK THE COSTUMES ARE REALLY IMPORTANT. IF WE DON'T FEEL THAT WE'RE LOOKING OUR BEST, WE DON'T PERFORM AS WELL AS WE CAN!' AGNETHA

'FRIDA IS EXTREMELY TALENTED. SHE COULD HAVE BEEN A PROFESSIONAL DANCER WITHOUT ANY DOUBT. SHE MADE A LOT OF PROGRESS AND THIS GAVE HER AN EVEN BIGGER INTEREST. WHEN WE MEET WE DANCE AND DANCE, WE CAN'T STOP DANCING.'
GRAHAM TAINTON ABBA'S CHOREOGRAPHER

The first part of the tour consisted of thirteen dates in several northern European countries. Surprisingly, no concerts were planned in Belgium or Holland, where ABBA had had considerable success.

NOVEMBER

Sunday	17	Copenhagen	Falkonerteater
Monday	18	Hanover	Kuppelsaal
Tuesday	19	Munich	Deutsches Museum

ABBA then played in Frankfurt, Berlin, Nuremberg (Germany), Innsbruck, Vienna (Austria), Zürich (Switzerland), Düsseldorf, Bremen and Hamburg (Germany). The last concert was on 30 November.

In Copenhagen, ABBA played to a full house, and the critics were favourable. The day after the premiere, Tore Ljunberg wrote in the daily newspaper *Arbetet*: 'Even if the sound level was too loud, the show was very well produced and the rhythm was brilliant.' Hans Fridlund said in *Expressen*: 'A dazzling show, both with colour and costumes, with very good choreography. The sound quality was perfect and the new songs are fantastic and very lively.' Thomas Walden remarked in *Aftonbladet*: 'The audience applauded politely, but there was no emotion, which is something I've often noticed in Denmark.'

The first two weeks of concerts had been disappointing. Apart from Copenhagen, ABBA played to half-empty houses. The Düsseldorf and Zurich concerts were cancelled because of low ticket sales. On top of this, Anni-Frid had a bad case of flu and feared that she would not be able to perform every night. However, thanks to their unfailing enthusiasm and energy, the four Swedes overcame these difficulties.

One German journalist wrote: 'Total entertainment. The shiny and glamorous ABBA performed a set that emphasized the visual. Björn sparkled in his overalls and his platform boots, higher than those of Dave Hill and Gary Glitter combined. The girls showed their bodies and sang in perfect two-part harmony. Vocally, ABBA have more resources than many other pop groups. Nevertheless, the audience's reception was lukewarm.' Gerald Büchelmaier wrote in *Bravo*: 'The high point of the show was the scant clothing. Until now, no group has bared so much of itself in Germany. The most courageous were Björn, in his glittery tights *à la* Mick Jagger and Anni-Frid in a skintight bolero and a mini-skirt slit into eighteen strips.'

The group kept something in reserve for the continuation of the tour. From a financial point of view, this first leg of the tour wasn't at all profitable. 'We thought that we would be turning some people away here and there,' explains Björn. 'Especially in Germany and in Austria, where our records were always at the top of the charts. We also thought that we would be singing in front of a younger audience. The majority of people in the crowd were at least twenty-five to thirty years old.'

After a long break and following a week's rehearsal at the Jarla theatre in Stockholm, ABBA went back on the road. From 10 to 22 January, they toured Scandinavia.

JANUARY

Friday	10	Oslo	Chateau Neuf
Saturday	11	Stockholm	Konserthuset
Sunday	12	Lund	Olympen
Friday	17	Copenhagen	Tivoli Konsertsal
Saturday	18	Gothenburg	Scandinavium
Monday	20	Helsinki	Finlandia Hall
Wednesday	22	Umeå	Universum

This second part of the tour was much more successful. The group played to packed houses every night. After the Oslo concert, Mats Olsson wrote in *Expressen*: 'ABBA has become a real stage group. In concert, "King Kong Song" is much more aggressive and has got more rhythm than on record. "Man In the Middle" is another song which works really well on stage, just as "I've Been Waiting For You", the highlight of ABBA's show, sung by Agnetha, sends shivers down your spine.' Critical opinion was divided, though, and the day after the show at the Konserthuset in Stockholm, Björn Levin wrote in daily newspaper GT: 'On stage, ABBA do no more than they do on record. The songs all follow each other, there are highs and lows – happy pop music, but nothing remarkable. The songs are nice to listen to, but after an hour it gets quite tedious.' *Aftonbladet* was more positive: 'Well that's it then – international group ABBA have achieved their breakthrough in Sweden. If you thought that the group's popularity was beginning to fade then you were wrong. They're more popular now than ever. When someone writes the history of seventies pop music, ABBA will come out on top.'

Björn has bad memories of the show they did in Stockholm: 'It's the worst onstage moment that I have ever experienced. It happened on "King Kong Song". When we came to one of the percussion breaks in the song, one of the girls started singing in the wrong place. One half of the band followed her,

'SOME OF THE TOURS WERE FULLY EQUIPPED WITH TWO OR THREE OR EVEN FOUR SAMPLES OF EACH COSTUME, SO THAT THEY COULD BE SHIFTED.' OWE SANDSTRÖM ABBA'S COSTUME DESIGNER

ABBA on stage in Germany

Liseberg, Gothenburg

the other half played on like it was supposed to be, and after a while it was just chaos. There were a lot of colleagues in the audience, and it was all so embarrassing. We didn't even manage to finish the song properly, everyone just stopped playing, one after the other!' (The Complete Recording Sessions, 1994.)

After the Stockholm concert, Agnetha, Björn, Benny and Anni-Frid met American producer Sid Bernstein (ex-producer of the Beatles in the USA). He couldn't stop showering them with praise: 'They're the Swedish Beatles. They've got a different style of song, they're young and are physically very attractive. That's very important in the United States!'

In Gothenburg, the Scandinavium theatre holds only 7,000 people; this greatly displeased director Bertil Rönnberg, who wanted to move the stage to allow a few thousand more people in. The day after the concert, Hans-Eric Åhman wrote in Göteborgs-Posten: 'A joy to both the eyes and the ears. This was a very classy show. There wasn't a single dull moment. The songs that hit you most are "I've Been Waiting For You", where the girls sing so high that it gives you goose pimples, and the gentle, melodic "Hasta Mañana". The group finish with "So Long" and "Waterloo" and it has the desired effect. The applause carried on for a long time after the show had ended. ABBA are the best we have in Sweden right now.'

In February 1975, following the success of the Scandinavian tour, Stig announced that ABBA would be extending it with a series of concerts in the Swedish parks during the summer.

Rehearsals began again on 1 June at the Jarla theatre. This time, guitarist Lasse Wellander joined the Beatmakers. During the show, which featured eighteen songs, Agnetha and Frida had several changes of costume, including some new creations by Owe and Lars: long dresses and short white tunics featuring blue and yellow cats.

JUNE

Day	Date	City	Venue	Time
Saturday	21	Skellefteå	Folkets Park	20.00
Sunday	22	Sunderbyn	Sunderby Loge	19.30
Wednesday	25	Hudiksvall	Köpmanberget	21.00
Thursday	26	Björneborg, Finland	Folkets Park	22.00
Friday	27	Borlänge	Folkets Park	21.00
Saturday	28	Eskilstuna	Folkets Park	22.00
Monday	30	Stockholm	Gröna Lund	20.00

JULY

Day	Date	City	Venue	Time
Tuesday	01	Linköping (cancelled and rescheduled for 8th July)		
Wednesday	02	Gamleby (cancelled and rescheduled for 9th July)		
Thursday	03	Malmö	Folkets Park	21.00
Friday	04	Storebro	Folkets Park	22.00
Saturday	05	Kristianopel	Masten	22.00
Sunday	06	Gothenburg	Liseberg	20.00
Monday	07	Borgholm	Slottsruinen	20.00
Tuesday	08	Linköping	Folkets Park	21.00
Wednesday	09	Gamleby	Folkets Park	21.30

Gröna Lund amusement park, Stockholm

Liseberg, Gothenburg

The two concerts in Linköping and Gamleby were postponed due to Agnetha having a bad case of tonsillitis – she was taken to Danderyd hospital with a temperature of 39.6°. Agnetha recalls: 'The evening in Malmö was a nightmare. My legs were shaking and 10 minutes before going on stage I broke down in tears in the dressing room. Luckily, I managed to keep going until the end of the show. Our doctor, Åke Olsson, was waiting backstage in case something happened to me.'

The day after the concert in Skellefteå, a disappointed Ricki Neuman wrote in *Aftonbladet*: 'We were waiting for something really exciting. There was lots of electricity but not much contact. No rapport between the artists and the audience. Even on stage there was no real communication. Except for Björn's comment about his wife: "She's got a really romantic voice and the sexiest bottom in Sweden!"'

Anders Björkman, in *Expressen*, had a quite different opinion: 'The whole show was a pleasure to watch. It was a real party, with fireworks, smoke and bubbles, all competing with the setting sun. The ABBA circus is without doubt a star attraction.' But Mia Gerdin wrote in *Dagens Nyheter*: 'I heard them sing, I saw them move, but they gave me the impression that they were lifeless. The ABBA show was a mixture of absurd contrasts.'

Despite these criticisms, the tour was a triumph. The audiences in the parks were full of admiration. Being used to more traditional shows, people were astonished when they witnessed the innovative special effects. The group attracted more than 100,000 spectators, with a record audience of 19,000 at the amusement park Gröna Lund in Stockholm.

1975

3 January ABBA made their long-awaited return to Swedish television, appearing on a TV show called *Nygammalt*, presented by Bosse Larsson. The group performed 'So Long' and 'I've Been Waiting For You'.

7–8 January Björn and Benny were in the studio putting the finishing touches to a new version of 'Bang-a-Boomerang' for Swedish duo Svenne and Lotta. The couple were to take part in the Swedish Eurovision heats the following February. Björn and Benny, not having had the time to compose an original song for the competition, had suggested arranging the song at a slightly faster tempo. Svenne and Lotta would record Swedish and English versions of 'Bang-a-Boomerang'.

10 January ABBA opened the second leg of their tour with a concert in Oslo. Stig confessed to *Kvällsposten*: 'We would have really liked it if Swedish Television had made the most of this tour and filmed the show. But we didn't get any positive response. Only one producer was interested in doing a programme with ABBA, but that project fell through due to financial problems.'

30 January The four Swedes went to Germany to sing 'So Long' on the very popular *Disco 75* TV show. Polydor presented the group with four gold discs, to acknowledge sales of two million copies of 'Waterloo'.

1 February ABBA arrived in Paris for three days of promotion. The group sang 'So Long' on the show *Samedi est à Vous* and then went on to RTL radio for the programme *Super Club*, where they performed 'Waterloo' and 'So Long'. During their stay in the French capital, Agnetha, Björn, Benny and Anni-Frid gave several interviews and attended various photo sessions. They were invited on to Guy Lux's *Système 2* programme. The clip of 'So Long' would be screened on 9 February.

At the beginning of February, Stig announced to the Swedish press that ABBA would follow their European tour with a series of fourteen concerts in the Swedish parks the following June and July. By doing this he put an end to the resentment felt by certain journalists who had accused the group of neglecting the Swedish public after the cancellation of the summer 1974 tour.

15 February Svenne and Lotta performed 'Bang-En-Boomerang' (Swedish version) in the 1975 Swedish Eurovision heats. They finished in third place, but this didn't prevent the record from becoming a big hit in Sweden. The B-side, 'Kom Ta En Sista Dans Med Mig' is the Swedish version of 'Dance (While the Music Still Goes On)', from ABBA's *Waterloo* album.

Agnetha, Bjorn, Benny and Anni-Frid devoted the months of February and March to the recording of the new album. For the sleeve, photographer Ola Lager shot the group in the Castle Hotel in Stockholm and in a limousine hired for the occasion. 'The idea came from Ron Spaulding, my artistic director at the time,' explains Ola Lager. 'The car is a 1952 Rolls-Royce which belonged to financial genius Torsten Kreuger. My wife took charge of the styling. Actually, you can see her in a black dress in the photos taken at the hotel. The other extras were Lars, the manager of the hotel, and his staff.'

At the end of March, the two couples allowed themselves some time off before setting out on a very heavy promotional schedule. Agnetha, Björn and Linda flew off for a week's holiday in Crete, in the village of Ayios Nikolaos. Anni-Frid and Benny chose Los Angeles in sunny California. While there, they had the chance to meet up with their friend Björn Skifs, who was touring the United States at that time with his group the Blue Swedes.

10 April 'I Do, I Do, I Do, I Do, I Do' was released. In London, Epic-CBS sent three promotions men to all the capital's radio stations. The men, dressed in dinner jackets, arrived by limousine and delivered the single to the DJs together with a bottle of champagne. Despite these efforts, the record didn't reach higher than No. 38 in the charts. It has to be said that the British press took great delight in knocking ABBA. The *New Musical Express* wrote: 'The melody is desperately ordinary.' *Melody Maker* didn't go overboard either: '"I Do, I Do, I Do …" is so bad it hurts.' The welcome was clearly better in other countries. The record reached No. 2 in Belgium, No. 6 in Germany and in Denmark, No. 5 in South Africa, No. 3 in Holland and No. 1 in Australia.

14 April ABBA performed 'I Do, I Do, I Do, I Do, I Do' and 'S.O.S.' on the Dutch TV show *Top Pop*. The former was then No. 3 in the Dutch Top 40.

15 April ABBA were in Brussels for the recording of the RTB show *Chansons à la Carte*. The group performed 'Rock Me' at the beginning of the show, and 'I Do, I Do, I Do, I Do, I Do' later on in the programme.

In France, 'I Do, I Do, I Do, I Do, I Do' received a lot of radio airplay. The four Swedes arrived in Paris from Brussels and appeared on the programmes *Samedi est à Vous* and *Midi-Première*. ABBA were to be seen again on 1 June, in a clip recorded for Guy Lux's *Système* 2 show.

'SOMETIMES, WHEN YOU HAVE A CATCHY HOOKLINE, YOU FIND THAT THE REPETITION OF WORDS IS VERY EFFECTIVE. WE USED TO FEEL THE TITLES MORE THAN, YOU KNOW, ACTUALLY MAKING IT IMPORTANT WHETHER THEY MEANT SOMETHING OR NOT!' BJÖRN

Chansons à la Carte, Brussels

'Rock Me', Chansons à la Carte, Brussels

After having recorded the promotional video for 'Mamma Mia' in the studio, ABBA filmed clips for three other songs: 'I Do, I Do, I Do, I Do, I Do', 'S.O.S.' and 'Bang-a-Boomerang'. The latter was recorded in the centre of Stockholm. 'We have to thank producer Lasse Hallström,' Björn emphasizes, 'because he was one of the pioneers in the field of videos. MTV and the other music channels didn't exist in those days. We had seen a really badly filmed promotional video from the United States where a single camera had filmed just one view. Lasse convinced us that we could do distinctly better. He already had lots of ideas in his head. Even if we sometimes added some ideas of our own, it was Lasse who found all the concepts and developed the synopsis. Today, these clips seem out of date. In 1975, we were among the first to record them.'

21 April The long-awaited new album, entitled *Abba*, was released simultaneously throughout Europe. For the first time, the melodies, voices, arrangements and sound recording combined to give the impression of exceptional harmony. You could say that this is where Björn, Benny and Michael B. Tretow revealed the 'new', almost-perfect ABBA sound, instantly recognizable as their own. One should also mention the innovative track 'Intermezzo No. 1', previously entitled 'Bach-låten' (Bach's Song), Benny's subtle tribute to his favourite classical composer. In Sweden, the album was a considerable success, going straight in at No. 1 on the Kvällstoppen chart on 29 April, staying in the charts for a total of forty-one weeks and selling 550,000 copies.

Mats Olsson wrote in *Expressen*: 'What is interesting is that ABBA have refined their style. The songs are stronger and give an impression of homogeneity. There are no longer any weak tracks. Björn and Benny have no equals in recording catchy, instantly memorable melodies. The lyrics don't carry any

'THE ABBA SOUND IS THE GIRLS – THEY ARE THE ONES YOU HEAR. BJÖRN AND I MAY CREATE THE WORDS, BUT THEY ARE THE ONES WHO MAKE THE SOUND. TAKE THEM AWAY AND YOU HAVE NO MORE ABBA. I THINK WE PIONEERED THAT SOUND.' BENNY

strong message but ABBA have never claimed that they do. Their music is superior to others. It's at the same time *schlager* and pop. Especially "I Do, I Do, I Do, I Do, I Do", which is without doubt their best song: marvellous saxophones, a melody, superb couplets and Agnetha's voice layered over Anni-Frid's in the chorus. And as far as the girls are concerned, yes, it's possible that Anni-Frid has the better voice, but Agnetha has a special stamp which I find tremendously seductive ("I've Been Waiting For You", for instance). I often play the album and you probably will do so too.'

In Britain, the press persisted with comments such as 'ABBA cannot survive the Eurovision Song Contest'. *Disc* magazine wrote: 'Poor ABBA seem to have had a lot of good intentions with this album. Certainly, it contains some songs which would make excellent singles, like "Bang-A-Boomerang", "I Do, I Do, I Do, I Do, I Do" and the excellent "So Long", but the rest do not deserve a mention.' However, despite the bad press, the record reached No. 13 on the British charts. Björn remembers: 'In 1975, the welcome in Britain had completely changed as opposed to the previous year. We really had to fight to command respect among Anglo-Saxon artists. When we appeared on the programme *Top of the Pops*, the British unions told us we weren't allowed to use our playback tapes which had been recorded using foreign musicians. It left us two solutions: record a new version using the show's musicians or perform completely live. One day we were in Manchester for ITV with the group Queen. Their performance, using their tape, was magnificent, but ours was very average. When "Waterloo" was No. 1 they put us in the best hotels and drove us around in a Rolls. Later on, the quality of the rooms we were given and the transport we used had really gone downhill.'

6 May   ABBA were in the studio to record 'Medley'. Made up of three extracts of American folk songs, the track appeared on a German album entitled *Stars im Zeichen eines Guten Sterns*, for which all profits were donated to cancer research. 'We were asked if we would like to contribute a song to this album,' remembers Benny, 'and since it would take too much time to write a new song, we decided to record this medley of folk songs. It was fun to do it – we felt freer because it wasn't our own material, and I think it turned out quite well.' (*The Complete Recording Sessions*, 1994.)

22–23 May   Agnetha, Björn, Benny and Anni-Frid were in Hamburg to take part in the TV show *Disco 75*. After the recording, they were presented with gold discs acknowledging sales of 'Honey Honey' in Germany.

25 May   ABBA were in Paris to sing 'I Do, I Do, I Do, I Do, I Do' on the programme *Système* 2. The clip was recorded in advance and screened on 1 June. On the RTL charts, they climbed no higher than No. 26. However, the single was awarded a silver disc. (A little clarification is necessary as far as the French charts are concerned. Unlike a lot of countries, French chart placings were not based on record sales up until 1984. They were produced by the directors of programme planning for private radio stations and inevitably were not representative of sales or the tastes of the general public. They were also based on other factors: the tastes of the programme planners, affinities with record companies, publishing contracts, and so on. In ABBA's case, the group sold lots of records, were often played on the radio and on TV, but their chart positions didn't reflect this.)

27 May   The group were in Copenhagen to take part in the programme *Omkring Et Flygel*, on which they sang 'I Do, I Do, I Do, I Do, I Do', 'S.O.S.' and 'So Long', and hummed 'Alleycat'. During the afternoon there was a presentation of gold discs and a photo session at the famous Tivoli Gardens.

3 June   The single 'S.O.S.' was released simultaneously in Sweden and the United States. In Belgium, it was released at the end of the month and reached No. 1 on 5 July. There were excellent results, too, across the Rhine: the song, having reached No. 1, stayed in the German charts for more than seven months.

During the month of June, the Polish President, Edward Gierek, was in Sweden for a visit which lasted several days. In Poland, the press widely covered this visit and dedicated numerous articles to the host country. This led to one daily newspaper publishing a photo of ABBA along with the address of the Swedish fan club. In a few weeks, dozens of sackloads of post would arrive at the group's Stockholm headquarters containing letters, poems, pictures and hand-made objects paying homage to ABBA. Amusingly, the Polish fans, taking Björn to be a woman, portrayed him with breasts. In response to this tidal wave of interest, Stig took steps to distribute the group's records in Poland and East Germany. His concern was not only that the record companies in these countries were controlled by the state, but that the annual budget was allotted to limited imports. As Stig explained: 'We pressed 250,000 copies of the *Abba* album especially for Poland, while the demand was four times greater. As a result, these financial restrictions increased sales of ABBA's records on the black market.'

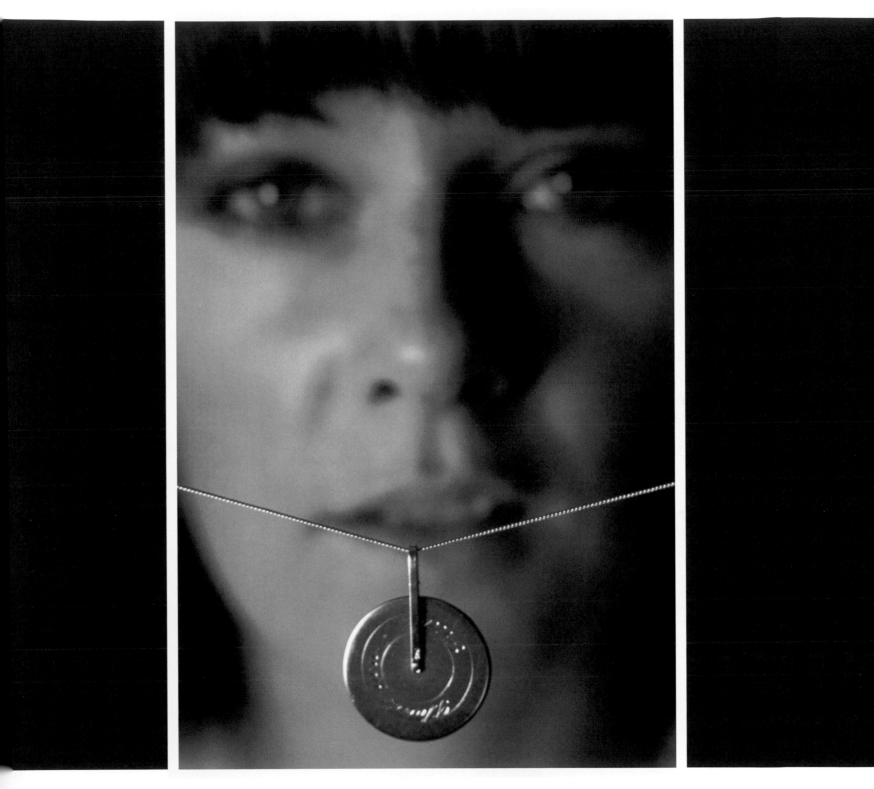

'WHEN I WAS THIRTY, I FELT VERY TRAPPED: I THINK IT'S SOMETHING MOST WOMEN GO THROUGH. I READ SOMEWHERE THAT AT TWENTY YOU MAKE UP YOUR MIND WHAT YOU WANT FROM LIFE AND AT THIRTY YOU CHANGE AND QUESTION EVERYTHING. EVERYTHING WAS UPSIDE-DOWN FOR ME. I HAD NO CONFIDENCE IN MYSELF. AT THE SAME TIME, YOU MUST GO ON WORKING. IT LASTED ABOUT A YEAR.' FRIDA

Promotional trip to Paris, February

'EVERYONE ELSE HAD DECIDED ALREADY THAT THIS WAS THE USUAL ONE-HIT WONDER OF EUROVISION. WE KNEW INSIDE – AND NOBODY ELSE DID – THAT WE HAD COME TO STAY. WE KNEW THE POTENTIAL WE HAD AS RECORDING ARTISTS, AS WELL AS SONGWRITERS.'
BJÖRN

Photo session in the Bois de Boulogne, Paris

11 June Agnetha, Björn, Benny and Anni-Frid travelled to Hilversum, in Holland, to record their first TV special outside Sweden. In this programme, presented by Eddy Becker and entitled *The Eddy-Go-Round-Show*, ABBA performed six songs, including 'Tropical Loveland', and gave an interview. Eddy Becker remembers: 'Everything was organized very easily. It was good to work with ABBA. Björn and Benny were confident and very professional. Agnetha and Frida were shy and nothing like your average celebrities. They were like two friends or work colleagues, they encouraged each other and joked between themselves. There was no rivalry there whatsoever.' After the filming of the show, a photo shoot took place in the gardens of the Hooge Vuursche Hotel. *The Eddy-Go-Round Show* was televised on 21 August.

24 July Vogue France released 'Bang-A-Boomerang' as a single with 'S.O.S.' as the B-side. After seeing the latter song soar up the charts of neighbouring countries, the French record company later pressed a second sleeve highlighting 'S.O.S.'.

2 August Agnetha took part in the TV show *Sommarnöjet*, recorded in Skansen park in Stockholm. The Swedish public had the exclusive opportunity to see the singer perform a new song, 'Dom Har Glömt' (They've Forgotten), a track which would be featured on her forthcoming solo album.

Agnetha, Björn, Benny and Anni-Frid then immediately embarked on a promotional tour of several countries, taking part in various TV shows. In Norway, they sang on the famous *Momarkedet* TV programme.

In the middle of August, Swedish weekly *Vecko Revyn* arranged a photo shoot on the island of Viggsö. The group, together with Linda, posed in front of the lens of photographer Lars Falck.

30 August Anni-Frid took part in the last of the *Sommarnöjet* shows. Frida performed two tracks from her forthcoming solo album in front of a live audience: 'Aldrig Mej' and 'Syrtaki'.

In Australia, ABBA were becoming more and more popular. Since 'Ring Ring' and 'Waterloo', every single had been a hit. While RCA were planning to release 'S.O.S.' during the month of September, an unprecedented phenomenon occurred. The video for 'Mamma Mia' was screened on the programme *Countdown*. Record stores, the TV station and the record company were immediately bombarded with phone calls and letters asking for the song. Stig appeared reluctant to give in to RCA's request for 'Mamma Mia' to be released as a single, fearing a saturation of the Australian market. It should be said that 'I Do, I Do, I Do, I Do, I Do' and 'I've Been Waiting For You' were still in the charts. However, he gave in to the tide of phone calls, telegrams and faxes sent by the record company. It was a good decision – as soon as 'Mamma Mia' was released in August, it climbed the charts at breathtaking speed. When RCA released the album *The Best of Abba* in November, it signalled the beginning of 'ABBAmania' in Australia. In the space of six months, the group sold 850,000 compilations and half a million copies of 'Mamma Mia'.

9 September Stig organized a party in a restaurant in the Östermalm district of Stockholm. During the course of the evening, he presented the group with a platinum disc for sales of the *Abba* album in Sweden. Svenne and Lotta were given a gold disc for their albums *Svenne And Lotta* II and *Oldies But Goodies*. The party ended with a concert by pianist Charlie Norman, accompanied by his son Lennie on bass and Ronnie Gardine on trumpet. The concert was recorded with a view to releasing a live album on the Polar Music label.

In the middle of September, Swedish TV began filming a 35-minute documentary about Stig Anderson. The SVT Örebro team would be following the producer and businessman on his forthcoming trips around Europe.

18 September Vogue Belgium released the compilation album *Greatest Hits*. For the majority of new fans, this was their chance to discover the group's early hits like 'People Need Love', 'Nina, Pretty Ballerina' and 'Ring Ring'. At the same time, the Belgian record company released 'Mamma Mia'. During ten weeks in the charts, the single peaked at No. 2. In France, Vogue released the compilation *Greatest Hits* with a different sleeve.

The belated release of 'S.O.S.' in Britain can be explained by the fact that Epic, noting a decline in ABBA's sales and popularity, hesitated for some time before releasing this new single on to the market. Nevertheless, it was a remarkable return to the British charts for the group, peaking at No. 6.

During September, Swedish TV screened a musical documentary entitled *Made In Sweden For Export*. This 45-minute programme, recorded in English, presented the most popular Swedish artists at that time. Among them were ABBA, Björn Skifs, Lill Lindfors, Merit Hemminsson and Sylvia Vrethammar. ABBA performed 'Mamma Mia', 'I Do, I Do, I Do, I Do, I Do' and 'So Long'. A limited-edition album was produced. The documentary was shown in January 1976 at the MIDEM (Marché International du Disque et de l'Edition Musicale) fair in Cannes and represented Sweden at the Golden Rose of Montreux competition in the spring of the same year.

In Sweden, the four members of ABBA were voted Artists of the Year by readers of *Vecko Revyn*. At a cocktail party, the magazine's editor, Birgitta Dahl, presented them with two prizes: a 'fantasy-surrealistic' painting by artist Hans Arnold and an envelope containing 5000 Swedish kronor. ABBA chose to donate this sum of money to a 'promising young talent', the opera singer Carl Johan Falkman, better known by the name of Loa Falkman.

20–21 September ABBA were in Italy for two days of promotion, including a TV show in Venice. The group then immediately flew to Germany to perform a live version of 'S.O.S.' on the TV programme *Musikladen*.

26 September ABBA were in Paris to record the shows *Samedi est à Vous* and *Ring Parade*, in which 'S.O.S.' was competing against other songs. 'S.O.S.' won the competition and the show was screened two days later. The viewers therefore had the chance to see a shorter version of the clip again on 19 October. During their trip to Paris, the group made several radio appearances (notably the show 5, 6, 7 with Jacques Ourévitch on Europe 1) and filmed *Les Rendez-vous du Dimanche* with Michel Drucker. This clip would be screened on 9 November. 'S.O.S.' was promoted well and was given frequent airplay. The song reached the top of the chart on France Inter's *Hit*, and it made a brief appearance for one week at No. 40 on RTL.

Anni-Frid recorded a duet with Swedish singer Björn Skifs. The song, entitled 'Med Varann' (With Each Other), featured on Björn's *Skifs* album.

15 October Stig went to Copenhagen to receive several gold and silver discs for ABBA's and Svenne and Lotta's record sales in Denmark. Stig was on top form and didn't mince his words: 'Swedish television is neglecting ABBA and it's intolerable! Since Brighton, we have been invited to appear on television just once, while in Britain, Germany and France we have done ten times as many TV shows.' Stig announced to the press that the group would be travelling to the United States in November and that Agnetha would have an operation on her tonsils in December.

In the United States, ABBA's standing was excellent. In 1974, 'Waterloo' had sold 800,000 copies and had been awarded the prize Most Played Song of the Year. The award was now given to them again for 'S.O.S.'. In the trade magazine *Cashbox*, Phil Alexander ran the headline 'ABBA – Hit Makers of International Success'. His article spoke highly of them: 'Since the Beatles, no group has known how to capture the attention of people in the music industry or the public like ABBA.' Of the new album he wrote: 'This record combines a rare technical nature and a rare modernism. A genre somewhere between the genius of Béla Bartók and that of Elton John.'

The group faced a tight schedule when they arrived in San Diego on 2 November. Jerry Greenberg and his associates at Atlantic Records collaborated with Stig so that these two weeks of promotion in the United States would be the most effective. The emphasis was put especially on TV appearances. For *The Mike Douglas Show*, the group were filmed singing from the exotic birds cage at San Diego zoo. The following day, ABBA took off for Las Vegas, where presenter Merv Griffin and composer Neil Sedaka (co-author of 'Ring Ring') welcomed the four Swedes live at Caesar's Palace. ABBA performed 'S.O.S.' and 'I Do, I Do, I Do, I Do, I Do'. Merv Griffin announced them as 'an international supergroup from Sweden'. Americans found Agnetha's first name too difficult to pronounce, and she became known as 'Anna'.

'I GATHERED ON THE [*FRIDA ENSAM*] ALBUM MANY OF THE KINDS OF THINGS I LIKE TO DO BUT WAS NOT ABLE TO DO INSIDE THE FRAMEWORK OF ABBA – WE ARE A GROUP. FOR THE SAKE OF MY OWN PERSONAL SATISFACTION, IT WAS BOTH FUN AND GOOD FOR ME TO DO MY OWN ALBUM. IT HAD NOTHING AT ALL TO DO WITH MY WANTING TO LEAVE THE GROUP.' **FRIDA**

After Las Vegas, they headed for Los Angeles where ABBA recorded three TV programmes: *American Bandstand*, *The Don Kirshner Show* (where they performed five songs, including 'Hey Hey Helen', which they rarely sang on TV) and *The Dinah Shore Show*. During the course of this trip, 20th Century Fox invited the group to take part in a musical film alongside Barry Manilow and Phoebe Snow.

The high point of this trip would be New York. ABBA performed 'S.O.S.' and 'Waterloo' on the very famous *Saturday Night Show*. The group met up again with producer Sid Bernstein, who had been at their concert in Stockholm the previous January. Having successfully handled the Beatles' career in the United States, he promised the four Swedes that he would take control of their destiny on the American continent. ABBA returned to Sweden on 16 November.

10 November Polar Music released Anni-Frid's solo album, *Frida Ensam*. The release was limited to the countries of Scandinavia. The enormous success of the album in Sweden (130,000 copies sold) led to several rumours that Anni-Frid was leaving ABBA. 'I've wanted to record a second solo album for a long time,' said Frida. 'This time, I had no commercial or time constraints. I was able to choose carefully the songs I liked with Benny. I took a great deal of pleasure in making this record.'

Vocally, Anni-Frid was on top form. Listening to the album, the richness and extent of her capabilities come through. She uses her voice like a musical instrument. Moreover, each song has a different 'colour'. Hans Fridlund wrote in *Expressen*: 'On this record, Anni-Frid Lyngstad sings more sensually than with ABBA. It's obvious that she possesses a characteristic stamp and unique musical phrasing.'

Visually, we also see a new Anni-Frid. 'At that time, the group had a very "sequins and glitter" side and an image "for everyone",' explained designer Rune Söderqvist. 'In the case of the *Frida Ensam* album, I found it interesting and original to bring out all of Frida's sensual side. In the studio, we constructed the set of a flat. Ola Lager took all the shots in black and white, and I hand-painted the picture we chose for the cover. For the artwork, I wrote everything by hand, on the front as well as the back. We took lots of care over the illustration of the record. I'm quite pleased with the results. You've never seen Frida like this!'

Harry Doherty wrote in *Melody Maker*: 'The album portrays Frida as a very strong and emotive singer and shows the true value of the music, that if sung properly and with enough feeling, it transcends all language barriers.'

14 November Epic-CBS released the single 'Mamma Mia' in Britain. The album *Abba*, which had come out nine months earlier, would finally enter the British charts thanks to the single, which would be the four Swedes' second No. 1 since 'Waterloo'. It can also be said that this song put ABBA back on the right track as far as their success in Great Britain was concerned. The music critics recognized the qualities of the group and had to admit that they weren't just a flash in the pan.

17 November The compilation album *Greatest Hits* was released. Exclusively for the Swedish market, Polar Music chose to feature the wonderful painting by Hans Arnold on the sleeve. The record entered the Swedish charts on 28 November and stayed at No. 1 for eight weeks. It would sell 300,000 copies in Sweden. 'Fernando' was added to later editions. In Britain, the record would be released in March 1976, with a different sleeve.

From 24 November onwards, Björn and Benny took part in recording sessions for Michael B. Tretow's first album, entitled *Let's Boogie*. During these recordings, lasting several months, all four members of the group would take part, providing vocals and several guitar and piano sessions.

'THE *FRIDA ENSAM* ALBUM HAS A SLEEVE PHOTOGRAPH SO SENSUOUS THAT IT WOULD MAKE THE LEANING TOWER OF PISA STAND TO ATTENTION.' **HARRY DOHERTY** *MELODY MAKER*

'"MAMMA MIA" IS VERY IMPORTANT TO ME BECAUSE THAT VIDEO REALLY BROKE IT IN AUSTRALIA AND AFTER THAT, IN '76, THINGS REALLY WENT ABSOLUTELY WILD AT ONE POINT. EVERY TENTH OF THE POPULATION, EVERY TENTH INHABITANT WOULD BUY AN ABBA RECORD, WHICH IS AN INCREDIBLE RECORD. I DON'T THINK THAT HAS HAPPENED ANYWHERE ELSE WITH ANYONE ELSE.' BJÖRN

1 December   CBS-Cupol released Agnetha's *Elva Kvinnor I Ett Hus* (Eleven Women In a House) album. It was the singer's last record on this label. Apart from 'S.O.S.', all the lyrics were written by Bosse Carlgren and the music composed by Agnetha. She also produced the entire album. Mats Olsson wrote in *Expressen*: 'I like Agnetha Fältskog. She has a voice which has gone straight to my heart since her first hit in 1967. I'd like to be able to say that it's a great album, but I can't. I like Agnetha when she sings sad ballads and songs of genuine sorrow. Here, she has to fight to be able to be heard (and she doesn't manage it!). Is it because the album wants to be taken seriously? Musically, it's quite an original record (good melodies, good arrangements and a different production to ABBA) which deserves genuine lyrics and not clichés pulled out of a hat. Fortunately, the second side makes up for the rest with tracks like "Mina Ögon", "Dom Har Glömt" and "Visa I Åttonde Månaden". I'd prefer to learn more about Agnetha rather than a crowd of fake people in a house which doesn't even exist!'

In view of the way that ABBA's career was taking off, Stig insisted that Agnetha and Frida did no TV promotion for their respective albums. He was relieved to see the end of the contract which tied Agnetha to her record company. From now on, he would be able to remove the credit 'Agnetha by courtesy of CBS-Cupol AB' from all the group's records.

4–5 December   The group were in Germany for the recording of a New Year's Eve show. There was a real party atmosphere as ABBA sang 'I Do, I Do, I Do, I Do, I Do', 'S.O.S.', 'Mamma Mia' and 'Waterloo' in front of an audience.

During December, Björn and Benny completed the recording of Ted Gardestad's new album *Franska Kort* (French Card), which they had begun in August. The record was co-produced by Michael B. Tretow. Frida contributed backing vocals on some songs.

8 December   Agnetha had an operation on her tonsils. After having to put the date back several times due to time constraints, she finally chose this time of year which was more favourable for resting. 'I couldn't wait any longer,' remembers Agnetha. 'Since childhood, I had suffered from repetitive tonsillitis and throat problems. Because of that, I almost jeopardized our participation in the Eurovision Song Contest in Brighton. On tour, I was always afraid of an infection. It became an obstacle to our career. Of course, the operation was painful, in view of my age. For the following two or three weeks I didn't say a single word. I was so afraid that my voice would change!'

10 December   The single 'I Do, I Do, I Do, I Do, I Do' was released in the United States. Its climb up the American charts was slow but sure: the song remained in the charts for eight weeks and reached No. 15 in May 1976.

The year finished brilliantly for ABBA. All the effort put into promotion paid off. In most countries, the group improved on their success or managed to pick up again where their popularity had been foundering.

In the United States, 'S.O.S.' sold more than a million copies. As a result of numerous TV appearances the group became better known and appreciated by American audiences. They also did a lot of TV and radio promotion in France, where, even if their songs did not always reach the top of the charts, as they did in Belgium, their records sold relatively well. After 'I Do, I Do, I Do, I Do, I Do' (silver disc), 'S.O.S.' received a gold disc, and the youth press (*Salut Les Copains*, *Stéphanie*, *Hit Magazine*) were becoming more and more interested in ABBA. It was a successful year in Belgium: 'I Do, I Do, I Do, I Do, I Do' reached No. 2, 'S.O.S.' No. 1, and 'Mamma Mia' had been at No. 2 since 12 December. They spent a total of thirty-one weeks in the Belgian charts. In Germany, 'S.O.S.' was voted Best Song of the Year. And in Britain, 'S.O.S.' and especially 'Mamma Mia' had put a smile back on the faces of British fans.

'ABBA'S HITS ARE SO MUCH BETTER THAN ANYONE THOUGHT AT THE TIME. MANY OF THEM STAND UP AS WELL AS THE BEATLES.'
TIM RICE

1976

The year began very well for the group. Their songs were in the charts in numerous countries and they had just won back the British market, reputed as being one of the most difficult in pop music.

It was a dream come true for Björn: 'Everywhere in the world, Britain is looked on as the home of modern pop music, particularly in relation to groups. In fact, it was the Beatles and the songwriting of Paul McCartney and John Lennon which encouraged Benny and I to start writing pop songs when we did. We thought if they can do it, then so can we.'

3 January Frida broke all records in Sweden with sales of her single 'Fernando', which stayed at the top of the charts for nine consecutive weeks. Even if the singer did no television promotion, the single became a favourite of the radio programmers and was already being called a Swedish classic.

11 January ABBA went to London to record the programme *Top of the Pops*. 'Mamma Mia' was in the British Top 5. Following problems previously encountered with British musicians, this time the group brought along bassist Kaj Högberg, drummer Ola Brunkert and guitarist Lasse Wellander. A new *Top of the Pops* version of 'Mamma Mia' was recorded in the studio on 12 January, with Swedish and British musicians. No one was satisfied with the results. Nevertheless, they used the tape for the show. To avoid problems like this happening in the future, the group would always send promotional films of their songs.

This visit to the UK marked the group's triumphant return to the top of the charts for the first time since 'Waterloo'. The journalists, who had previously been convinced that ABBA's success would be short-lived, suddenly started to sing their praises. Benny and Björn made the most of a press conference to say what they thought of the negative attitude of the British towards ABBA: 'This is the first time since "Waterloo" that we've been met with some sort of respect. We didn't get the image we deserved. Now people believe that we're not just a one-hit group. We never felt we should forget about conquering England, we just thought it was extremely difficult to reach the British people, but we have so much self-confidence that we thought that sooner or later it was bound to happen here. It was just a matter of time, because we had hits in Europe, in Australia and even in America.' With the *Abba* album not managing to get any higher than No. 13 in the charts, Benny tackled the problem of album sales: 'Except in Scandinavia and Australia, we're mainly selling singles. But the singles aren't really representative of everything we do. I wish we could also be appreciated as a band which sells albums. People only know one side of our work. When we make an album, we try to record ten or twelve very good singles.'

During this trip to Britain, Stig and ABBA met two important people from Australian television who were also rivals: Lyle McCabe, director-general of Reg Grundy Productions and Lynton Taylor, programme director for Network 9 (TCN-9). They had travelled to London especially to negotiate exclusive rights for a TV show to be filmed during the group's promotional visit that coming March. ABBA's success in Australia was so great and demand so high that Stig was able to make the most of the situation to up the bidding.

At the end of January, Agnetha, Björn, Benny and Anni-Frid recorded a 45-minute show called *Musikladen – The Best of Abba* for German TV. This show would be screened for the first time on 31 March on the regional channel NDR. Director and producer Michael Leckebusch remembers: 'I was convinced that Germany had to know more about ABBA. The phenomenon had only just begun. The four Swedes had two free days in their timetable and came to Bremen. They knew about my work, so there was no problem in getting them. There was no question of finance either since the entire show cost DM 6,000. It was a pleasure to work with them. They were calm, friendly, co-operative and very professional. We had to record ten songs in two days.

We added "S.O.S." [performed "live" in 1975] because of time constraints. The programme was broadcast in more than thirty countries.'

2 3 February The group were in the studio with director Lasse Hallström to record the promotional film for 'Fernando'. ABBA went for the simple approach, with lots of long shots of them sitting around a fire. This new track gave the fans the chance to see Benny playing the guitar. They made a small mistake with their English on 'Fernando', singing 'since many years …' instead of 'for many years …', which amused the British audience. At the same time, Lasse Hallström recorded the video for 'Dancing Queen', which was filmed at the Alexandra discotheque.

Gold disc for ABBA in Australia

MusikLaden TV special, Germany

22 February The French audience had their first chance to hear the new ABBA song 'Fernando'. ABBA were invited to appear on Guy Lux's *Système* 2 show, live from the Sporting-Club in Monte Carlo. Two days later, Agnetha, Björn, Benny and Anni-Frid were in Paris to appear on *Midi-Première*. 'Fernando' entered the RTL charts on 20 March and stayed there for three months, peaking at No. 3. The single was awarded a gold disc. It was ABBA's best performance in France since 'Waterloo'.

28 February The group were in Germany to record the programme *Disco 76*. During this time, Polydor released the single 'Fernando'. The track would stay in the charts for seven months. It reached No. 1 on 29 March. The German public had taken ABBA to their hearts. Since their victory in Brighton, the group's fans had seen several compilations released by Polydor: *Honey Honey*, *Best of Abba*, *The Very Best of Abba*, *Mamma Mia* and *Pop Power*.

4–14 March Agnetha, Björn, Benny and Anni-Frid paid their first visit to Australia. The welcome they received as they stepped off the plane took them by surprise. The girls were moved to tears. The airport was besieged by about a thousand fans, all shouting and chanting for the group. Even the police, complete with reinforcements, had trouble controlling the crowd. The following day, the newspaper headlines read 'ABBA Fever Hits Australia'. The television news even devoted 8 minutes to a report on what they called 'The most important musical event since the Beatles'. In his report, the journalist said: 'This continent hasn't been touched by a phenomenon like this since Hurricane Tracey.' The group had brought along Thomas Johansson (EMA-Telstar) on this promotional trip; he was in charge of organizing the future tour of Europe and Australia. Journalist Hans Fridlund was also with them. Each day he sent an update on 'ABBA in Australia' by telex to *Expressen* for the next day's paper.

After Melbourne, the group travelled to Sydney. In ten days, they took part in press conferences, autograph-signing sessions, radio interviews and TV shows (notably *A Current Affair*, *Bandstand* and *Celebrity Squares*). The Australians had been waiting so long for this visit and the welcome that ABBA received was so warm that the group found it hard to refuse the numerous requests which came in. There is a story that before ABBA's arrival, many Australians believed that Agnetha and Frida were two models who were there to enhance the group's image and that Björn and Benny had used two very accomplished but less attractive singers in the studio!

Frida at a press conference, Australia

One of the high points of this trip was the recording of a TV show. Two months earlier, several companies had been fighting over exclusive rights. It was eventually Network 9 who won the rights to record the programme. Stig had negotiated airline tickets and first-class accommodation in luxurious hotels for the whole entourage. The television company pulled off a real coup: when the programme was first shown, it was watched by 58 per cent of the viewing public, more than had watched the first moon landing in 1969!

In the televised show, the group performed their biggest hits, with several costume changes. There are actually two versions of the show. In the first, intended for selling abroad and entitled *Abba In Australia*, outside shots

THE BASIC
THING IS
TO BE VERY
HONEST,
NOT TO
SELL AS
MANY
RECORDS
AS POSSIBLE.
THE MAIN
THING IS
TO DO
WHAT YOU
THINK IS
THE BEST
YOU CAN
DO ALL
THE TIME.'
BENNY

'Tropical Loveland', *Musikladen* TV special, Germany

'THE CLOTHES ARE DESIGNED BY OWE SANDSTRÖM AND LARS WIGENIUS. WE MEET REGULARLY. WE TALK AND SKETCH, I OFTEN COME UP WITH IDEAS. WE TRY TO REACH AN AGREEMENT AMONG OURSELVES ABOUT SOMETHING ALL OF US THINK IS GOOD. WE TOTALLY TRUST OWE AND LARS IN QUESTIONS OF QUALITY AND MATERIALS.' FRIDA

were mixed in with studio recordings of the songs. Agnetha, Björn, Benny and Anni-Frid were shown at Sydney zoo, on a boat on the Hawkesbury River, having a barbecue at the water's edge and trying to throw a boomerang during the song 'Tropical Loveland'. The second version, for Australian audiences, was filmed entirely in the studio and entitled *The Best of* ABBA. The show was screened numerous times in Australia and was bought by several television companies around the world.

At the end of ABBA's visit, Vicki Jones, publicity manager for Sydney's TCN-9, declared: 'I have never worked with such an agreeable group of people. Their schedule made them go at a killing pace – but they never once complained. And they were always on time for every appointment. The sort of image they present on screen – friendly, warm, bright, intelligent people – is exactly what they are.' Tony Culliton, the producer/director of the TV special, added: 'They were incredibly easy to get along with. They took direction well, but being professionals, had some suggestions of their own which always worked well. Complete modesty is the group's most refreshing quality.'

13 March   'Fernando' reached No. 1 in Belgium. The record stayed in the charts for four months. A survey revealed that ABBA were the most popular group in Belgium.

23–24 March   ABBA recorded two new tracks at the Metronome studios: 'Knowing Me, Knowing You' and 'That's Me'. Of 'Knowing Me, Knowing You', Benny says: 'I think this ranks as one of our five best recordings.' And 'That's Me' is still one of Agnetha's favourite songs. (*The Complete Recording Sessions*, 1994.)

26 March   The compilation album *Greatest Hits* was released in Britain. It was one of the first records to benefit from a television advertising campaign. There were four unreleased songs on this album: 'He Is Your Brother', 'People Need Love', 'Another Town, Another Train' and 'Nina, Pretty Ballerina'. The album had already sold so many copies through advance orders that it went straight into the charts. *Greatest Hits* stayed at No. 1 for nine weeks.

3 April   The album *Frida Ensam* reached No. 1 in Sweden. It remained on the Svensktoppen chart for forty weeks.

5 April   ABBA attended *Expressen*'s Spring Party, at the Operakällaren restaurant in Stockholm. The group celebrated Agnetha's twenty-sixth birthday at this event, together with Stig and numerous other guests.

During April, ABBA made a brief promotional visit to France. The group performed 'Fernando' on the programmes *Ring Parade* and *Midi-Première*. Vogue released a new pressing of the *Greatest Hits* compilation, with 'Fernando' as a bonus track. After several months, the record was awarded a gold disc.

Expressen published some astounding figures at this time: 'Since the group's visit to Australia, "ABBAmania" has grown even further. The four Swedes have now managed the achievement of having five singles and two albums in the charts at the same time. "Fernando" is at No. 1 and "Ring Ring" is a new entry on the chart at No. 4. "Rock Me" is at No. 5, "Mamma Mia" is at No. 20 and "S.O.S." is at No. 22.' 'Fernando' would actually stay at No. 1 for fifteen weeks. The record for the most weeks at No. 1 in Australia was held by the Beatles with 'Hey Jude', which was at the top for sixteen weeks. In the album charts, *Abba* was at No. 1 and *The Best of Abba* at No. 2. The TV programme *The Best of Abba* was screened several times in Australia. Public demand was so great, however, that the television stations went so far as to buy footage from German and French television. An Australian TV crew was even sent to Stockholm to make a programme called *Abba In Sweden*.

In the United States, ABBA's records were often released in a different order to the rest of the world. While 'Fernando' was having great success all over Europe, 'I Do, I Do, I Do, I Do, I Do' was at No. 15 in America. On 3 May,

'Fernando', ABBA In Australia TV special

Blaupunkt advertising campaign, Sweden

Atlantic released 'Mamma Mia' as a single. It got as high as No. 32 in the charts. Album sales were not as encouraging, since the Abba album hadn't even made the Top 150.

3 May The TV show Made In Sweden For Export (featuring ABBA, Björn Skifs, Sylvia Vrethammar and Lill Lindfors) was shown at the Golden Rose Of Montreux festival. The BBC won first prize.

8 May 'Fernando' managed to knock 'Save Your Kisses For Me', by the 1976 Eurovision winners Brotherhood of Man, off the No.1 spot in the British charts.

ABBA's Eurovision win inspired many imitators. First there was the Brotherhood of Man – two boys and two girls who tried to be 'the new ABBA' but, despite their Eurovision success, didn't manage to keep up the momentum. Then there were the two couples who made up Bucks Fizz, winners of the 1981 Eurovision Song Contest. In Holland, there was Teach-In, Luv' and, especially, the group Champagne, with their songs 'Valentino' and 'Oh Me, Oh My, Goodbye'. These groups tried to copy the ABBA image and sound, but the magic was always missing.

19 May An awful rumour that ABBA had been involved in a plane crash at Berlin's Tempelhof airport caused panic among German fans. Two days later, Polydor Germany's representative told newspaper Expressen: 'After having called Polar Music, I have spent the whole day trying to deny this stupid rumour, but it has already reached neighbouring countries. The bigger it gets, the more distorted it becomes. In Denmark and Holland, they're talking about three members of the group being killed in a plane crash. They're adding that Frida was the sole survivor but that she's now unable to sing any more because she is so badly injured.' Björn said of the situation: 'I can't explain these rumours. Agnetha and myself have often stated that we travel separately by plane because of the children. Maybe someone wanted to make fun of us?'

18 June ABBA paid tribute to a very special couple. King Carl XVI Gustav of Sweden would be marrying Silvia Sommerlath the following day. A huge gala had been organized at the Stockholm Opera House. The event was televised live and featured a host of prestigious Swedish stars like Birgit Nilsson, Kjerstin Dellert, Sven-Bertil Taube, Alice Babs and Elisabeth Söderström. ABBA were also among the artists performing. The group chose to perform the obvious song: 'Dancing Queen'. In honour of the occasion, Agnetha, Björn, Benny and Anni-Frid swapped their stage gear for costumes from the eighteenth century. Their performance captured the imagination of the audience and television viewers alike, but the press laid into ABBA in their

reports. Björn explains: 'They complained about us on the one hand for having written "Dancing Queen" for the future Queen Silvia, which wasn't the case because we had started recording this song a year earlier. On the other hand, the journalists used the gala to throw open the question of us performing live again. They were annoyed with us because we were the only ones to use playback during the show, whilst the other artists sang with the Royal Orchestra. We would have loved to have used the court musicians, but how could they really have reproduced the sound of our song?' At the end of the gala, the King, his fiancée and their entourage went on to Drottningholm Palace, where a grand banquet was held. The 300 guests, including the four members of ABBA, were invited to a huge dinner-dance at the Operakällaren restaurant.

July Björn, Benny and Thomas Johansson of EMA-Telstar travelled to London to make plans for a concert in 1977. Björn had the massive Earl's Court Arena in mind, having attended a Rolling Stones concert there, but they eventually settled on the Royal Albert Hall.

During the summer, the Australian television station Network 7 sent a camera crew to Sweden. Having failed to secure exclusive rights to Abba In Australia, the company had decided to make an hour-long programme entitled Abba In Sweden. Journalist Ian Meldrum interviewed the four members of ABBA on a boat moored in Stockholm port. Numerous clips were filmed around the capital, as well as an interview with Stig and radio presenter Ulf Elfving. For the songs, the company purchased footage from the TV show Musikladen – The Best of Abba. The show Abba In Sweden was screened in Australia on 30 September.

August ABBA recorded five adverts for the Japanese company National. The recording took place in Stockholm, in the ballroom of the Grand Hotel, with the outside shots being filmed near Drottningholm Palace. The song 'Fernando' had been reworked with new lyrics to promote the brand name National. Each little advert featured one of a range of products, from a hi-fi to various other household appliances. The Japanese company invested a million Australian dollars in the twelve-month campaign for Australian television, mainly in Melbourne and Sydney. 'Lots of companies wanted to use our name or a photo of ABBA in their advertising,' explained Stig. 'I was always against it. We made an exception with the company National because it gave us the opportunity to finance part of the Australian tour, and the products didn't do any harm to the group's image. It's more acceptable to see ABBA singing the praises of hi-fi equipment than tights or sweets!' Despite this declaration from Stig, the group were still seen publicizing Lois jeans and Blaupunkt and taking part in the Australian environmental campaign Keep Australia Beautiful.

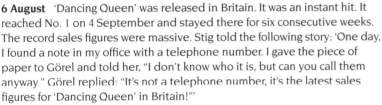

6 August 'Dancing Queen' was released in Britain. It was an instant hit. It reached No. 1 on 4 September and stayed there for six consecutive weeks. The record sales figures were massive. Stig told the following story: 'One day, I found a note in my office with a telephone number. I gave the piece of paper to Görel and told her, "I don't know who it is, but can you call them anyway." Görel replied: "It's not a telephone number, it's the latest sales figures for 'Dancing Queen' in Britain!"'

13 August Vogue released the 'Dancing Queen' single in France and Belgium. The song reached No. 1 in Belgium on 21 August and would stay in the charts for fourteen weeks. This record introduced the whole world to the group's new logo. 'This was the second time that I'd worked with ABBA,' remembers Rune Söderqvist. 'Together with photographer Ola Lager, we thought that they needed an identifiable logo, since the record companies around the world were just doing anything with the design. For a long time I'd been talking to them about a real ABBA logo, easily identifiable and easy to use on any publicity material. I showed them about ten different slides with the reversed "B", each one totally different. I remember that Benny thought that the logo was "too industrial". I told him that this was my job and that he could trust me. I was subsequently proved right. The new logo was adopted from the "Dancing Queen" single onwards. Stig, who understood how powerful it could be, asked me to put it at the top of the record sleeve. This would mean that ABBA's albums could be instantly found on the shelves of the record stores.'

For the first time, Swedish Television was to dedicate a whole programme to ABBA. The documentary, entitled *Abba-Dabba-Dooo!!*, coincided with the launch of the new *Arrival* album and showed a different side of the group. In the middle of August, the four Swedes were filmed and interviewed by Per Falkman on the island of Viggsö. During the same month, several recording sessions took place at the Metronome studios, and Björn and Benny had the chance to complete tracks like 'My Love, My Life', 'Why Did It Have To Be Me' and the instrumental piece 'Arrival'.

16 August Polar Music released the 'Dancing Queen' single. Eight days later, the song was No. 1, staying at the top of the charts for fourteen weeks. More than 150,000 copies were sold in Sweden. 'In the beginning, we had decided not to release the track before the *Arrival* album,' explained Stig. 'But we changed our minds following the hundreds of requests which came in from everywhere. Everyone wanted to buy "the wedding song"!'

18 August Mats Olsson wrote in *Expressen*: 'Is "Dancing Queen" going to be a new worldwide hit, after the enormous success of "Fernando"? I don't know! But the song doesn't have the immediate effect of "Ring Ring", "Waterloo" or

"Mamma Mia" on the listener. On the other hand, though, it's certainly ABBA's best production so far. The attention to tiny detail and the girls' way of singing are becoming ABBA's trademark.' Anni-Frid remembers: 'I loved the song from the very beginning. Coming back from the studio, Benny played the backing track for me. It was so beautiful that I started to cry. I mean, even without lyrics or voices on it, it was outstanding.' As for the song's rhythm, Björn and Benny never concealed the fact that they were influenced by George McCrae's hit 'Rock Your Baby'.

21 August *Musikladen – The Best of Abba* was screened nationwide in Germany. Polydor made the most of the occasion by releasing the double compilation album *The Best of Abba*. The sleeve featured a series of stills from the TV show. In the programme, the group were interviewed and performed their biggest hits, changing costumes for each song.

26 August Vogue released the *Golden Double Album*. The French and Belgian fans had their first chance to hear 'Love Isn't Easy (But It Sure Is Hard Enough)', one of the group's early songs.

During September, the group continued filming for *Abba-Dabba-Dooo!!*. The crew made short film clips for some of the songs and interviewed each member of the group. The sections of ABBA singing live with an orchestra were recorded in a studio at the end of September.

1 September Agnetha, Björn, Benny and Anni-Frid attended the premiere of Lasse Berghagen's show at the Cabaret Berns in Stockholm.

2 September The centre of Stockholm witnessed a demonstration which said a great deal about ABBA's popularity in Sweden. At the beginning of the afternoon, a group of young people, with placards and a portable cassette player, marched around the streets of the capital announcing that the group ABBA would be visiting the steps of the Konserthuset at 4 o'clock that afternoon. The area around the theatre was soon invaded by several hundred people chanting: 'ABBA, we want to see ABBA!' The police, realizing the extent of the problem, finally put up barriers to contain the crowd. But the ABBA fans were disappointed when it all turned out to be a joke.

☆ ☆ ☆ ☆

Görel Johnsen, Stig, Benny & Ted Gärdestad at the Polar Music offices

'I DON'T THINK ANYONE CAN SPECULATE IN THE WAY THE MEDIA SAY WE DO. IT WOULDN'T WORK, BECAUSE IT WOULD BE A FALSE FEELING.' STIG

Baldersgatan 1 was Polar Music's new address and home of the music-publishing company Sweden Music. Baldersgatan is a quiet street. The streets of the area are heavily patrolled at night, not in order to protect ABBA's headquarters but because many of the neighbouring buildings are foreign embassies.

The Polar Music premises were very spacious. Agnetha, Björn, Benny, Anni-Frid, Stig and their nineteen staff would now be able to work more comfortably. On entering the hall, one would find the staircase and the old lift. Both served all four floors of the building. The staircase also allowed access to the basement and loft. In the basement were a sauna and a relaxation room. The ground floor was used principally by the four members of the group. There was a rehearsal room containing the very latest audiovisual equipment. This is where Agnetha and Anni-Frid worked with choreographer Graham Tainton. A few doors further down were Björn and Benny's offices, a meeting room where the team could receive journalists, and finally the fan club's office. Polar Music always made a point of taking care of the fans from all over the world. Christina Bernhag and Sussie Wågeborg managed all this superbly. 'There is a lot of work,' said Christina. 'I receive about 10,000 letters each week. In Sweden alone we have 75,000 members. Membership is free. We try to offer fans items at reasonable prices: posters, T-shirts, etc. Agnetha and especially Anni-Frid call in to see us regularly to read the post and sign photos.'

On the first floor were the offices of Stig and his assistant Görel Johnsen, the telex room, and also the administrative and financial centre, run by Gudrun Anderson and Hans Bergkvist (a childhood friend of Björn's and ex-driver for the Hootenanny Singers). The two top floors were home to an insurance company, independent of the Polar Music company. Behind the noise of the phones and the telex machine, the atmosphere was hushed and studious. Every Friday afternoon, Stig, Björn and Benny, and sometimes Agnetha and Anni-Frid, would meet to discuss offers received during the week, finances, investments and other projects. Everything was decided in a very democratic way. Stig placed a lot of importance on the family way in which the business was run.

☆ ☆ ☆ ☆

'THERE WAS A DEFINITE MUSICAL TRADITION THAT WE SHARED IN SWEDEN, WHERE WE GREW UP WITH GERMAN, ITALIAN AND SWEDISH AS WELL AS ANGLO-SAXON MUSIC, WHICH NO ENGLISH OR AMERICAN POP MUSICIAN WOULD BE EXPOSED TO.' BJÖRN

'THEY WERE EASY AND ALWAYS VERY NICE TO WORK WITH, THEY WERE PROFESSIONALS. BEFORE A PHOTO SESSION THERE WAS ALWAYS A DISCUSSION BETWEEN ME AND THE GROUP.'
OLA LAGER
ABBA'S FORMER PHOTOGRAPHER

29 September   Director Leonard Eek finished filming the documentary *Abba-Dabba-Dooo!!* in the Swedish National Television studios. The group sang live, with a seven-piece orchestra, in front of a teenage audience.

During this time, Agnetha, Björn, Benny and Anni-Frid recorded five hour-long programmes to be transmitted on Radio Sweden's P3 station during the Christmas and New Year period.

2 October   Swedish National Television organized a brief press conference to present the documentary *Abba-Dabba-Dooo!!* to journalists. Agnetha, Björn, Benny and Anni-Frid were there, as well as Leonard Eek, producer and director of the programme. The Swedish press claimed that Agnetha had 'a new smile' – that she had had the gap between her teeth filled in, a gap which had been there since she had begun working in the business. Agnetha eventually set the record straight in *Expressen* on 5 October: 'I have had absolutely nothing done to my teeth since I was eleven years old!'

7–8 October   The four members of the group were invited to go to Poland. ABBA had recently been named Most Popular Group in Eastern Europe. This would be the first time that international artists had performed on the other side of the Iron Curtain. The trip was carefully organized by the Warsaw Travel Office, the Office for Artists, and national television. The Polish government chartered an 'ABBA special' plane to bring Anni-Frid, Björn and Benny, together with about a hundred European journalists, to Warsaw. Agnetha, travelling separately, left the previous day with her father.

A Polish television crew made an entire programme out of the event. More than two hundred journalists and photographers from Russia, Hungary, Czechoslovakia and East Germany were waiting for ABBA at Warsaw airport for a press conference. This was followed by a coach tour of the Polish capital and a visit on foot to the old town. The group then went to the national television studios to record the show *Studio 2 – Abba Special*. They performed eight songs, including six tracks from the new album. After 4 hours under the lights, Agnetha, Björn, Benny and Anni-Frid went back to their hotel for a short while. The day was not yet over, though; there was a second press conference to come. The journalists' questions were quite amusing: 'Why do you sing in English?'; 'Mr Andersson, is Stig your father?'; 'Miss Folkog and Miss Lintatt [the Polish pronunciations], what is your attitude to love?' – Agnetha, hugging Björn, replied, 'This!' Frida, for her part, announced: 'I like making love!' During this interview, Stig told the journalists that the total budget granted by the Polish State for international records was going to be used entirely for 800,000 copies of the *Arrival* album. Everyone in the room applauded.

10 October   After a brief detour to Stockholm, the group took off for two weeks' promotion in the United States. Starting in Los Angeles between 10 and 18 October, ABBA sang on *The Merv Griffin Show*, *The Tony Orlando Show* and *The Dinah Shore Show*. During the last of these programmes, Dinah invited Benny and Anni-Frid to get married in front of the American TV cameras. The couple politely replied: 'We will get married when we have the time, and in the place we want to. At least not in front of the television cameras.'

18–24 October   ABBA took part in two television programmes in Vancouver before moving on to New York to take part in the *Midnight Special* and *Wonderama* shows. On *Wonderama*, a children's entertainment programme, the group sang 'Mamma Mia', 'S.O.S.', and 'Fernando'. During the interview afterwards, Björn talked about the next single, 'Dancing Queen', which was going to be released in the United States on 18 November. Benny amused the children on the set by speaking in Swedish. The trip ended in Philadelphia with *The Mike Douglas Show*. The four members of the group had been named Top TV Entertainers of the Year by the *Sun* and were presented with their prize during the show by actor Anthony Newley. Agnetha and Björn travelled straight back to Sweden, while Benny and Anni-Frid returned to New York for a few days to visit the museums and art galleries.

11 October Polar Music released the long-awaited album *Arrival*. There were advance orders of 250,000 in Sweden. Rune Söderqvist had the idea of photographing the group with a helicopter. This took place at the Barkarby military airfield, north-west of Stockholm. The album entered the Swedish charts at No. 1 on 19 October and stayed there for twelve weeks.

Sivert Bramstedt wrote in *Dagens Nyheter*: 'Beautiful arrangements and new sounds. The voices bring out the characteristic music and strike a perfect balance. The group ABBA invite us to escape.' Mats Olsson was less kind in *Expressen*: 'Björn and Benny have crafted a new style for ABBA, far removed from little pop songs. This is beautifully produced, but too much attention has been paid to technique, which leads to it taking over. ABBA sound here like the result of a meeting between 10cc and the Beach Boys. The lyrics are the weak part. They are nearly all disappointing and are empty of any feelings or ideas. Two tracks, "My Love, My Life" and "Knowing Me, Knowing You" are a concentration of ABBA's faults. Is Stig Anderson to blame? Couldn't Björn and Benny have offered us something else? Don't they have any feelings?' However, Christer Borg wrote in *Kvällsposten*: 'Björn and Benny demonstrate, once again, their exceptional capacity at writing international hits. Technically, *Arrival* can equal any of the best albums in pop music.'

Arrival was a very important album in ABBA's career. Considered one of their best, it proved how much ABBA had developed both musically and artistically, with help from Michael B. Tretow, who had pushed the technical side of the recordings even further. The diversity of the tracks was another thing which made the album original, especially the instrumental title track. At the time of its release, 'Intermezzo No. 1' caused a big surprise because it was so innovative, mixing classical and electronic music. Björn and Benny had created a 'hymn', directly inspired by Swedish folk music. In *Expressen*, Mats Olsson described it like this: 'Swedish violins meet electronics. It really made me think of a caravan of camels which had lost its way in Dalecarlia [a province in the middle of Sweden] on a summer's evening.' During the coming weeks, the album would be distributed in thirty-four different countries.

12 October *Arrival* was released in France and Belgium. Vogue was the only label which gave the album a different presentation: the outer and inner photos were swapped over and the cover had a gatefold sleeve. The record's release could not have been timed better: 'Dancing Queen' was at No. 2 on the France Inter chart and at No. 20 on the RTL radio chart. The track 'Arrival' was covered in France by Petula Clark (as 'La Vallée'), Michèle Torr (as 'J'aime') and also by Daniel Balavoine and Frida (as 'Belle').

25 October Polydor Germany released the *Arrival* album and the 'Money, Money, Money' single simultaneously. The single reached the No. 1 position and remained on the charts for six months. *Bravo* wrote: 'With *Arrival*, ABBA have once again hit the target as far as the public's musical taste is concerned.'

In October, due to the success of 'Dancing Queen', the *Greatest Hits* album returned to the top of the British charts. The album would go on to be one of the all-time bestsellers in Britain, staying in the charts for a total of two and a half years and selling more than three million copies.

In November, Benny and Anni-Frid left their flat in the old part of Stockholm (Gamla Stan) to move into a villa on the island of Lidingö. In 1969, this house was used in the Swedish film *Miss and Mrs Sweden*.

1 November Polar Music released the 'Money, Money, Money' single in Sweden. The following day, Vogue launched the single in France and Belgium. ABBA gave their fans an extra 'gift' with the single: the previously unreleased track 'Crazy World' on the B-side. The song, performed by Björn, had been recorded in October 1974 but had recently been reworked.

5 November SVT2 screened the documentary *Abba-Dabba-Dooo!!* The next day, *Expressen* said: 'The programme was an effective mixture of interview and music, it flowed well and had a good pace. Anni-Frid showed us a personality which is more interesting than when she sings. All four members were very convincing in their affirmation that they totally believe in what they do, that they have never speculated about their careers and that they always try to give their best.' As an indication of ABBA's popularity in Sweden, half the country's population (4.5 million viewers) watched the broadcast.

The same day, Epic released *Arrival* in Britain. The album had already sold 300,000 copies through advance orders, beating the Carpenters, who had previously held the record for advance orders with 225,000 copies for their album *Horizon*. *Arrival* went straight into the British charts at No. 6. The *Daily Express* organized a competition with a hundred copies of the album as prizes; an impressive 21,640 entries were received.

This time, the British press reacted favourably to the album. *Music Week* wrote: 'With different, gentle and easily recognizable songs, ABBA show that good pop is best. On top of this they have brought a new kind of sophistication to the genre.' Bob Woffinden wrote in the *New Musical Express*: 'ABBA are irrepressible. *Arrival* matches expectations, and is their most accomplished set to date. Their lyrics, though improving steadily, remain weak; no doubt Benny and Björn are aware of the problem.' Garth Pearce wrote in the *Daily Express*: 'Their lyrics are innocent and naïve. But their innocence only makes them more attractive. People have always preferred the innocent over the sophisticated.'

The release of the album was followed by the single 'Money, Money, Money' on 11 November. The choice of single was not unanimously appreciated, though, with some people slating the song for being 'German-cabaret style revisited'. The *New Musical Express* called it 'patent rubbish'.

Captivated by its melody, Mike Oldfield covered the track 'Arrival' in 1980, along with the helicopter idea for the sleeve of his single. The British media described the release of *Arrival* as 'the musical event of the autumn'. This response was far removed from the reception given to ABBA during the first half of 1975. As Garth Pearce wrote in the *Daily Express*: 'The worst they could do was to win the Eurovision competition. They were regarded in the beginning as a very lightweight pop group and were not treated seriously in the press. And in 1974 it seemed wrong that they looked so clean and fresh. Pop music then needed to be aggressive and rebellious, performers needed to have long hair and beards.' Julia Barnes of the CBS press service said: 'There was a time when it was extremely difficult to place anything about ABBA in an English newspaper except for the *Record Mirror*. Today the papers literally fight to speak with ABBA. If I could convince ABBA to come to London I could easily fill four days with interviews and as many days with photo shoots for various newspapers.'

This time, the album's launch was accompanied by a massive promotional campaign, with ABBA travelling to England for four days. Epic-CBS planned a spectacular arrival for the group on 15 November, in keeping with the album's sleeve. Immediately after arriving at Heathrow Airport, the four Swedes were supposed to have boarded a helicopter to take them to the Mayflower Queen, a boat anchored in the middle of the Thames. A press conference and luncheon awaited them. However, the record company hadn't counted on the notorious English fog, which descended on the capital that day. The group finally arrived an hour late in a limousine. The reception was very grand. Agnetha, Björn, Benny and Anni-Frid wore their famous white overalls. During the press conference, the group spoke a lot about their future tour of Europe and Australia, but questions about money, success and the so-called 'hit-making machine' dominated the interview. The British journalists were especially impressed by the way that ABBA managed to perfectly combine music and good business sense. There was endless champagne and numerous awards. BBC DJ Simon Bates presented them

'ABBA WERE NOT MORE IMPORTANT FOR THE SWEDISH ECONOMY THAN VOLVO AND SAAB TOGETHER. THAT IS SOMETHING SOMEBODY ELSE MADE UP. I DON'T KNOW WHY THAT EVER OCCURRED. WE MADE A LOT OF MONEY, BUT NOT TO THAT EXTENT.' BENNY

'WE GOT HEAVILY CRITICIZED, ESPECIALLY HERE IN SWEDEN DURING THE 1970s, WHEN THERE WAS A STRONG LEFT-WING MOVEMENT. SO, WE RECEIVED SEVERE CRITICISM ABOUT SELLING A LOT OF RECORDS, EARNING A LOT OF MONEY AND SO FORTH. WE COULDN'T SEE ANY SENSE IN TRYING TO FIGHT BACK. IT WAS BETTER TO CONCENTRATE ON WHAT WE DID – RECORDING MUSIC.' FRIDA

with thirty-two gold, platinum and silver discs for the group's sales in Britain, plus a diamond disc for the 1,250,000 copies sold of *Greatest Hits*. The festivities were brought to a close by Epic-CBS announcing to the group that, only four days after the single's release, 'Money, Money, Money' had already sold 300,000 copies.

In Australia, ABBA pulled off an unprecedented achievement by having three albums simultaneously in the Top 30. The compilation *The Best of Abba* had already sold 860,000 copies, and even before its release the *Arrival* album had sold 750,000 copies through advance orders. Australian TV had screened *Abba-Dabba-Dooo!!* on 26 October, long before other television companies around the world would do so.

The *Melbourne Star* wrote: 'There is no doubt that *Arrival* is ABBA's best album and that they're going to earn lots of "Money, Money, Money".' The *Sydney Gazette* said: 'They definitely have a style which is instantly recognizable. This could be the reason why they are the kings and queens of current pop.'

Even Stig Anderson, who never concealed his taste for making money, couldn't believe it. 'I was astounded,' he said. 'A few years ago, I promised Björn and Benny that with my help they would one day be famous outside Scandinavia. But I could never have imagined such success. We are now selling well everywhere, except for China, North Korea and Vietnam.' On the other hand, ABBA fell victim to intense piracy. A stock of 700,000 pirated albums were discovered in Australia. The records, of an inferior quality, had the same sleeves as the originals but in black and white.

20 November   ABBA were back at the top of the Belgian charts. 'Money, Money, Money' was the fifth single by the group to reach No. 1 in Belgium.

23 November   ABBA made a brief visit to Holland. The four Swedes were invited to take part in the TV show *Een Van De Acht*, presented by Mies Bouwman, on which they performed 'Money, Money, Money', 'Dancing Queen' and 'Why Did It Have To Be Me', wearing their famous kimonos. Before the recording of the programme, the group were presented with numerous gold and platinum discs at a press conference.

24 November   ABBA were in Paris to record two songs for *Les Rendez-Vous du Dimanche*. The first of these, 'Money, Money, Money' was screened on 28 November, while the second, 'When I Kissed the Teacher', would be screened on 2 January. 'Money, Money, Money' had just entered the RTL charts. It stayed there for twelve weeks, reaching No. 1 on 22 January 1977.

Rehearsals for the 1977 tour began at Grünewaldsalen, a room at the Konserthuset in Stockholm. Curiously, the tour wouldn't include Stockholm, although there were two concerts at the Scandinavium in Gothenburg. The 20,000 tickets sold out several hours after they went on sale. Stig told the press at this time: 'I have said to everyone that ABBA are not available for anything between April and October next year. Björn and Benny must have peace and quiet to write new songs for the new album.'

27–31 December   Swedish radio station P3 broadcast a series of five programmes recorded that September: A *för Agnetha Fältskog*, B *för Benny Andersson*, B *för Björn Ulvaeus*, A *för Anni-Frid Lyngstad* and *The Abba Story*. On New Year's Eve, Agnetha, Björn and some of their friends were out drinking champagne at the Alexandra club, before it closed for the last time. Their friend Alexandra Charles, the owner of the club, would later open another establishment bearing the same name.

If 1975 had been a turning point for ABBA, 1976 was without doubt a year of great success, and one of the most important of their career. With such strong songs as 'Mamma Mia', 'Fernando' and 'Dancing Queen', the group had carved out a place for themselves among the world's biggest music stars and discredited the people who had claimed that ABBA were just a one-hit wonder.

In the United States, sales of the *Greatest Hits* album exceeded 500,000 copies. *Cashbox* magazine had just awarded them the prize Top LP and Singles Artists of the Year. ABBA had also received awards galore in Britain. The figures spoke for themselves: 1,250,000 copies sold of *Greatest Hits*. The *Arrival* album, released at the beginning of November, had already sold 450,000 copies and sales of 'Dancing Queen' were approaching 850,000. The *Sun*, having already named them Top TV Entertainers of the Year, awarded them the prize of Top Artists of the Year. Three ABBA tracks were in the paper's Top 10 chart, voted by the readers. Another tribute came from broadsheet *The Times*, which published a long article analysing ABBA's career.

In Britain, ABBA's huge popularity was clearly demonstrated by what had happened in November, when it was announced that two concerts would take place on 14 February 1977 at the Royal Albert Hall. Tickets had gone on sale by mail application only. For the 11,212 available seats, the organizers received an astonishing 3,500,000 ticket applications! It was therefore no exaggeration when David Hamilton introduced ABBA on *Top of the Pops* in December as 'the hottest group in the world'. Showbusiness professionals in Britain often used Stig as an example of successful management. Garth Pearce wrote in the *Daily Express*: 'Stig has built up a relatively small organization that ABBA themselves control 100 per cent. ABBA is actually a model, and there are many within the British music industry who have begun to reassess their views after seeing how ABBA is run. What England needs is one or two Stig Andersons.'

In Sweden, sales were also surprising for a country with a population of only nine million people. The *Arrival* album (which had been at the top of the chart for the last ten weeks) had already sold 770,000 copies. The *Greatest Hits* compilation had sold around 300,000. *Expressen's* annual survey revealed that its readers considered *Abba-Dabba-Dooo!!* to be the Best Television Programme of 1976; the prize would be presented to the group the following spring. Last but not least, a journalist declared that ABBA were the second-biggest Swedish export after Volvo.

In other countries, sales of the *Arrival* album were also exceptional: 800,000 copies in Australia, 225,000 in Denmark, 130,000 in Norway and 52,000 in Finland. In Holland, the cassette *The Best of Abba* was the biggest seller of all time. In Belgium, *Arrival* was awarded a gold disc. In France, the compilation *Golden Double Album* received a gold disc and *Arrival* would receive a platinum disc a few months later. In Turkey, the public voted ABBA Group of the Year.

Mick Farren of the *New Musical Express* summed up the general attitude of the British press towards the four Swedes thus: 'I'd dismissed ABBA until a couple of my noble colleagues pointed out just how complex the ABBA backing tracks were. They were right. It took quite a while to strip away the eager, healthy vocal sound. Once that's done, you're actually left with pop structure in the grand manner of the Beatles or Phil Spector.'

'"MONEY, MONEY, MONEY" WAS A MASTERPIECE AS GOOD AS BEETHOVEN AND BACH. IT IS BANAL SONGS SUCH AS THEIRS WHICH HELP FURTHER MANKIND'S UNDERSTANDING OF MANKIND. THE SONGS WERE BRILLIANTLY CONSTRUCTED. ABBA IS ART.'   PHILIP HAUENSTEIN MUSIC LECTURER

'THEY ARE A LIVING LEGEND. IN BRITAIN, IT'S ROUGHLY RECKONED THAT ONE IN EVERY TEN HOMES HAS AN ABBA RECORD IN THE FAMILY VINYL COLLECTION.' **HARRY DOHERTY** *NEW MUSICAL EXPRESS*

1977

At the beginning of the year, ABBA were awarded numerous prizes for their chart successes during 1976. In Britain, the *New Musical Express* announced that ABBA were now selling more records than either Paul McCartney or Rod Stewart. While *Arrival* was named Best Album of the Year by *Hitmakers* magazine, the readers of *Record Mirror* voted ABBA as their Top Group. The *Daily Express* wrote: 'ABBA are the biggest pop act since the Beatles.' In Holland, 'Dancing Queen' was named the Top Single of 1976. In Portugal, the same trophy went to 'Fernando', and Benny and Björn were awarded the prize for Top Producers and Top Songwriters.

Agnetha and Björn had been talking privately for some time about the possibility of having a second child. So as not to interfere too much with ABBA's career, they decided that it would be best if they planned the birth. After having consulted Stig, as well as the other people around them, they agreed that the most appropriate time would be at the end of the year. The couple, who had been living in Vallentuna for several years, had recently moved to the island of Lidingö, north-east of Stockholm.

4 January The *Arrival* album was released in the United States. It reached No. 20 and would remain in the charts for a total of fifty weeks. *Arrival* was the first ABBA album to be awarded a gold disc on the other side of the Atlantic.

12 January Björn, Benny, Stig and Thomas Johansson travelled to London to finalize details for the British concerts and especially for the shows at the Royal Albert Hall.

In response to journalists who constantly talked about 'ABBA's fortune', Stig announced: 'We are always investing money. For instance, we have just bought an art company, AH-Grafik, and also an art gallery. We're also planning on building a recording studio. Because of costs and timing, it would be much easier if we could work in our own studio. As far as the tour is concerned, it's going to cost between 1.3 and 1.5 million Swedish kronor. We won't make any profit from it at all, but it's important that the fans see ABBA on stage. It's also excellent promotion for the group and will generate record sales.'

In Stockholm, Agnetha and Anni-Frid were supervising the preparation of stage costumes with Owe Sandström and Lars Wigenius. Rehearsals had just resumed at the Europa Films studios in Bromma, near Stockholm. There was just a two-day break to record the promotional film for the next single, 'Knowing Me, Knowing You'. Lasse Hallström recorded the video in the snow, on the island of Lidingö. The indoor shots were filmed in a studio. Once again, the director's trademark style was evident, with long fixed shots highlighting the faces and profiles of the group. ABBA come across as being more sensual than in previous videos.

22 January 'Money, Money, Money' reached No. 1 on the French RTL chart; this was the first time that ABBA had reached the top of the radio station's chart. The song would go on to receive a gold disc. The group had appeared on Michel Drucker's *Les Rendez-Vous du Dimanche* show on 2 January. The clip, showing ABBA dressed in their kimono outfits performing 'When I Kissed the Teacher', had been recorded during the group's flying visit to Paris the previous November.

After rehearsing for several weeks during December and January, ABBA started their European tour, leaving Stockholm for Oslo on the evening of 26 January. The first concert took place at the Ekebergshallen two days later. The climax of the European tour would be the Royal Albert Hall shows on 14 February. (See '1977 Tour' chapter.)

'IT WAS SAID
THAT WE WERE
ALWAYS FALLING
OUT AND IT
WAS ABSOLUTELY
NOT TRUE.
I CANNOT EVEN
REMEMBER AN
AGGRESSIVE
MOMENT
BETWEEN US.'
FRIDA

'ARTICLES HAVE
SPECULATED
THAT FRIDA
AND I HATED
EACH OTHER
FROM THE START,
WHICH IS,
IN FACT, PURE
NONSENSE.
DURING OUR
ABBA CAREER,
WE ALWAYS
SUPPORTED
EACH OTHER
ON STAGE.
IF ONE OF
US WASN'T
ON FORM,
THE OTHER
STEPPED IN
AND TOOK
OVER.'
AGNETHA

2 February The *Sun* published an article exposing alleged 'tensions' within the group. 'Secret Catfights of ABBA's Angels: It is all harmony on stage. But away from the public eye, tensions within ABBA often boil over into full-scale rows. In particular, the two girls go for each other's throats in spitting, screaming catfights.' According to the article, 'Agnetha is obsessional about being on time for rehearsals and being ready in costume on time for their stage appearances. Frida is constantly late. Agnetha, on the other hand, is not as quick on the uptake as Frida. She needs more rehearsals. She doesn't seem to grasp the musical points being made by Björn and Benny as quickly as Frida. In rehearsal, Frida's exasperation with Agnetha's slowness bubbles over and the two girls really let fly at each other.'

At the time, the group were playing in Berlin. Björn and Benny were keen to keep the article hidden from Agnetha and Frida before they went on stage. After the concert, the girls were stunned by the news. 'None of this makes sense,' said Benny, 'none of us have made any statements like this.' Björn added: 'On tour, we are together all the time. Sometimes you can get on each other's nerves and might say something you shouldn't. It would be very strange if that didn't happen. But there is no conflict within the group!' Agnetha said: 'I started crying when I read all these lies about me. Especially when I think that this all gets repeated around the world. Frida and myself have very strong personalities, but we have never come to blows. We're the best friends in the world and we tell each other everything.' Anni-Frid seemed to look at the matter with detachment and a sense of humour: 'I almost burst out laughing. Nobody could really believe that the members of a group would stay together when they're quarrelling, scratching each others' eyes out and spitting at one another!' Following the article, proceedings were taken out against the *Sun*. Afterwards, it seemed that whenever sales dropped, or if the news lacked a titillating story, the British and international press would dust off this story and use it again. Of the four members of the group, it was Agnetha who was ultimately most affected by all these remarks.

The German fans couldn't wait for the tour to reach their country. Polydor made the most of the situation by releasing the single 'Knowing Me, Knowing You'. This would be the seventh ABBA single to reach No. 1 in the German charts. Once again, the group decided to feature an unreleased track on the B-side: 'Happy Hawaii'. The original piano-guitar demo had a Fats Domino feel, with vocals by Björn and the title 'Why Did It Have To Be Me'. It was Benny's idea to try an arrangement with Hawaiian guitars. Stig wrote some lyrics to go with the title 'Happy Hawaii' and the vocals were given to Agnetha and Frida. Once the song was finished, the group all thought that it was too slow for the *Arrival* album. After having tried a country version entitled 'Memory Lane', they decided to go back to the first recording with Björn on vocals, and 'Why Did It Have To Be Me' was included on the new album. This is a perfect example of how Björn and Benny would work, tirelessly searching for original sounds and new arrangements, while still using their own melodies as a base. 'Happy Hawaii' was used in an Australian cartoon film series which animated some of ABBA's songs. (*The Complete Recording Sessions*, 1994.)

4 February Epic-CBS released the 'Knowing Me, Knowing You' single in Britain. Videos would be indispensable to ABBA this year, as the group were doing no television promotion. The 'Knowing Me, Knowing You' video was excellent. It seemed to correspond perfectly with the image the public had of the two couples – even if the four Swedes didn't smile quite as much as in previous clips!

13 February Vogue released 'Knowing Me, Knowing You'. In Belgium, the song shot straight up to No. 2 on 26 February and stayed in the charts for eleven weeks.

14 February ABBA performed in London at the Royal Albert Hall. At the end of the two concerts, the four Swedes were tired but happy as their dressing rooms were invaded by friends, various showbusiness people and journalists. Benny was still suffering from shock: 'I remember a moment in the middle of the Albert Hall night when I thought, "Good grief, Benny, this is you sitting here playing at the Albert Hall." For a little while, I could not believe it was me there. It was very hard for me to sit steady on my stool.' Anni-Frid added: 'I managed to control my nerves. At the end of the show, when the audience went wild, it was a real pleasure to be on stage!' Agnetha had a different impression: 'I was terribly nervous during the first show. I felt really strange and couldn't move, I couldn't calm myself down.' Björn concluded by saying: 'Some people say that London audiences are difficult. Maybe they are at first, but after that: wow!'

'WHEN PEOPLE COME TO ME AND SAY: "BUT REALLY, OWE, THEY LOOKED TERRIBLE IN THOSE COSTUMES!" I SAY, YES, BUT YOU MUST GO BACK TO THE 1970s, IT WAS FASHION!' **OWE SANDSTRÖM**

16 February Prince Rainier and Princess Grace of Monaco presented ABBA with the Carl Allen Award for Best Vocal Group of 1976. The ceremony took place at the Lyceum Ballroom in London.

17 February The group returned to Stockholm. Agnetha, Björn, Benny and Anni-Frid had a week to recover and to prepare for their departure for Australia.

18 February 'Knowing Me, Knowing You' was released in Sweden and in Holland, where the single would reach No. 3.

The group and their entourage spent a lot of time discussing the idea of making a documentary film about the tour. The prospect of a TV show called 'ABBA In Concert' had been abandoned, and eventually, the idea of a full-length film in 35mm Panavision was proposed. Everyone seemed enthusiastic apart from Benny, who still had bad memories of filming in Africa with the Hep Stars. Stig's main argument in favour of the film was that this would be the perfect opportunity for the many fans who hadn't had the chance to go to a concert to see ABBA on stage. Because this was now going to be a full-length film, Lasse Hallström had to bring along more equipment and increase the number of people on his team. It was the director who suggested the idea of having a mini-screenplay and using some actors in the film. (See 'Abba – The Movie' chapter.)

25 February ABBA flew from Stockholm to Sydney, via London. There was a reception organized at Stockholm's Arlanda airport before their departure. The Australian ambassador to Sweden, Lance Barnard, came along to congratulate Agnetha, Björn, Benny and Anni-Frid and to wish them well for their series of concerts in his country.

27 February In Australia, the euphoria – which had been dubbed 'ABBA-mania' by the media – had reached fever pitch. The record company were rubbing their hands with glee, as nobody had achieved better record sales or chart positions since the Beatles. The song 'Knowing Me, Knowing You' was at No. 9 in the charts and the 'I've Been Waiting For You'/'King Kong Song' single, originally released in 1975, had re-entered the Australian charts three weeks earlier. Keith Cronau, from RCA, had obtained Stig's permission to release a new edition of the *Ring Ring* album with a different sleeve. The album earned three platinum discs as a result.

Press conference in Australia

Vogue Records promotional poster

3–12 March ABBA gave eleven concerts in the main cities of Australia: Sydney, Melbourne, Adelaide and Perth. A total of 145,000 people came to see the group. This was the most important tour on the Australian continent since the Grateful Dead and the Rolling Stones.

13 March ABBA and the majority of their team returned to Stockholm. Stig had just received a telex informing him of the group's sales in South Africa and Rhodesia. *Greatest Hits* had sold more than 50,000 copies. *Arrival* was still No. 1 in the charts, having sold 25,000 copies in South Africa and 15,000 in Rhodesia.

1 April CBS in Sweden released an album entitled ABBA – *Our Way* by Nashville Train. The group was in fact made up of Roger Palm (drums), Rutger Gunnarsson (bass), Janne Lindgren (guitar) and some of the other musicians who worked with ABBA. The instrumental version of their song 'Please, Change Your Mind', was used in the opening credits of the film *Abba – The Movie*.

2 April 'Knowing Me, Knowing You' reached the top of the British charts and stayed there for five weeks.

9 April Björn and Benny's dream came true. A telex arrived, announcing that ABBA had reached No. 1 in the United States with 'Dancing Queen'. Agnetha remembers: 'We were in the office when all of a sudden we heard someone shouting: "ABBA are No. 1 in the U.S.A!" We immediately opened a bottle of champagne to celebrate the event!'

19 April ABBA shared the front page of *Expressen* with skier Ingemar Stenmark. The previous day at the newspaper's Spring Party they had been awarded the Golden Wasp (the wasp is *Expressen*'s logo) for *Abba-Dabba-Dooo!!*, which the newspaper's readers had voted Best TV Programme of 1976. *Expressen* announced that the Swedish ABBA fan club now had more than 200,000 members. In Britain, figures were equally impressive, with 40,000 people having already subscribed.

26 April Atlantic released 'Knowing Me, Knowing You' in the United States. The single stayed in the American charts for fifteen weeks, peaking at No. 14.

At the beginning of May, Björn, Benny and Michael B. Tretow travelled to Los Angeles to meet Tom Hidley, whose mission was to construct ABBA's future recording studio, together with architects Michael Borowski and Jan Setterberg. The Polar Music studio was going to be built in an old Stockholm cinema, the Riverside. Meanwhile, Anni-Frid was taking part in the recording of Claes af Geijerstam's *Starlight* album at the Glen studios.

17 May Björn, Benny, Anni-Frid and some of their friends went to see the Eagles in concert at the Gröna Lund amusement park in Stockholm.

The Japanese label Discomate Records released 'Dancing Queen' as a single and chose 'Tiger' for the B-side. The single took ABBA to the top of the Japanese charts for the first time, an event which coincided with the release of the *Arrival* album in June.

28 May 'Knowing Me, Knowing You' reached No. 8 on the RTL chart. The single received frequent airplay on the main French radio stations, with the video being screened on television four times.

31 May Björn and Benny began recording ABBA's next album at the Marcus Music studio in Stockholm. The first track, entitled 'A Bit of Myself', would eventually become 'The Name of the Game'. The two musicians had to work to a very tight schedule since the album was planned for release during December, to coincide with the release of *Abba – The Movie*. At Polar Music, there was even talk of the possibility of a double album, with one of the two discs being a live recording of ABBA on stage in Australia.

The majority of June was devoted to filming additional scenes for the full-length film *Abba – The Movie*. Lasse Hallström and his team filmed these scenes in Stockholm and the surrounding area. Australian actors Robert Hughes and Tom Oliver flew over especially from Sydney.

1 June There were studio sessions for the new song 'Eagle'. Björn had given it the provisional title 'High, High'. 'The words came to me quite quickly,' he explains, 'after having read *Jonathan Livingstone Seagull*, the book by Richard Bach. People often said that the song was a homage to the group the Eagles, but that's not the case. I wrote the lyrics on Viggsö, in silence, surrounded by nature, water and space.'

2 June Anni-Frid went to see Lasse Berghagen's new show at the Gröna Lund amusement park in Stockholm. On the same day, Agnetha and Björn announced to the press that they were expecting their second child at the end of the year.

30 June The Swedish press announced that Agnetha would have to pay Danish composer Per Hviid 5000 Swedish kronor. Seven years earlier, he had accused Agnetha of plagiarizing his work in her song 'Om Tårar Vore Guld'. The compensation payment put an end to this prolonged controversy.

During the first two weeks of July, Lasse Hallström finished the filming of *Abba – The Movie*.

11 July Björn and Benny joined the Hootenanny Singers for a one-off concert at the Västervik Visfestival (Song Festival), where 1400 people came to watch Hansi Schwarz, Tony Rooth, Lars Frosterud and the two ABBA musicians.

☆ ☆ ☆ ☆

Throughout the summer, Björn and Benny alternated studio recording sessions with long periods of writing. The two musicians would spend hours searching for arrangements which would be just right for their melodies. The same applied to the lyrics, with them trying every idea and combination possible. 'We considered that the sound of the words was more important than their meaning,' Björn later commented. 'When we found a catchy hookline, we thought that the repetition was very effective!'

For the forthcoming album, however, they used this technique far less. The latest compositions had a new sound and different arrangements to their previous records. The lyrics were also more developed. They were slightly ambiguous ('Eagle', 'Move On'), or more profound ('One Man, One Woman', 'The Name of the Game'). Benny emphasizes the shift in approach: 'I find that it's easier to retain a liking for the songs that we recorded from this period onwards. The lyrics tend to be better and the melodies are stronger. "One Man, One Woman" is probably my favourite track off *The Album*, apart from "Thank You For The Music".' (*The Complete Recording Sessions*, 1994.)

In the studio, the two musicians had trouble trying to fit together the songs from the mini-musical which featured in their stage show, despite the fact that they had already been performed live on numerous occasions. However, Björn and Benny had composed 'Thank You For the Music', 'I Wonder (Departure)' and 'I'm a Marionette' specifically for the stage, with strong cabaret-style arrangements designed to reinforce the visual effect. The songs therefore had to be adapted for the record.

☆ ☆ ☆ ☆

'NINETY PER CENT OF THE SONGS SO FAR HAVE BEEN RECORDED WITH BACKING TRACKS, AND THE MOOD HAS BEEN THERE BEFORE THE LYRICS HAVE BEEN ADDED.' **BJÖRN**

During August, the Japanese label Discomate Records released 'That's Me' as a single, with 'Money, Money, Money' on the B-side. In anticipation of its release, Lasse Hallström had recorded the video for 'That's Me' the previous July, on the island of Viggsö. Several shots which hadn't been used in either 'Money, Money, Money' or 'Knowing Me, Knowing You', were added to the final cut.

2 August   Due to the lack of ABBA scoops, with the group working on the album and Agnetha being pregnant, the Swedish press turned their attention to the financial side of Polar Music. The headlines declared: 'Polar Music is the most profitable company in Sweden'. Since Brighton, profits had been invested in the following: the purchase of AH-Grafik, a wholesale company dealing in art (3 million kronor); the film *Abba – The Movie* (3 million kronor); the Polar Music recording studio (3–4 million kronor); the purchase of various buildings (5 million kronor); the purchase of land and various shares; the purchase of the Wimab company in Umeå, importing and selling sports goods.

5 August   *Expressen* ran the headline: 'ABBA and Anders Wall exchange pop music for oil'. In the article, Arne Lamberg explained how the group were paid in Eastern Europe. Stig and ABBA, helped by financial adviser Anders Wall, had created the company Sannes Trading. This firm, which had its head office in Gothenburg, owned an office in Warsaw and sub-offices in East Germany, Romania, Czechoslovakia and Russia. When a new album was

9 September   Alfred Haase arrived in Stockholm to spend the weekend with Benny and Anni-Frid. A week later, the singer confided to the *Gothenburg Post*: 'I wasn't strong enough to go with Benny to the airport. I was so tense before I met my father. When he arrived, we kissed each other but I don't remember what we said. I was very nervous and so was he. He told me everything. He hadn't known that my mother was expecting a child. And I'd always been told that he had been killed on his way back to Germany. When I was small, I used to think that he was out there somewhere and that one day we'd meet. He told me a lot about my mother. The first time he met my mother, in Ballangen, she was carrying a bucket of milk. They saw each other every day until it was time for him to leave.' Anni-Frid added: 'My father has now gone back to Karlsruhe and all the tension has come back. The other night I was crying for hours. It's very hard to suddenly discover that you have a father when you're thirty-two years old.' At the end of the interview, her face lit up: 'I've got a thirty-year-old half-brother, Peter, and a thirty-four-year-old half-sister called Karin. My father and I are so alike. We've got the same features, the same crooked index fingers and identical feet.'

At the beginning of September, Lasse Hallström recorded the videos for 'The Name Of The Game' and 'Take a Chance On Me'; The former was filmed in the garden and on the veranda of Björn and Agnetha's house.

'TECHNICALLY, AGNETHA IS A SOPRANO AND I'M A MEZZO-SOPRANO. SO I HAVE THE DEEPER VOICE AND SHE HAS A HIGHER-PITCHED VOICE.'   FRIDA

released, Polar Music would send a team out to those countries. The records were pressed and sold in that territory and the group were paid in currency. The money went through Sannes Trading, who would buy, among other things, oil, vegetables and tinned food. These products were then transported to Sweden where they were resold. The company would then pay the money back to Polar Music.

11 August   The headlines announced: 'ABBA leave Sweden to escape jealousy and financial pressure.' At every press conference from now on, journalists wouldn't fail to ask the question: 'With taxes being so high, do you ever think of leaving Sweden?' Benny replied by saying: 'We know very well that we wouldn't be able to live in peace anywhere else. In Stockholm, Frida and myself often go to the theatre, cinema or go to see a show. Nobody comes to bother us. We really appreciate that. That kind of freedom is priceless.' Björn was always firm on the matter: 'We will never leave Sweden. Where would we go? This is our home and we love it. Swedish taxes are high, but it's not as if we have any financial worries. And we don't even have expensive tastes. We have houses, summer cottages, boats and even an island. We don't need much more.'

Anni-Frid's private life was suddenly turned upside down by the astonishing news that her father, who she believed to have died at the end of the Second World War, was still alive and living in Karlsruhe, Germany. The discovery was the result of an article which had been published in German pop weekly *Bravo*. On 25 August, the magazine had featured a biography of the four members of ABBA. Andrea Buchinger, one of the group's fans, had read the article and recognized the name of her uncle, Alfred Haase. She immediately telephoned her cousin Peter, who asked his father if he had known a certain Synni Lyngstad during the time he had spent in Norway in 1944. Alfred Haase's thoughts were suddenly taken back thirty-three years to the time of his relationship with Synni. As a result of the article, Alfred contacted Polar Music immediately. One of the female office staff, who spoke fluent German, took his call and passed on the information to Anni-Frid, who discovered that her father was still alive. Once she had recovered from the shock, she invited her father to come to Stockholm.

Anni-Frid with her father, Alfred Haase

Opening of the AH-Grafik art gallery

13 October Vogue released the single in France. It reached No. 23 in the RTL chart, stayed there for two weeks, and then fell again. The video was screened for the first time in France on 30 October on *Les Rendez-Vous du Dimanche*. The group had more success in Belgium, though, where the single spent fourteen weeks in the charts and peaked at No. 2, the same position that it reached in the Netherlands.

17 October Polar Music released 'The Name of the Game'. It had already sold 140,000 copies through advance orders. The record had been exclusively previewed three days before its release on P3 radio. Anni-Frid had been invited onto Ulf Elfving's *Skivspegeln* programme, where she spoke at length about the new album and *Abba – The Movie*. The single spent eighteen weeks in the Swedish charts, peaking at No.2.

Mats Olsson wrote in *Expressen*: ' "The Name Of The Game" is a gentle song which doesn't have the immediate impact of ABBA's previous singles. It has a slow rhythm and all the instruments can be heard. Its best quality is the sad little melody and the two sections where the group carry on singing without any musical accompaniment. The worst part of the song is the trumpet, reminiscent of the Beatles' "Penny Lane" period. The B-side, "I Wonder", is a beautiful ballad which was recorded live on stage in Sydney. Frida sings with a lot of emotion. The song's melody has got all the qualities of a stage musical and shows how Björn and Benny are always willing to try something new. A good record and a new sound for ABBA.'

Stig and his wife Gudrun had just bought a huge villa on the island of Djurgården, in the centre of Stockholm. They would leave their old house in

'I'D SAY AGNETHA IS MORE THE INTERPRETER OF WHAT SHE'S DOING AND FRIDA IS MORE THE NATURAL SINGER.' BENNY

12–16 September Björn, Benny, Frida and Michael B. Tretow left Stockholm for the Bohus Studio on the west coast of Sweden. As well as mixing 'The Name of the Game', they did some work on the soundtrack of *Abba – The Movie*. Agnetha stayed in Stockholm. This led to new rumours suggesting that the singer was seriously ill. Agnetha responded by saying: 'I'm not ill at all. My doctor just recommended some peace and quiet. I'm not holding up the release of the new album, either. We have quite simply scheduled my recording sessions for the mornings and I rest for the remainder of the day. There have been far too many lies going around since I became pregnant and these rumours have got to stop.'

23 September Atlantic released 'Money, Money, Money' in the United States. The single did quite badly in comparison with the previous singles, failing to reach higher than No. 56 on the Top 200.

During October, RCA released 'The Name of the Game' in Australia. The B-side, 'I Wonder (Departure)' had been recorded on 3 and 4 March during the concerts at the Sydney Showground. Benny just reworked the piano parts in the studio. This was the first time that a live ABBA track had been released on vinyl. The fans were delighted, especially since the prospect of a live album seemed to be back on the cards. However, Björn was not keen: 'I hate live albums myself. It's boring to hear "reproductions" of songs that sound much better in the studio. That kind of thing only works with artists who somehow reinterpret their material on stage.' (*The Complete Recording Sessions*, 1994.)

10 October Polydor Germany released 'The Name of the Game'. The single rose no higher than No. 7. Since 'S.O.S.', every one of the group's singles had been up tempo and had reached No. 1; the performance of 'Name of the Game' suggests that the Germans preferred ABBA's more fast-paced songs.

Nacka during December. Meanwhile, Stig travelled to New York to negotiate the renewal of ABBA's contract with Atlantic.

19 October *Expressen* announced that the singles 'S.O.S.' and 'Money, Money, Money', as well as the *Arrival* album, had entered the charts in Russia.

In Stockholm, the recording of the new album was moving along more quickly than expected. Agnetha, whose pregnancy was approaching full-term, announced: 'I've finally finished recording the vocals. The last few sessions were very uncomfortable. I had to sing while lying in a deckchair.' Because she had been told to rest, she was unable to attend the opening of the group's art gallery. Several artists and art lovers attended the cocktail party which marked its opening. Anni-Frid, Benny and Björn were also there. The gallery displayed paintings by Miró, Arman and Vasarely, among others.

1 November The press announced: 'Paintings stolen off ABBA's walls'. The AH-Grafik gallery had been burgled. The total value of the items stolen was 300,000 Swedish kronor. Tom Anderson, the gallery's director, announced: 'We discovered the theft yesterday morning. It must be the work of professionals. The items stolen were obviously carefully chosen. However, I'd like to know why the robbers also destroyed a part of the gallery.'

5 November ABBA reached No. 1 in Britain with 'The Name of the Game' and stayed at the top of the charts for the rest of the month. *Sounds* magazine commented: 'A satisfying emotive chord sequence and the usual superb vocal harmonies.' By releasing 'The Name of the Game' as a single, ABBA seemed, once again, to have made the right decision. The single's success in most countries was undeniable. Nevertheless, with the length of the single being 4 minutes 54 seconds, the group were risking the song either being cut short on the radio, or, even worse, being left off the playlists altogether. In the end, though, the unusual length of the single didn't seem to pose too many problems.

Meanwhile, the press were still tirelessly searching for ABBA stories to fill their columns. When they weren't talking about ABBA's fortune, they either wrote about Stig's lifestyle or focused on the art collection and gold records which decorated the walls at Polar Music. *Record Mirror* organized a pseudo-trial in which journalist Tim Lott accused ABBA of 'making bland and sickly music, of insulting their audience with an embarrassing stage act, and of having become a mechanical hit machine'. This attack was all the more uncalled for as, in an interview with Lott, Björn had just admitted: 'We didn't make any money at all from that tour. In fact, we lost, despite every concert being sold out.' Björn even added: 'We didn't enjoy it much anyway. It was boring – all that time confined to hotel rooms. It's healthy to stand on stage and perform, but I just can't understand how some groups tour for eight, nine, even ten months – it would kill me.' Talking about the conception of the show, he said: 'I think if we did it again, we'd concentrate more on the music than on the cabaret, make it not so much a show as a musical concert.' With the group's sixth single at the top of the charts, some other British journalists began to ask if ABBA were 'the new musical phenomenon after the Beatles' or just 'a hit-making machine'.

At the end of the year, the first issue of *Abba* magazine was published in Britain. Officially authorized by the group, it was issued in response to the ever-growing demand for information from the public and the fans. Along with the Beatles, ABBA were now among the very few artists to have their own monthly magazine on sale in the shops.

7 November 'The Name of the Game' entered the Australian charts, staying for nineteen weeks but peaking at No. 6. Even if ABBAmania had abated slightly, the four Swedes were still front-page news. According to a journalist, one Australian household in three owned a copy of the album *The Best of Abba*; he concluded his article by asking: 'Is the word "popular" strong enough for a group like ABBA?'

21 November Anni-Frid, Björn and Benny appeared on the Swedish television programme *Nöjesliv*. The three members of the group talked about the new album and *Abba – The Movie*. In a world exclusive, the programme also featured a clip from the film.

22 November A private screening of the film was organized at the Look cinema in Stockholm. Chris Kuhn (from Svensk Filmindustri) was responsible for selling the film to foreign buyers. The screening was attended by seventy-five publishers and film distributors. Two days later, a contract was signed between Polar Music, Reg Grundy (the film's co-producer) and Warner Brothers U.S.A. Svensk Filmindustri also sold the rights to Denmark, Norway, Finland, Germany, Belgium, Holland and Israel. The Reg Grundy company were in charge of distribution in Australia and New Zealand, while Warner Brothers released the film elsewhere.

In the United States, Atlantic, who had just had their contract with Polar Music renewed, decided to release 'The Name of the Game' on 28 November. The single entered the *Billboard* 100 on 24 December.

4 December At 9 p.m., Agnetha gave birth to a boy, who was named Christian Peter. The baby was 54 centimetres long and weighed 3.78 kilograms. Although the mother was said to be doing well, she was very tired. Björn told *Expressen*: 'She started having pains the night before. At 3 o'clock in the morning, Agnetha was really suffering. I took her to Danderyd hospital. She went through hell and was in labour for 18 hours. During the last few months, she had been told by the doctor to lie down as much as she could, since there was a risk of losing the child.'

Photo session for Abba – The Album

5 December It was announced that twenty-five of the group's gold discs had gone missing. They had been stolen when Björn and Agnetha had moved to the island of Lidingö. When the couple were making plans to move from their home in Brevik to a 1940s villa in the Gåshaga area of Lidingö, they had called a removal company called Freys Express. Bo Lindahl, one of the people in charge of the company, explained what happened: 'Björn and Agnetha called on our services when they were moving. Because the date was changed at the last minute, we were unfortunately unable to carry out the work due to lack of staff. We therefore contacted another company to take care of moving their furniture. When they were unpacking at their new house, Björn noticed that twenty-five gold discs were missing, as well as an electric drill.' Stig said: 'The cost of a gold disc is no more than about 350 Swedish kronor, but it could easily be sold for much more. I don't think we'll get any of the stolen goods back. It's a shame, because the sentimental value is much higher.'

6 December Stig Anderson, Gudrun and director Lasse Hallström travelled to Sydney to attend the premiere of *Abba – The Movie*. Benny and Anni-Frid were on holiday in the United States.

9 December Christian Peter Ulvaeus, in his parent's arms, made the front pages of the Swedish papers. Bengt H. Malmqvist was the only photographer permitted to take official shots of the baby at Danderyd hospital. These photos were also published in the foreign press.

12 December   Polar Music released ABBA's new album throughout Scandinavia. Intended to accompany *Abba – The Movie*, it was entitled *Abba – The Album*. The sleeve was the work of Björn Andersson and Rune Söderqvist. Rune explained: 'From the very start, Stig Anderson wanted the album to promote the film and the film to promote the album. It was therefore necessary to create something which was relevant to them both. I thought that it would be original not to just feature a photo of the group but to use the contents of the film as an illustration. Firstly, I did a sketch of the four ABBA members' heads, which Björn Andersson then painted. I added to that all the tiny characters from the film. In Britain, they added a bluish background because they didn't think that a white sleeve would be commercial enough.'

Abba – The Album marked a new stage in the group's career. As usual, the production was brilliant and the arrangements very sophisticated. This time, however, the tracks were longer and the lyrics more profound. Among the nine songs were 'The Name of the Game' and a studio version of 'I Wonder (Departure)', as well as another track from the group's mini-musical 'The Girl With the Golden Hair' (performed in concert on the 1977 tour) – 'Thank You For the Music', a song which would go on to become an ABBA classic.

Advance orders for the album were impressive: 600,000 copies in Sweden and 200,840 in Norway. Four factories were used to press and package the album for Scandinavia alone. The album's international release had been postponed until the beginning of 1978. This was for the simple reason that in some countries, advance orders were so high that there wasn't enough time to press sufficient copies.

15 December   *Abba – The Movie* was released in Australia. The premiere had taken place the night before at the Hoyts Plaza Theatre in Sydney. Stig, Gudrun, Lasse Hallström and actor Robert Hughes attended the premiere. Robert remembers: 'When the film finished, everyone went beserk. I was really worried because they were pushing my wife Robyn around [she was in the later stages of pregnancy]. There were teenagers tearing, ripping our clothes and the limos were gone. Mrs Grundy [Joy Chambers] had taken the car. Finally, we jumped into Tom Oliver's limo to make a getaway.'

In Sweden, children doing door-to-door newspaper deliveries were given a flexidisc entitled ABBA *Live 77* for Christmas. The gold vinyl record featured five tracks from the group's Australian concerts: 'Fernando', 'Rock Me', 'Why Did It Have To Be Me', 'Money, Money, Money' and 'Waterloo'. This was Polar Music's idea, carried out in association with a newspaper publisher.

16 December   *Expressen* paid homage to ABBA with the first in a series of cartoon strips retracing the group's career. One episode of T*he* ABBA S*tory* was printed in the newspaper each day. The idea and text came from Peter Himmelstrand, with the pictures being drawn by Kjell Ekeberg. The cartoon, in a total of twenty-one episodes, was also published in Denmark, Norway, Finland and Germany. Peter Himmelstrand was well known to the group. A journalist and musician, he had written the words for the Festfolket show in 1970, as well as several songs for Agnetha and Anni-Frid.

26 December   The Swedish premiere of *Abba – The Movie* took place. For this exclusive evening, the Nybroplan district of Stockholm had been turned into a Hollywood boulevard. Limousines made their way along Strandvägen and pulled up outside the China cinema. As the numerous celebrities made their way along the red carpet, their names were announced by loudspeaker to the crowds outside. Thirteen policemen were on hand to handle security. This was Agnetha's first public appearance since Christian had been born, and she seemed tired but happy. After the screening of the film, Claes af Geijerstam got up to make a speech and invited the four members of the group onto the stage to present them with a golden gong. At the end of the gala, the guests were taken by bus to Stig's new house, the Ekarne villa on the island of Djurgården, for a private party.

30 December   *Abba – The Album* went straight into the Swedish charts at No. 1. Mats Olsson wrote in *Expressen*: 'The group changes and develops with each album. If you compare this with older songs like "So Long" or "Hasta Mañana", it's hard to believe that it's the same group. As far as lyrics, production and content are concerned, "Eagle" is the best song that ABBA have ever composed. The group have lacked fantasy and ambiguity in their songs for a long time, but this song features them both.' In *Vecko Revyn*, Lars Stahre wrote: 'Lots of fans will find the record more complicated than the group's previous ones. It's an ambitious attempt which is very elaborate but the sound is still ABBA. Agnetha sings "Thank You For the Music" like a cabaret singer from the 1930s. You can easily imagine the audience singing along.'

A few days before the end of the year, Vogue made an exception in Belgium by releasing a limited number of copies of the new album. The record company had put pressure on Polar Music to release the record at the same time as the film, which had just opened in Brussels and Antwerp. Flemish TV company BRT screened the entire 'Name of the Game' clip from the film on its weekly cinema programme.

A year which had been rich both professionally and personally for ABBA was drawing to a close. Even though no one could deny the success of the four Swedes, the press still didn't miss a single opportunity to attack them. Unable to criticize their professionalism, they pulled the group apart in other ways. *Abba – The Movie* was a prime example. 'I am weary of the so-called experts panning us like this all the time,' said Björn. 'They have a right to their own opinion, of course. But I can't help noticing that their opinions are not reflected by the millions of people all over the world who regularly buy our records and battle over tickets for our concerts.' Stig added: 'The achievements of ABBA are there for all to see. The critics can make what they like of them and say what they like, but they can't take anything away from ABBA's unique position in the world of music.' Stig, who always placed great emphasis on sales figures, must have been overjoyed with the news that the *Arrival* album had beaten sales records in a large number of countries, for example Sweden, where 739,218 copies had been sold, Britain (1.5 million copies), Germany (600,000 copies) and Australia (1.2 million copies). In the United States, sales of the 'Dancing Queen' single and *Arrival* album had just passed the million mark.

As further evidence of ABBA's success, there were an increasing number of artists covering their material. Polar Music was aware of 544 different versions of their songs in twenty-four different countries. 'Waterloo' was at the top of the list with ninety-two different versions!

Premiere of *Abba – The Movie* in Stockholm

'THE WORLD IS A DEPRESSED PLACE AT THE MOMENT AND MANY PEOPLE WANT TO BE HAPPY. ABBA HAVE A VERY PRETTY IMAGE. IT'S VERY ATTRACTIVE. EVERYONE LOVES EACH OTHER AND ALL THAT … PEOPLE NOW ARE READY FOR THAT TYPE OF IMAGE AND ABBA BECAME MUCH MORE THAN ANOTHER HIT GROUP.'
NICKY CHINN CO-WRITER FOR SWEET, MUD AND SUZI QUATRO

1977 TOUR

Even before the 1977 tour had begun, things were looking good. Tickets for the group's shows had sold out everywhere, and the 3.5 million ticket applications for the two concerts at the Royal Albert Hall in London had left journalists astonished.

However, the group weren't hiding the fact that they were apprehensive. 'We've been working on this tour for a long time,' Benny announced. 'We have to prove that we are as good on stage as we are on record. There's no room for mistakes. The press are waiting to catch us out and they won't let us off lightly!' Björn added: 'We're always pleased to meet our audience but we don't really like touring. I can't understand all these groups who spend half the year on the road. It kills creativity if you spend your life in planes, airports or hotel rooms. I can't compose in those conditions!'

ABBA, together with Thomas Johansson, Stig, Görel Johnsen, the musicians, and their stage and costume designers had been working flat out for several months preparing for this tour. Rehearsals had begun in December 1976 at Grünewaldsalen, a room in the Konserthuset in Stockholm, and had relocated to the Europa Films studios in January.

The final result was a show which lasted roughly 2 hours, consisting mainly of fast-tempo numbers. ABBA broke new ground, however, by including a mini-musical entitled 'The Girl With The Golden Hair'. It lasted for about 20 minutes and was the story of a young girl who dreams of becoming a singer, only to become a victim of her own success as soon as she achieves it. 'Benny and I became interested in the musical form at a very early stage in our career,' says Björn, 'and when we were about to go out on this tour, we thought it would be fun to have a sequence of songs that were a bit more theatrical than our other material. I remember that someone asked us why we didn't extend it to a full-length musical. Well, I don't think the story was quite good enough for that!' (*The Complete Recording Sessions*, 1994.)

'THE FIRST YOU KNOW IS WHEN YOU DRIVE OUT FROM THE AIRPORT AND YOU SEE THE STREETS ACTUALLY LINED UP ALL THE WAY FROM THE AIRPORT TO THE CITY. YOU DON'T EVEN BELIEVE YOUR EYES. AND THEN YOU UNDERSTAND THIS IS ACTUALLY A RECEPTION FOR US, NOBODY ELSE. IT'S NOT THE PRESIDENT COMING.' **FRIDA**

'FOR THE 1977 TOUR, BJÖRN AND BENNY WANTED MARBLE STATUES ON STAGE, CARRYING THOUSANDS OF RED ROSES. WE COULDN'T CARRY MARBLE STATUES AROUND THE WORLD, SO WE USED PLASTIC ONES FILLED WITH SAND, AND SILK ROSES.'
OWE SANDSTRÖM ABBA'S COSTUME DESIGNER

'I DRAW MY INSPIRATION FROM ALL OVER THE WORLD: FROM CABARET PERFORMANCES, OLD MOVIES, EVEN FROM NATURE.'
OWE SANDSTRÖM
ABBA'S COSTUME DESIGNER

'The Girl With The Golden Hair' is based around four songs: 'Thank You For the Music', 'I Wonder (Departure)', 'I'm a Marionette' and 'Get On the Carousel'. It is all held together by a master of ceremonies who could have come straight out of *Cabaret*. The role was played by Francis Mathews, a twenty-four-year-old English actor. During the tour, he spoke to journalist Lottie Molund: 'Thomas Johansson was looking for an English-speaking actor and contacted my agent. I had just finished playing at the Welsh National Theatre in Cardiff. This is the first time that I've been on stage in front of 10,000 crazy teenagers. It's a weird feeling. It's a shame it's such a shallow story, because it would have been great to have had some real lines and a real person to play.' The other surprise in the show was an unreleased, tongue-in-cheek song called 'I Am an A', where the four members of ABBA jokingly introduced themselves.

During the show ABBA performed twenty-five songs: 'Tiger' – 'That's Me' – 'Waterloo' – 'S.O.S.' – 'Sitting In the Palmtree' – 'Money, Money, Money' – 'He Is Your Brother' – 'I Do, I Do, I Do, I Do, I Do' – 'Dum Dum Diddle' – 'When I Kissed the Teacher' – 'Knowing Me, Knowing You' – 'Rock Me' – 'I Am an A' – 'I've Been Waiting For You' – 'Mamma Mia' – 'Fernando' – 'Why Did It Have To Be Me' – 'Intermezzo No. 1' – 'Thank You For the Music' – 'I Wonder (Departure)' – 'I'm a Marionette' – 'Get On the Carousel' – 'So Long'. Encore: 'Dancing Queen' – 'Thank You For the Music'.

The musicians were:
Keyboards: Anders Eljas, Wojciech Ernest.
Guitars: Finn Sjöberg, Lasse Wellander.
Bass: Rutger Gunnarsson.
Drums: Ola Brunkert.
Percussion: Malando Gassama.
Sax and flute: Lars O. Carlsson.
Backing vocalists: Lena Andersson, Lena-Maria Gårdenäs, Maritza Horn.
Sound engineer: Claes af Geijerstam

EUROPE
Fifty-two people were employed by ABBA for the seventeen concerts in Europe. Thirty tons of equipment were needed for the shows.

26 January
The group arrived in Oslo during the evening. The technicians and equipment had arrived several days earlier.

27 January
Polar Music organized a reception in honour of the 150 directors and marketing people who worked for ABBA around the world. They had all been invited to the first concert of the tour. They were also here to present the group with various awards. During the day, Anni-Frid and Benny visited the Edvard Munch museum.

28 January – Oslo, Ekebergshallen
The first concert, with an audience of 5300, including Queen Sonja and Prince Harald of Norway. After the show, the royal couple went backstage to congratulate the group and to present them with gold and platinum discs for Norwegian sales of the *Greatest Hits* and *Arrival* albums.

29 January – Gothenburg, Scandinavium
The group visited Liseberg during the afternoon. Agnetha, Björn, Benny and Anni-Frid were invited to leave their handprints and signatures in cement, as is the tradition for any stars who visit the amusement park. The prints were later cast in bronze.

Mats Olsson reviewed the concert in *Expressen*: 'Björn and Benny as writers of a musical? Why not! The audience were presented with what you might call "a pocket opera". It's a clumsy story but is ground-breaking for ABBA.

'BEING ON TOUR WAS BORING REALLY, IT'S DIFFICULT FOR PEOPLE TO UNDERSTAND THIS, BUT THEY SEE THE GLAMOROUS SIDE OF IT, PEOPLE CHEERING AND ALL OF THAT. BUT REALLY, APART FROM BEING ON STAGE FOR 2 HOURS, THE REST OF IT WAS *COMPLETELY* BORING. THAT'S WHY WE TOURED SO LITTLE.'
BJÖRN

'Why Did It Have To Be Me'

Agnetha and Anni-Frid look really beautiful in their blond wigs and they sing, dance and do pirouettes. The whole stage is white and they have glittering costumes. The group perform their best songs. The orchestra really goes for it and they lift the roof off when Björn and Frida sing "Why Did It Have To Be Me", which is a great swinging rocker of a song. The sound is almost perfect and Agnetha has become more daring. It's an elaborate show with good, hand-picked musicians.'

30 January – Gothenburg, Scandinavium
People were charging 500 Swedish kronor for tickets on the black market. The 20,000 tickets had gone on sale the previous 30 November and had sold out in a day! These were the only two concerts which the group did in Sweden. Many journalists and Swedish artists had attended the previous evening's concert. One of the headlines declared: 'A new sexy, sophisticated Anni-Frid wins over the audience!'

31 January – Copenhagen, Brondbyhallen
Heavy fog forced ABBA to travel overland between Gothenburg and Copenhagen instead of by plane. The group were all very stressed because they had no time to rehearse or even to rest. The concert eventually began half an hour late.

1 February – Copenhagen, Brondbyhallen
The second show in Copenhagen helped to ease the worries and criticism from the previous evening. This time, the acoustics were perfect and the group had calmed down. Björn told journalist Lottie Molund: 'It's much better now. In Oslo, 15 minutes before we went on stage we were all paralysed with nerves and couldn't even speak to each other. When you're working in the studio, you eventually feel completely isolated from the audience. I'd forgotten how fantastic it is to be on stage!'

2 February – Berlin, Deutschlandhalle
The *Sun* published an article alleging a deep rift between Agnetha and Frida. The group were deeply hurt by the claims.

3 February – Cologne, Sporthalle
ABBA were invited to attend a private reception given by President Walter Schiels in honour of Gerald Ford, President of the United States. The four Swedes declined the invitation.

4 February – Amsterdam, Jaap Eden Hall

5 February – Antwerp/Deurne, Arena Hall
It was announced that 7000 tickets had been sold, even though the hall was half that capacity. The group were a great success. However, Belgian magazine *Youpi* was not impressed: 'Their lack of stage experience and audience contact has been perceived by many as a disappointment. The music is too loud for the voices, the show is too static, the songs lack rhythm, and there is little loyalty to the purity and great quality that we are used to in ABBA's recordings. The group will have to do a lot more preparation for their shows if they want to be really successful.'

6 February – Essen, Grugahalle

7 February – Hanover, Eilenrieder Halle

8 February – Hamburg, C.C.H.
There was a press conference at the Plaza Hotel. ABBA were presented with a number of gold discs for sales of the 'Fernando' single and the albums *Abba*, *Best of Abba* and *The Very Best of Abba*. They also received a bronze trophy called the *Bravo-Otto 76* on behalf of the magazine's readers. The trophy was presented by Harald Funk, one of the group's young fans.

10 February – Birmingham, Odeon
The 3000 ticket holders were searched by the police on their way into the hall after IRA attacks on two pubs in the centre of town. The first concert on British soil went off perfectly. The four members of the group had noticed that their British audiences were older than in Scandinavia or Germany.

11 February – Manchester, Free Trade Hall
Some British critics couldn't resist having a dig at the group. Ray Coleman described the show as 'a cold and clinical disappointment' in *Melody Maker*, and Tony Parsons, in the *New Musical Express*, said it was 'crass, glib and contrived'. But John Blake in the *Evening News* called ABBA 'the greatest thing since the Beatles. With Anna and Frida looking as they do, I, for one, would be happy even if they didn't sing a note.'

12 February – Glasgow, Apollo
Richard Williams wrote in *The Times*: 'Their arrangements are their real secret; no one in the field can match their outstanding imaginative deployment of pianos, synthesizers and tuned percussion, derived from the innovations of Brian Wilson and Phil Spector.'

14 February – London, Royal Albert Hall (2 shows)
One of these concerts was filmed with the intention of making a TV programme. Tired but happy, Agnetha, Björn, Benny and Anni-Frid made the most of the event by celebrating with friends at the end of the day's second concert. Stig was euphoric: 'It's a new victory. We'll all be dreaming about it tonight!'

The following day, the *Financial Times* said: 'A group which has sold 30 million singles and 14 million albums have to be taken seriously. To be able to review ABBA, you have to strike a balance between their emotional potential and their recording capability. Emotion is completely lacking here.' The *Guardian* was hardly more positive: 'Musically, they haven't progressed very much since their victory in Brighton. They've written some practical numbers for this concert which sound good but don't mean very much. As for their rock opera, in its current state it's best forgotten.' Sheila Prophet wrote in *Record Mirror*: 'You can't criticize their musicianship – everything is immaculate, like a well-oiled machine. But they play common denominator rock … music watered-down and sweetened until it's bland enough to offend nobody. Then they take this bland mixture, chop it into neat 3-minute segments, tart it up to disguise the lack of substance, polish it until it shines … and sell it by the million to people who'll never look beneath the glittering surface.'

AUSTRALIA
The group, together with their musicians and technical personnel, travelled in a Boeing 727 throughout the Australian tour. Lasse Hallström and his technicians also travelled with them. The 30 tons of equipment had been transported to Australia by three Hercules planes. Sixty-five extra people (including seventeen Australian violinists) were added to the team for the eleven concerts the band gave in Australia.

27 February
ABBA arrived in Sydney at 9.15 p.m. and were welcomed by more than a thousand hysterical fans. However, to avoid causing a crush, the four Swedes left for their hotel via a secret door after a photo session for the press.

28 February
ABBA gave an important press conference in the hotel's main conference room at 11.30 a.m. The group's record company RCA presented them with a number of gold and platinum discs in recognition of sales in Australia and New Zealand.

'The Girl With the Golden Hair' mini-musical

'THERE WERE CONFLICTS BETWEEN US. THERE WERE FOUR STRONG WILLS INVOLVED AND IT WOULD HAVE BEEN STRANGE IF THERE HAD NOT BEEN DISAGREEMENTS. I DON'T THINK THAT THERE'S ANYTHING ODD IN THAT, NOR DO I THINK THERE'S ANYTHING TO SPECULATE ABOUT – BECAUSE THERE'S CONFLICT IN ANY WORKPLACE.' FRIDA

'I'm a Marionette'

1 March
The group gave several interviews and began rehearsals on the specially erected stage at the Sydney stadium. There had been torrential rain for the last few days in the Sydney area and there was talk of cancelling the concert.

2 March
More rehearsals. The group received a telegram from Australian Prime Minister Malcolm Fraser inviting them to travel with him on his private jet to Canberra to meet the Queen, who was on a visit to Australia. The group were forced to decline the invitation due to time constraints.

3 March – Sydney, Showground Arena
The first concert, in front of an audience of 20,000 in torrential rain. The stage was a giant pool of water despite the protective canvas covers. The audience, soaked to the skin, gave the four Swedes an incredible ovation. During the song 'Waterloo', Anni-Frid slipped and found herself sitting on her bottom. 'I was just a bit shaken by the fall,' she said at the end of the concert. 'But that was nothing compared to all the fans who were dancing and singing along with us in the rain. That was a real show of loyalty!'

4 March – Sydney, Showground Arena
A second concert which was just as triumphant as the first. The rain had finally stopped.

5 March – Melbourne, Myer Music Bowl
There was a civic reception at the town hall during the afternoon and Agnetha, Björn, Benny and Anni-Frid signed Melbourne's golden book. Outside, the crowds were so dense that the road had to be closed to traffic. In true royal style, the four members of the group made an appearance on the central balcony. During the evening, ABBA performed before an audience of 14,000, although this number could easily have been doubled by those people listening to the concert outside the stadium.

6 March – Melbourne, Myer Music Bowl
All tickets were sold out for both concerts (one at 2.30 p.m. and the other at 8.30 p.m.). Some songs had been taken out of the programme, mainly the ones featuring Björn, who was suffering from food poisoning.

7 March
Pat Bowring wrote in the *Melbourne Sun*: 'The group on stage was certainly not as sterile as many overseas critics had led us to believe. ABBA on stage contains more life than expected. The setting was magnificent. Frida is undoubtedly the focal point of the group on stage: a raw earthy rock singer, prancing and provocative. She provided a contrast to the cool and slightly aloof Anna, whose performance is more restrained.'

8 March – Adelaide, West Lakes Football Stadium
In the stadium that evening were 21,000 fans; another 10,000 were dancing and singing in the car park outside.

10 March – Perth, Entertainment Centre
ABBA gave two concerts, one at 6 p.m. and the other at 9 p.m. An anonymous phone call from a woman threatening that 'a bomb is going to kill ABBA' disrupted the first show. The security team evacuated the backstage area. Actor Robert Hughes remembers: 'Everyone was off stage, except for Benny who was playing "Intermezzo No. 1". He hadn't been told what was going on. At the end of the number, he was concerned because no one came back on stage. There was a long, awkward silence. And then there was an announcement that everyone had to leave. The venue was searched from top to bottom. After 20 minutes, the 8000 ticket holders took their seats again and the show carried on.'

11 March – Perth, Entertainment Centre
A trip on the River Swan during the morning and a concert at 8 p.m. in the evening.

12 March – Perth, Entertainment Centre
Two concerts, one at 3 p.m. and the other at 8.30 p.m. Since the acoustics were so good at this venue, lots of songs were filmed and recorded during the five Perth shows.

Having played to a total of 145,000 people in only eleven concerts, the Australian tour was a triumph.

Rehearsals, Australia

ABBA introduce themselves in the song 'I Am an A'

'YOU MAY SEE ME HAVE A BALL, JUMPING UP AND DOWN AT MY PIANO BENCH. YOU MAY EVEN HEAR ME SING SOME BACKING HARMONY. BUT YOU'LL NEVER CATCH ME SINGING SOLO. THAT REALLY SOUNDS TERRIBLE.' BENNY

'WE ALWAYS KNEW THAT LASSE HALLSTRÖM HAD GREAT TALENT. HE WAS VERY GOOD WITH MUSIC AS WELL. AND I ALWAYS THOUGHT HE WOULD GO ON TO SOMETHING BIGGER, ABSOLUTELY.' BJÖRN

ABBA THE MOVIE

It was originally intended that *Abba – The Movie* would be a documentary about the group's tour, filmed in 16mm. The idea of a TV special was then put forward, and one of the group's two concerts at the Royal Albert Hall in London was filmed by Lasse Hallström and his team. The project eventually became a full-length film, recorded in 35mm Panavision in Australia and Sweden.

Actor Robert Hughes remembers how it all came about: 'I had heard about the audition from my agent. We were told it was only going to be a 16mm documentary showing ABBA on tour and relaxing in between shows, and the radio announcer would be a linking device. I went to the screen test and met the director Lasse Hallström. He said: "I want you to do some impromptu acting." Then it turned out they were going to do some tests in 35mm Panavision and it was pouring with rain. We went to North Sydney and in the rain I walked across the flyover of the approach to Sydney Harbour Bridge on the north side. It looked fabulous and the decision was made to shoot in Panavision and to produce a major film.'

THE PLOT

Ashley, a young DJ working for an Australian radio station, finds himself with the difficult task of interviewing the Swedish group ABBA during their Australian tour. Inexperienced and without his press pass, he finds it impossible to break through the barricade of bodyguards surrounding the group. After following ABBA from town to town, he finally meets the four 'inaccessible' stars by chance in a hotel lift. Exhausted but happy, he makes it back to the radio station just in time to broadcast his report. As it goes out on the air, ABBA are leaving Australia, at the end of their triumphant tour.

FILMING

In total, 50 hours of rushes were filmed by Lasse Hallström. Robert Hughes explains: 'It was an unlimited budget. It was crazy – we just sort of went out with cameras and did things. There was no script. Robert Caswell was supposed to write the script and he was really upset because everything was moving too fast and he didn't have time to write anything. Nothing had been written down. Lasse came up with ideas on the spot. He didn't actually tell the band members that I was an actor playing a part, so I didn't really get to talk to them until the end of the tour in Perth.'

Australia, 3–12 March 1977

Several songs were filmed at each concert. However, many clips were filmed at the Entertainment Centre in Perth, since the acoustics were better there than in the other outside stadiums. Numerous outside scenes were filmed during the daytime (airports, stadiums, press conferences, interviews with fans, street and crowd scenes).

'WE WERE SO OCCUPIED WITH DIFFERENT PROJECTS LIKE RECORDING AND TOURING AND SO THE ONLY CHANCE HE REALLY HAD TO MAKE A MOVIE WITH US WAS TO RECORD IT DURING A TOUR; IN OTHER WORDS HE HAD TO WRITE SOME KIND OF STORYLINE AROUND THE GROUP TOURING, WHICH HE DID VERY CLEVERLY. IT WAS VERY SIMPLE BUT, I THINK, ENJOYABLE.' BJÖRN

Sweden, June, July and August 1977

Filming continued in Stockholm and the surrounding area. Actors Robert Hughes and Tom Oliver flew over especially from Australia. The production team arranged for a complete collection of ABBA products to be brought over: books, plates and mugs, cushions, shoes, and so on. The principal scenes filmed in Sweden were:

Ashley in his car and the shop scenes showing ABBA items for sale: Stockholm city centre.

The group in their hotel room: Sheraton Hotel.

The group on Viggsö island.

'Thank You For the Music', the film's closing sequence: Marcus studios.

Ashley's dream sequence during 'The Name of the Game': Lovön island, near Drottningholm (picnic and horse-riding scenes); the island of Djurgården (scenes on board the boat, ABBA playing golf, scenes with the photographers); Europa Films studios (psychiatrist's chair, dinner-table and saloon-bar scenes and scenes in the lift).

POST PRODUCTION

Lasse Hallström, Malou Hallström and Ulf Neidemar took care of the editing. The cartoon characters in the opening section of the film were created by Animagica AB following an idea by Rune Söderqvist. The live recordings were reworked and remixed for the soundtrack. Some tracks were also dubbed in the studio between 8 and 16 September 1977.

THE FILM'S RELEASE

Australia, 15 December 1977: *Abba – The Movie*
Sydney (Hoyts Regent Theatre), Melbourne (Palace Theatre), Parramatta (Astra Theatre), Canberra (Center Cinema).

The Netherlands, 17 December 1977: *Abba, de film*
Amsterdam (Amsterdamse city theatre and Calypso), Den Haag (Apollo 1), Rotterdam (Luxor), Nijmegen (Scala), Heerlen (H '3'), Maastricht (Royal), Den Bosch (Casino 1), Haarlem, Groningen, Utrecht.

Finland, 23 December 1977: *Abba-elokuva*
Helsinki, Turku.

Sweden, 26 December 1977: *Abba – The Movie*
Stockholm (China and Fanfaren cinemas), Gothenburg, Malmö, Eskilstuna, Halmstad, Helsingborg, Jönköping, Kalmar, Karlskrona, Karlstad, Kristianstad, Lund, Södertälje, Umeå, Uppsala, Västervik, Västerås, Växjö and Örebro. The film was also released in Norway and Denmark during this period.

Britain, 16 February 1978: *Abba – The Movie*
London (Warner West End) and large towns nationwide.

Germany, 17 February 1978: *Abba*
The film was released in forty-five German towns.

France, 19 April 1978: *Vive Abba*
The film was released in Paris at four Parisian cinemas: Lord Byron (original version), Cluny Palace (original version), Maxeville (French version) and Les Images (French version). It was also released in Lyon, Marseille, Bordeaux and Lille.

Japan, 15 July 1978: *Abba – The Movie*
Tokyo and large Japanese towns.

'THERE WERE DROVES OF PEOPLE EVERYWHERE. IT WAS ABSOLUTELY UNREAL AND INCREDIBLE. THE WAY THE FILM DESCRIBES THAT IS REAL. IT WAS VERY CLEVER TO MAKE US MYSTERIOUS AND UNAPPROACHABLE BECAUSE THAT'S EXACTLY WHAT WE WERE TO THAT REPORTER.' BJÖRN

REVIEWS

Sweden

Jan Andersson, *Aftonbladet*: 'The film reinforces ABBA's image as pop idols and becomes almost delusive. Unfortunately, you don't learn anything about them.'

Lasse Bergström, *Expressen*: 'Lasse Hallström's film lies somewhere between Hollywood and Broadway. It's extremely professional and works well.'

Tony Kaplan, *Arbetet*: 'The worst Swedish comedy to be screened here in ten years. Bad and humourless.'

Jan Aghed, *Sydsvenskan*: 'The longest promotional film ever made. It's imposing and boring.'

Eva af Geijerstam, *Dagens Nyheter*: 'A long, meticulous promotional film showing the current enormous popularity of the group in Australia.'

Jönköping-Posten: 'Perfect as far as promotional films go. But as a full-length film it's terrible.'

Gaby Wigardt, *Svenska Dagbladet*: 'After having seen *Abba – The Movie*, I can certify that the quartet are a phenomenon. But I don't think you could really call this a full-length movie. If it is, then it really is a bad film.'

England

Cecil Wilson, *Daily Mail*: 'One good reason for devoting a whole 95-minute film |to ABBA| is that these Swedish idols project a wholesome, natural vitality and look as if they wash. Another is that they sing better music and better English than most of their British rivals.'

Derek Jewell, *The Times*: 'This movie will stun you. Were ever a group more wholesomely handsome? ABBA themselves – such impact! See it and marvel.'

Sunday People: 'One forgets that this is virtually a 90-minute commercial ... the overwhelming likeableness of ABBA is astutely rammed home.'

Arthur Thirkell, *Daily Mirror*: 'Now the fans can enjoy the sight as well as the sound of the wholesome Swedes ... It's a film that is pure as freshly churned butter.'

Guardian: 'Everything is fine about ABBA except the film they have made. It is awful.'

New Musical Express: 'This full-blown epic is shockingly bad, providing the ABBA fan with an embarrassingly feeble plotline to offset the preponderance of ABBA music.'

France

Pierre Murat, *Télérama*: 'The thin plot is no more than a pretext to glorify ABBA, the biggest record sellers since the Beatles, so it seems. It's a nice film and the sight of the four Swedes performing their hits is pleasing on the eye. The fans will love it.'

Philippe Adler, *L'Express*: Even if you don't know anything about music, you should go and see this one. Not for the thrown-together plot but for everything else: the happy, appealing, lively music and the often passionate tale of a group on tour. And also, of course, for Agnetha and Anni-Frid.'

Belgium

Juke Box: 'The best thing is to hear the songs again, songs which give each of us a very distinctive feeling. On the other hand, it's a big disappointment. The only heat coming from this film is the temperature in Australia, and it seems quite appropriate that the group come from the polar region!'

'SEEING THE FILM CAME AS A BIT OF A SHOCK. IT IS HARD TO RECOGNIZE YOURSELF UP THERE ON A GIANT SCREEN IN PANAVISION.'   BJÖRN

'WE WRITE A SONG THAT WE'RE PROUD OF, RECORD IT THE BEST WAY WE CAN, AND RELEASE IT BECAUSE WE THINK IT'S VERY GOOD. BUT I HAVE NO CRITERION THAT IT HAS TO BE ART.' BENNY

1978

Stig and the four group members had decided to channel all their energy during 1978 into promotion of the new album and the film, as well as into writing new songs.

In the UK, Agnetha, Björn, Benny and Anni-Frid had been named Top Artists of the Year by British newspaper the *Sun*. A television crew was sent over to Stockholm to film the group at Glen studios on 10 January.

13 January Epic-CBS released *Abba – The Album* in Britain. The album had already been certified platinum and advance orders were estimated to be worth more than £1 million. The group's British record label took a different approach to other countries, releasing the album in a gatefold sleeve with a slightly bluish background instead of a white one. The photos inside the sleeve were different, too, and the tracks which were featured in the group's film were marked with a small symbol.

The critics were harsh. *Melody Maker* said, 'This is probably ABBA's weakest album since they hit the big time', adding that the mini-musical was a 'mistake'. The review in *Rolling Stone* was slightly more constructive: 'Side two is a real attempt to do something different, and, if not everything works, the effort is still laudable.' *New Musical Express* described 'Thank You For the Music' as 'the sort of tearjerker that turns up in provincial pantomimes' and claimed that the album 'could turn out to be ABBA's least satisfactory'. Sheila Prophet wrote in *Record Mirror*: 'ABBA on record shows up all their best features – their songwriting talent, their instrumental proficiency, their ability as arrangers, their vocal precision, without uncovering their worst – their clumsy stage presence, their lack of humour and their showbiz shoddiness.'

16 January Polydor released 'Take a Chance On Me' as a single in Germany. It entered the charts almost immediately and reached No. 3, staying in the charts for a total of twenty-five weeks. ABBA would be in Germany during February for the release of their film. A journalist from *Bravo* magazine wrote of *Abba – The Album*: 'What strikes me above all about ABBA is that they always give us honest records. Unlike other artists who lack substance, they do not fill their albums with unimportant little songs but give us strong authentic material throughout.'

At the end of January, Björn, Benny, Frida and Stig travelled to the MIDEM fair in Cannes to promote *Abba – The Movie*. Agnetha stayed in Stockholm with Christian. The three members of the group stopped off in Paris on 21 January to take part in Guy Lux's *Loto Chansons* programme. They were interviewed by the presenter and a clip of 'Take a Chance On Me' was shown. Sales of the album in France were already looking promising. Pierre Lescure wrote in *Music Media* magazine: 'Since "Waterloo", every single has sold 300,000 copies in France. The group's fantastic commercial and financial achievements are due to both their inexplicable success and a rigorous and continuous marketing technique. The magic is in the general impact of the group and their music.'

15 February Agnetha and Björn travelled to London for the British release of *Abba – The Movie*. Benny and Anni-Frid had arrived the previous day, giving them the opportunity to spend more time in the British capital.

16 February The premiere of the film took place at the Warner West End 2 cinema, near Leicester Square. There was a big crowd outside the cinema and the atmosphere was electric. Among the journalists, photographers and celebrities present were Pete Townshend, Keith Moon and John Entwistle from the Who, actress Connie Booth and composer Biddu. After the screening

Both: *Les Rendez-Vous du Dimanche TV show, Paris*

'FRIDA IS A LADY WITH ENORMOUS STYLE. EVERYONE USED TO SAY THAT AGNETHA WAS THE ONE THAT EVERYONE FANCIED, AND SHE WAS A BEAUTIFUL WOMAN. BUT I ALWAYS THOUGHT THAT FRIDA WAS JUST AS VITAL.' **TIM RICE**

of the film, there was a press conference and a reception at the Café Royal in Regent Street.

ABBA were only in the British capital for a short time. Among their various promotional activities were numerous interviews, including one with Dave Lee Travis from BBC Radio One, and a photo shoot at the Crockford Casino. One of the high points of the trip was a reception at the Lyceum Ballroom, where ABBA were presented with the Carl Allen Songwriting Award by Princess Margaret.

Abba – The Album went straight in at No. 1 in the UK on 4 February and stayed at the top spot for nine weeks; the 'Take a Chance On Me' single, which had only just been released, was already at the top of the singles chart.

The film received mixed reviews, however. ABBA were criticized for not managing to achieve 'the transition of music to the big screen', despite the fact that the film's technical quality was undeniable and its production exceptional. After all, *Abba – The Movie* was only intended as a documentary showing the group on stage during their tour.

17 February Agnetha, Björn, Benny and Anni-Frid, who were unable to attend the German premiere of *Abba – The Movie*, had decided to promote the release of the film by taking part in a TV show called *Am Laufenden Band*, presented by Rudi Carrell. During their two-day trip to Germany, ABBA also did some photo shoots and gave a press conference. The four Swedes were presented with various awards from teenage magazines, voted for by their readers, including the silver Otto award from *Das Freizeit Magazin* and the bronze Otto from *Bravo*. On Rudi Carrell's show, ABBA performed 'Take a Chance On Me' and took part in games and interviews. Anni-Frid's father, Alfred Haase, also participated in the show.

In between promotional trips, Björn and Benny continued work on the next album. The idea of writing a musical, which had been put forward the previous year, had been abandoned for the moment. Details of chart positions for 'Take a Chance On Me' began to arrive in Stig's office: No.1 in Belgium, No. 2 in Holland, No. 8 in Spain, No. 1 in Japan and No. 12 in Australia.

During this time, Lasse Hallström filmed several videos for the new album: 'Eagle', 'Thank You For the Music' and 'One Man, One Woman'.

4 March Agnetha and Björn presented the ABBA Prize trophy to seven-year-old Agnetha Hjort at a junior skiing competition which the group had sponsored that year. The event had been named the ABBA Prize, with the winner receiving a trophy and a cheque for 100,000 Swedish kronor.

11 March 'The Name of the Game' reached No. 12 in the United States. This was ABBA's best chart position since 'Dancing Queen'. *Abba – The Album* had been released on 24 January and was slowly climbing up the American charts.

Two weeks later, Stig travelled to the States in preparation for the release of *Abba – The Movie* and the single 'Take a Chance On Me'. ABBA's producer also finalized details with Atlantic and Scotti Brothers for a massive promotional campaign entitled 'ABBA Month'. 'By and large, the U.S. still remains for us to conquer,' admitted Stig. 'We've racked up good sales over the past few years, but we still haven't broken down the heaviest doors, so to speak. To be frank, we're not the household name over there we'd like to be.'

In the middle of March, the four members of the group permitted themselves a week's holiday, Björn and Agnetha deciding to stay in Sweden, while Benny and Anni-Frid went on a skiing holiday in Austria.

3 April A team from German pop magazine *Bravo* arrived in Stockholm. Photographer Wolfgang 'Bubi' Heilemann had reserved a studio for an extended photo shoot with the group. The mood was relaxed, despite the fact that Agnetha was suffering with flu. ABBA wore the new costumes which had been created by Owe Sandström – silk tunics with painted animals on them – as well as some of their stage clothes from the 1977 tour.

12 April Agnetha, Björn, Benny and Anni-Frid travelled to Paris for several days of promotional work. On the first evening, they recorded the show *Les Rendez-Vous du Dimanche* in Studio 11 at Buttes-Chaumont. Michel Drucker dedicated half his programme to the group and the release of their film, entitled *Vive Abba* in France. He interviewed the group and showed some clips from the film. ABBA also performed 'Take a Chance On Me' in the studio, although this version was slightly different to the single – it had an acapella ending. The programme was screened on Sunday 16 April.

During their stay in Paris, ABBA met the press, posed for photographers and also took part in Jean-Loup Lafont's radio show, *Basket*, on Europe 1. The group were presented with a Golden Basket award by the host in recognition of their excellent score on the programme the previous year.

In the middle of April, the Swedish Tourist Office launched a massive campaign to promote Sweden overseas. Two different posters were printed, one featuring ABBA ('ABBA welcome you to Sweden') and the other featuring the Swedish Royal Family. Bertil Harrysson, director-general of the Swedish Tourist Office, explained: 'The posters and brochures we have had printed are going to be distributed all over Europe. We wanted to portray a modern image of Sweden. ABBA very kindly agreed to take part in the campaign. It also served as good publicity for the group.'

At the end of April, the four members of ABBA agreed to be interviewed by Mats Olsson for a feature in *Expressen*. Each member of the group was more candid than usual, really opening up to the interviewer, as the following extracts demonstrate:

Frida: 'Sometimes I get tired of ABBA. But then I think about it and realize that ABBA is what I do best. I want to be prepared for the future. I don't know what I'll do. For the time being I'm carrying on with taking singing and dancing lessons. I'd like to do another solo album but it's hard to find good songs. Besides, I'd like Benny to produce it and he doesn't have the time. I've had enough of the negative climate in Sweden. Especially as far as showbusiness is concerned. People seem to be more open outside Sweden, which is very stimulating. When I get back here I get very frustrated by this negative attitude.'

Benny: 'Swedish folk music and Elvis Presley are where my real musical roots lie. As long as we enjoy working together as ABBA, then we will carry on. The writing gets harder and harder. It's easy to find ideas in the beginning but the rest of it is hard. Maybe we expect too much of ourselves. If I had the time, I'd like to produce other artists. My big dream is to produce John Lennon. I have no idea of what would come out of that or even of what I would do, but in my opinion he is the greatest rock singer in the world. And as regards writing a musical, we're not ready yet and we don't have the time.'

Agnetha: 'I think that Björn would like four or five children. But I said: no more. I had a difficult pregnancy. I almost lost Christian during the seventh month. I don't know if it's my age but I've started to question myself. Time is going by so fast. I'll soon be thirty. On a positive note, ABBA has given me my independence. I come from an unassuming family. Four of us would sleep in the same room. On the negative side of things, I don't like people thinking of me as a part of ABBA instead of for the person that I am and I also find our nice image embarrassing. The media created that. We're ordinary people. We can be just as bad as anyone else. The interest in my bottom in Australia and Britain is ridiculous. I didn't realize they were filming my backside so much. On stage, we like what we wear. Benny often has ample clothes to hide his … um … chubbiness, while Frida and myself think it's nice to wear things which show off our femininity.'

Björn: 'Even if ABBA were to split up, Benny and I would carry on working together. I sometimes feel out of it in Sweden. But at the same time, Agnetha and myself are very family-orientated. We couldn't leave our parents and friends here in Sweden. We don't feel any pressure to release an album a year. We do one when we have something ready. If we're satisfied with it, then we release it. And we're delighted when it sells well. I get very angry when the newspapers write more about what we earn than our music. I agree that we earn a lot of money but we also pay a lot of tax. But they rarely write that.'

'THE OPENING OF THE POLAR STUDIOS CHANGED A LOT IN OUR WORK. IT WAS MADE TO OUR SPECIFICATIONS. IT CONTAINED ALL THE THINGS WE NEEDED, AND WE COULD GET HOLD OF THEM FAST, SO WE COULD WORK MUCH MORE SMOOTHLY THAN WE DID BEFORE, IN OTHER STUDIOS. SO, IT WAS VERY EASY TO RECORD THERE. WE HAD THE BEST EQUIPMENT IN TOWN, AT THAT TIME. IT'S STILL A GREAT STUDIO!'
MICHAEL B. TRETOW ABBA'S SOUND ENGINEER

Having fun on Olivia

Building the Polar Music studios

30 April 'Take a Chance On Me' reached No. 8 on the RTL charts. In France, due to a lack of promotion, the film *Vive Abba* didn't do very well at the box office. It was taken off within three weeks of its release.

1 May ABBA flew to the United States. Polar Music, together with Atlantic, had invested $1 million in the ABBA Month campaign. To help matters along, Stig had also signed a contract with Scotti Brothers, who had previously promoted Barbra Streisand, John Denver and Leif Garrett. During their stay, Agnetha, Björn, Benny and Anni-Frid took part in numerous television and radio shows and met the press. *Newsweek* and *Time* magazine published extended features on the group. Special signs, posters and window displays were installed in record stores. A television and radio advert for *Abba – The Album* was also planned. On top of all this, there was also a 7-metre-high display board on Sunset Boulevard in Los Angeles.

8 May The two couples took part in Olivia Newton-John's television show. This was the high point of ABBA Month. On the programme, the group performed some of their hits and sang with Olivia and Andy Gibb. In one long sequence, the six artists did fun improvisations of various songs, ranging from the Beach Boys' 'Barbara Ann' to an operatic aria, performed by Frida. The first screening of the show was on ABC on 17 May.

Stig explained: 'Olivia said that she liked us a lot. Our participation in this programme is just the first step in a collaboration. We're going to do the same thing in September when she comes to Sweden. Polar Music are going to take care of the distribution of her records in our country.'

10 May ABBA arrived in Düsseldorf to record the TV show *Star Parade*. The group performed 'Eagle', 'Take a Chance On Me' and 'Thank You For the Music'.

18 May The cream of Swedish showbusiness – artists, musicians, technicians and record-company executives – attended the opening of the Polar Music studios. Stig and his wife Gudrun greeted the guests at the entrance to the studios. Inside, Agnetha, Björn, Benny, Anni-Frid and Michael B. Tretow showed guests their new musical 'laboratory'. Built in an old cinema, the Riverside, it was one of Europe's most advanced recording studios.

7 June Vogue released the single 'Eagle'. Some countries, such as Germany, Japan and France, fearing that the song was too long to be played on the radio, had asked for a shorter version. The song was therefore cut from 5 minutes 47 seconds to 3:36. The single, which had already been released in several countries, did very well, reaching No. 2 in Belgium, No. 8 in Germany, No. 4 in Holland and No. 9 in Spain.

ABBA är här!

Agneta, Frida, Benny och Björn.

Ha dom hemma hos dej. Alla fyra!

Störtsköna dockor med ABBAS häftiga scenkläder till. Precis som i verkligheten. Res med ABBA på världsturné! Klä dom för scenen och låt dom uppträda.

Lev med i deras spännande liv på lek!

MATCHBOX

Lesney AB, Ringögatan, 417 07 Göteborg.

10 June Benny and Anni-Frid flew off for a three-week holiday in Barbados. Björn and Agnetha had decided to spend some time with their children on the island of Viggsö.

12 June *Abba – The Album* reached sales of one million in Britain. A customer in Reading, Mrs Bonner, was presented with a congratulatory telegram, signed by all four members of the group, for having purchased the millionth copy.

At the beginning of the summer, toy company Matchbox released four dolls styled on the members of the group. Each one was 24 centimetres tall and had moveable limbs. Agnetha and Frida had implanted hair, while Björn's and Benny's hair was moulded and painted. A set of stage clothes was available separately. The dolls didn't resemble the four members of ABBA at all!

3 July On his return to Sweden, Benny went to Västervik with Björn and Clabbe af Geijerstam to take possession of his new boat, a Storebro Royal Cruiser 38. It was 12 metres long and cost around a million Swedish kronor. The three men took to sea immediately to sail the boat back to Stockholm. Benny and Anni-Frid continued their holidays sailing along the Swedish coast until the end of July.

8 July 'Take a Chance On Me' reached No. 3 in the USA. The single had sold a million copies, and *Abba – The Album* was steadily climbing the charts. The famous American weekly magazine *People* sent photographer Marvin E. Newman to Sweden to produce a full report on the group. Most of the photos were taken in the Stockholm archipelago, on a boat and on the island of Viggsö. The magazine printed a long article on ABBA at the beginning of September.

19 July Benny and Frida attended the tennis championships in Båstad, on the west coast of Sweden. Judging by the crowd's reaction when they arrived, it seemed that the couple's appearance was more important than Björn Borg's!

At the beginning of August, after seven weeks of holidays, the two couples returned to work for what was their first proper session in the new Polar Music studios. Björn and Benny tried as hard as they could to put the finishing touches to 'Summer Night City', a new track intended for the forthcoming album. This song is a good example of a track which was difficult to complete. Assisted by Michael B. Tretow, the two musicians spent the week trying every mix imaginable. Unable to find an alternative for the new single, Björn and Benny decided to use 'Summer Night City'. In an effort to make the song sound more forceful, the two musicians decided to cut the 45-second introduction. Björn commented later: 'The song deserved a better treatment.'

21–23 August Lasse Hallström recorded the video for 'Summer Night City'. The inside shots were filmed in the Europa Films studios amid people dancing to create a discotheque atmosphere. For the outside shots, the director chose a waterfront location in central Stockholm. Agnetha and Anni-Frid were filmed on Benny's boat and together with their partners on the quays and in the streets near the Grand Hotel. Filming began during the early evening and continued until the small hours. The entire event was covered by photographer Torbjörn Calvero.

At the end of August, a Soviet delegation travelled to Sweden to meet Stig and to discuss the possibility of distributing ABBA's albums and *Abba – The Movie* in the principal towns of the U.S.S.R. The group had achieved great success in the Soviet Union, with their promotional videos being regularly shown on television. The Polish TV special *Studio 2* had also been screened. Yet their records and cassettes were still only available on the black market. In reply to this huge demand, Polar Music at first agreed to license the pressing of 200,000 records. Several other countries of the Eastern bloc were to be granted licences during the year (via Sannes Trading), allowing them to press a specific number of ABBA albums locally: Poland (500,000 copies), Czechoslovakia (300,000 copies), East Germany (200,000 copies), Bulgaria (100,000 copies) and Hungary (50,000 copies).

6 September Polar Music released the 'Summer Night City' single. The B-side, 'Medley', was an old track, recorded in May 1975, and had only been previously released on a German album entitled *Stars im Zeichen eines Guten Sterns*. The proceeds from the sales of this album went towards the fight against cancer. 'Medley' was slightly remixed for its international release. Mats Olsson wrote in *Expressen*: ' "Summer Night City" has got the word "hit" stamped all over it. The lyrics have no real importance, paying homage to a summer's night in town, and reliving how liberating a night like this can make you feel. Musically, it's the same as ever, but more so. ABBA's strong point is being able to find something different for each new record, while still keeping the recognizable sound which is ABBA's and ABBA's alone. It has been said that the song is a plagiarism of the Bee Gees, but ABBA's sound is fresher and more original than that.'

'Summer Night City' entered the Swedish charts on 22 September, reaching No. 1 on 6 October. It signalled the long-awaited return of the group to the Swedish singles chart, as Polar Music had decided not to release the singles 'Take a Chance On Me' and 'Eagle', due to the enormous success of *Abba – The Album*.

8 September Epic-CBS released the single in the UK, where its success was guaranteed by advance sales of 250,000 copies. Despite this fact, the single rose no higher than No. 5 in the British charts. This was a surprise, as ABBA's singles had always made the Top 3 over the past three years. Reviews were not favourable, with ABBA now being accused of following the 'disco' trend. *Record Mirror* wrote: 'The calculating Swedes have produced a piece of disco muzak', while the *New Musical Express* said: 'ABBA go disco – the song's by no means as memorable as earlier stuff'. Björn retorted: 'Everyone's doing it – it's the pulse of the seventies!'

15 September Vogue released 'Summer Night City'. Although the single took off slowly in France, it was virtually an instant hit everywhere else, reaching No. 3 in Belgium, No. 5 in Holland, No. 6 in Germany, No. 2 in Austria, No. 1 in Ireland, No. 1 in Denmark, No. 2 in Finland, No. 28 in Spain, No. 13 in Australia and No. 37 in New Zealand.

' "SUMMER NIGHT CITY" NEVER ACTUALLY CAME OUT THE WAY IT SHOULD SOUND. WE HAD FIFTY MIXES OF IT. IT'S STILL A GOOD SONG AND A FAIRLY GOOD RECORDING, BUT NOT THE WAY IT WAS SUPPOSED TO BE.' MICHAEL B. TRETOW

Press conference at the Publicistklubben, Stockholm

'YEARS AGO, I PROMISED BJÖRN AND BENNY THAT, WITH MY HELP, THEY WOULD CARVE A PLACE OF HONOUR FOR THEMSELVES IN THE WORLD, BUT EVEN I NEVER EXPECTED ANYTHING LIKE THIS. PEOPLE HAVE BEEN TRYING TO EXPLAIN WHY IT HAS HAPPENED. I DON'T KNOW WHY, AND I DON'T THINK ANYBODY WILL BE ABLE TO PUT THEIR FINGER ON IT.' STIG

Recording sessions for the next album continued at Polar Music studios. The two couples were working on the tracks 'Lovelight', 'The King Has Lost His Crown' and 'Dreamworld'.

6 October Benny married Anni-Frid in Lidingö church. The ceremony took place amid as much secrecy as possible, with only three other people present: the priest and the two witnesses – a church employee and the couple's housekeeper. Benny said: 'We felt it was the right moment to marry but it had to be a quiet ceremony, because we didn't want it to be like Björn and Agnetha's wedding, where there were so many people that it was just too crowded. Not that we didn't want our fans to know about it, but we both felt that our wedding was very personal, and we didn't want it spoilt by anything like that.' Those close to the couple were not left out, however; the following evening, a dinner was held at Benny and Anni-Frid's Lidingö villa. Among the twenty or so guests present were Agnetha, Björn, Stig and Gudrun, Görel Johnsen, Björn Skifs, Clabbe af Geijerstam, Alexandra Charles and Michael B. Tretow. No one could believe it when the news of the wedding was announced during the simple meal.

12 October Stig, Agnetha, Björn, Benny and Anni-Frid invited several hundred journalists to attend an unusual press conference at the Publicistklubben, in the Stockholm parliament buildings. Instead of the aim being to promote something, as was usually the case, it was to clarify ABBA's position with the press. They set the tone from the start, declaring: 'We are often the object of personal attacks and rarely have the opportunity to defend ourselves directly.' Agnetha announced: 'The main thing for us is our music. Unfortunately, this is usually seen as secondary. Instead, so many stupid things are written which are mostly untrue.' The roles were reversed for a change, with the members of the group asking the journalists questions. Anni-Frid asked them: 'What do you want from us? Have we made too much money?' Benny explained: 'The journalists who say that our music is the result of calculated planning would change their minds if they were involved in our hard work sessions.' The journalists finally had the following to say in their own defence: 'We do respect people's private lives. We don't make up stories like the British and German press.'

Promotional visit to Japan

18 October ABBA arrived in Paris for two days of promotion. During the afternoon, they went to Studio 102 at the Maison de la Radio for rehearsals of *Top Club*, a daily TV show presented by Guy Lux. The programme had very high viewing figures – it was screened just before the 8 o'clock news. Agnetha, Björn, Benny and Anni-Frid were guests of honour the following week (23 – 28 October). They recorded six songs in one evening, changing costumes between each filming session, and were interviewed several times by the presenter. 'Money, Money, Money' was used as the opening music. The following day, ABBA were due to sing 'Summer Night City' on a *Top Club* Special. But because of a strike by the technicians of the S.F.P. (French Production Society), the recording was cancelled. During the evening, Alain Boublil organized a dinner, in the presence of Mireille Mathieu, at the famous restaurant Le Grand Véfour. The group returned to Stockholm the following day.

25 October – 10 November ABBA continued with the recording and mixing of two new tracks for the forthcoming album: 'Angeleyes' and 'If It Wasn't For the Nights'. Polar Music made an announcement to the press that the album would not be ready before spring 1979. At the end of October, Stig and Görel Johnsen travelled to Tokyo to finalize details of ABBA's pending visit to Japan.

11 November ABBA travelled from Stockholm to Los Angeles to take part in a live performance of *The Dick Clark Show* on 15 November, and to receive platinum discs recognizing sales of the albums *Greatest Hits* and *Abba – The Album* in the United States. ABBA did no promotion for 'Summer Night City', as the single had not been released in America.

16 November The group left the States and flew to Tokyo. Stig, Görel Johnsen and representatives of record label Discomate had planned ten days of promotion to consolidate ABBA's success in Japan (their previous visit had been in November 1972). Görel told the Swedish press: 'The Japanese are growing to like ABBA more and more, especially since the screening of the TV shows *Olivia* and *Studio 2*, from Poland. "Summer Night City" has just been released as a single – with a "Welcome ABBA" caption printed on it – and three albums are currently in the Top 20: *Arrival*, *Greatest Hits* and *Abba – The Album*.'

The timetable was very tight and the group had very little free time during their trip. On 20 November, ABBA gave a press conference at the Hilton in Tokyo. They took part in several radio shows and previewed a new track, 'The King Has Lost His Crown'. Agnetha, Björn, Benny and Anni-Frid also participated in several TV shows and recorded an *Abba Special*. In this hour-

ABBA TV special in Japan

long programme, the group, sometimes surrounded by dancers, performed thirteen songs – some recorded live with a backing orchestra – and unveiled the new song 'If It Wasn't For the Nights'. Japanese television made a whole feature on this ten-day promotional trip, including backstage footage from the *Abba Special.*

27 November The group landed back in Stockholm. At the end of their trip, Agnetha told *Expressen*: 'The timetable was very intense. But I have never seen such efficient people. We didn't see much of Japan apart from the hotel and the radio and TV studios. During the ten days we only had an hour and a half of free time, but we enjoyed ourselves!'

6 December The group flew to London for three days of promotion. They were accompanied by musicians Ola Brunkert (drums), Christian Veltman (bass) and Janne Schaffer (guitar). ABBA recorded two TV shows: *The Mike Yarwood Christmas Show*, on which they performed 'If It Wasn't For the Nights' and 'Thank You For the Music', and *Jim'll Fix It*, presented by Jimmy Savile. On the latter, two of the group's fans had the opportunity to meet their idols; they were chosen from 50,000 people who had written letters to the BBC. During the programme, the four members of the group announced two pieces of important news: their participation in the Unicef gala the following

January, which would take place at the United Nations building in New York, and the filming of a *Snowtime Special* the following February, a show which would be co-produced by the BBC and several other European television companies. During this brief trip to Britain, the group also attended Rod Stewart's concert in Leicester.

On their return to Stockholm, Björn and Benny shut themselves away in the studio to finish off a new track, 'Chiquitita'. It went through numerous phases before becoming the song which is so well known and loved. Originally entitled 'Kålsupare', the song quickly evolved into 'In the Arms of Rosalita' and then finally became 'Chiquitita'. From the start, it had a slightly 'dancy' feel, with castanets here and there giving the melody a Latin touch. The guitar and piano segments, as well as the lyrics, were fine-tuned until they were perfect. The two girls recorded the vocals over and over again until finally,   it was Agnetha who retained the solo parts.

Perhaps one of ABBA's real strengths was the length of time they spent in the studio. The journalists who called the group a hit-making machine would have changed their minds if they had been in the studio with them. They would have witnessed four perfectionists working until they were exhausted in order to achieve the best results possible. People close to them knew how passionate they were about their recording sessions and how tiring these sessions were. Agnetha's and Frida's contributions were considerable. Michael B. Tretow would later say: 'We had enormous fun in the studio, all the time, but we worked very hard. Everything became so easy and those girls were so terrific at singing. They could do almost anything with their voices. They loved working in the studio.'

A fruitful year was drawing to a close for ABBA, Stig and their team. Everyone had worked hard and the results had proved that their efforts weren't in vain. In Sweden, sales of *Abba – The Album* had reached 753,000 copies. In France and Belgium, the album had been awarded platinum discs. In Britain, the group had broken all records: *Abba – The Album* had sold over a million copies, and they had been at the top of the charts for nine weeks with 'Take A Chance On Me', ABBA's seventh No. 1 in the UK. *Abba – The Movie* was the seventh most successful film of the year, after *Star Wars*, *Grease* and *Saturday Night Fever*.

'IF BENNY DOESN'T LIKE A LYRIC THAT I HAVE WRITTEN, WE DON'T USE IT. IT'S AS SIMPLE AS THAT. I JUST THROW IT AWAY AND WRITE SOMETHING NEW UNTIL IT PLEASES BOTH OF US. AND IT'S THE SAME WHEN WE WRITE THE MELODIES.' BJÖRN

In the United States, despite the opinions of some journalists, ABBA Month had been a success. The *Greatest Hits* album had been awarded a platinum disc, as had *Abba – The Album*, which notched up forty-one weeks in the charts, peaking at No. 14. The single 'Take a Chance On Me' had been awarded a gold disc – it reached No. 3 during its eighteen weeks in the charts.

Benny at the Polar Music studios

ABBA in Paris, October

'TO ME THE POP CHARTS REALLY HAVEN'T BEEN THE SAME SINCE ABBA'S DEMISE. IT WAS THE FIRST TIME I'D HEARD GORGEOUS HARMONIES AND ANGELIC CHORUSES THAT MADE YOU FEEL REALLY ELATED. I LOVED THE FACT THAT THEY WENT ON TO MAKE DISCO, LIKE "VOULEZ-VOUS", THEY FULLY UNDERSTOOD IT.'
ANDY BELL ERASURE

4 January Agnetha, Björn, Benny and Anni-Frid flew to New York to take part in the Music For Unicef gala to mark the beginning of the Year of the Child. Unicef (United Nations Children's Fund) is a humanitarian organization founded to help children in third-world countries. All the artists who took part in this show, which was presented by the Bee Gees, performed free of charge and all agreed to donate the rights of their songs to Unicef. Among the artists taking part were Olivia Newton-John, Earth Wind and Fire, John Denver, Rod Stewart and Donna Summer. The event was filmed on 9 January by American TV station NBC, and would be broadcast in seventy countries to an estimated audience of more than 300 million viewers. ABBA had decided to give 'Chiquitita' its worldwide premiere and this gala was obviously an excellent platform for the new song. At the end of the show, all the artists came back on stage to sing together 'He Is Your Brother'. Christina Kallum wrote in *Expressen*: 'All four members of the group – dazzling in their black stone-encrusted costumes and perched on a moveable podium in the middle of the hall – were a big success. "Chiquitita", ABBA's new song, has all the qualities of another hit and will also raise several millions for Unicef.' Curiously, Atlantic didn't release 'Chiquitita' as a single in the United States until the end of the year.

The group used their few days in the United States to meet the press and give interviews. Stig announced: 'The new album will be ready in the middle of April. I am currently in the process of negotiating a tour which will include the USA and Canada. We will give twenty-five concerts in the biggest towns of North America.'

10 January Stig and ABBA threw a party on the thirty-eighth floor of New York's Plaza Hotel, in the presence of the Swedish ambassador to the United States, Wilhelm Wachtmeister, as well as the Swedish ambassador to the United Nations, Anders Thunborg. The evening concluded at the famous Studio 54 nightclub. The following day the whole team returned to Stockholm.

16 January The Swedish newspapers ran the headline: 'ABBA Divorce: Agnetha and Björn Split'. The news came completely out of the blue. For many people it was as if a fairy tale had come to an end. The group's image of two happy couples had been shattered. In an exclusive interview with Mats Olsson in *Expressen*, Agnetha and Björn explained the situation:

Agnetha: 'What has happened only concerns the two of us. There's no point talking about what went wrong with our marriage. The fact is that Björn and myself can no longer live together.'

Björn: 'It's important to say that this is an amicable divorce, if you can call it that. In the beginning, it was all very romantic and we were in love. But after we got married, bit by bit we began to move apart. Our tastes and opinions started to differ more and more. We thought that a second child would bring us closer together.'

Agnetha: 'Christian doesn't know anything about what's going on because he's too young, but Linda understands. In the end the three of us sat down to talk about it. It's almost a month since we separated and I think she prefers to see that her two parents are happier now. And anyway, I only live 7 minutes away from Björn. The news isn't a surprise to Benny and Frida because they're close to us and can see how we work.'

Björn: 'It's not very nice to talk about all this in public. Which is why we won't be talking about our divorce any more in the future like we have done here. It's important that we stress that ABBA is not going to break up. The group means so much to us.'

On the set of *Gå På Vattnet Om Du Kan* – director Stig Björkman, Lena Nyman, Anni-Frid & Thomas Pontén

Nevertheless, despite Agnetha and Björn's declarations, the Swedish and international press continued to speculate on the reasons for their separation and the future of the group.

On the same day, the new single 'Chiquitita' was released simultaneously in Sweden and many other countries. The group's fans were doubly pleased with the single's B-side, 'Lovelight', since the song wasn't to be included on the forthcoming album.

Christer Faleij wrote in *Aftonbladet*: '"Chiquitita" is typically ABBA: the arrangement, the sound, the singing, nothing has been left to chance. Therefore, there is no surprise. When I listen to such perfection, I don't feel anything. Is this what ABBA are going to give us in the future or will Björn and Benny be able to do something new? The B-side, "Lovelight", opens with some great bars of guitar but doesn't contain any other surprises.' Mats Olsson wrote in *Expressen*: 'The song isn't bad but it's nothing unusual. ABBA had been accused of following the "disco" trend with "Summer Night City". This ballad of 5 minutes and 26 seconds is rather long to be a single. Apart from that, as usual, it's a good-quality song, well made and well produced.'

17 January Stig travelled to Cannes for the MIDEM fair. It gave him the opportunity to announce ABBA's autumn tour and to meet the representatives who were working for the group around the world.

For some time, Björn and Benny had been running short of ideas for writing and producing new songs. This bad patch was understandable: Agnetha and Björn's divorce, travelling, a busy promotional calendar and pressure to complete the new album, due for release in April, – all these had obviously affected the two musicians' inspiration. It was therefore quite natural that they decided to leave the Swedish winter behind them and recharge their batteries and compose new songs in the sunshine of the Bahamas. They took off for Nassau on 22 January. Björn later announced in an interview:

'Atlantic Records suggested that we rent a house in the Bahamas. We had the chance to listen to other music there, which was very stimulating. The pleasure of writing and playing soon came back.' Several tracks first came to light there, including 'Kisses of Fire' and 'Voulez-Vous'. Björn and Benny were so pleased with the latter that they decided to record it at the Criteria studios in Miami on 1 February, together with Michael B. Tretow. The musicians from the disco group Foxy took part in the recording. Björn, Benny and Michael returned to Stockholm on 3 February.

29 January Agnetha recorded a new solo song, 'När Du Tar Mig I Din Famn' (When You Take Me In Your Arms). Agnetha – who hadn't written a song for four years – had specially composed this track for her forthcoming compilation album, *Tio År Med Agnetha* (Ten Years With Agnetha), which CBS-Cupol were going to release throughout Scandinavia. After having written an English lyric, with the title 'I'm a Fool Again You See', the singer gave the job of writing the Swedish text to Ingela Forsman.

3–5 February Anni-Frid was in Seville, Spain, for the filming of a full-length movie entitled *Gå På Vattnet Om Du Kan* (Walk On Water If You Can). The film was based on the book *Orlanda Och Världen* (Orlanda and the World). Orlanda (played by Swedish actress Lena Nyman), is a young literature student who falls in love with Anders (Thomas Pontén), a Swedish diplomat based in Argentina who is married to Anna (Anni-Frid). Although the story is based in South America, the filming took place in a wonderful villa in Seville. During a break in filming, director Stig Björkman said: 'I've been thinking about Frida for a long time. I'd seen her on television, in ABBA's videos, and I'd read some interviews. She seemed to be very intelligent and talented. She read the script and found the role serious and thought it would be interesting for her cinema début.' Frida confided: 'The fact that I was chosen came as a surprise to me. I've wanted to try something new outside ABBA for a long time. Even if I only had a small role, the first day of filming was very tough.'

'I THINK ALL FOUR OF US COULD SEE THE POTENTIAL IN THE GROUP WAS STILL THERE, SO WHY LET OUR PRIVATE LIVES RUIN SOMETHING THAT IS STILL GOOD?' BJÖRN

10 February 'Chiquitita' reached No. 2 on the British charts, where it would remain for two weeks, unable to knock Blondie's 'Heart of Glass' off the top spot. The *Daily Mirror* announced Agnetha's engagement to Swedish psychologist Håkan Lönnqvist. Agnetha responded quickly: 'Håkan is the psychologist whom Björn and myself consulted when we were having problems. Over time, he became one of our best friends. It saddens me to read all this speculation.'

14 February Agnetha, Björn, Benny and Anni-Frid took off for Leysin, Switzerland, where they were to record the TV show *Abba In Switzerland*, part of the *Snowtime Special* series being produced by the BBC. Soon after taking off from Stockholm, the plane was forced to turn back because of a technical problem caused by the bad weather. ABBA finally landed at Geneva airport an hour late. Leaving the plane, the group were invited to board a helicopter, since the BBC wanted the group to arrive in Leysin in the style of their *Arrival* album sleeve.

At 7 p.m., the group gave a press conference in the hotel's discotheque. Inevitably, questions concentrated on the divorce:

Agnetha: 'I don't want to talk about the divorce this evening. It's a private matter and we've already explained ourselves in an interview. Also, the man who has been named as my new fiancé is just one of our old friends. The only man in my life at the moment is my son Christian.'

Björn (visibly irritated): 'I assure you that Agnetha and myself work very well together but that we could no longer live together. Your questions always used to be about money. Now all you talk about is our divorce. It's a matter between Agnetha and myself. I'd be grateful if you would please stop speculating about our private lives.'

Benny: 'I can assure you that the group will carry on. Even if we were all divorced, ABBA is ABBA!'

At the end of the interview, the four Swedes were presented with a silver trophy, the *Bravo* Otto 78 (voted for by readers of the German magazine) by Thomas Heidenreich, one of the group's fans, as well as gold discs for 'Chiquitita' in the UK (650,000 copies had already been sold).

At 9 p.m., the group went to the Leysin ice rink, where the television crew filmed ABBA while they skated on the ice. Despite several falls, Agnetha, Björn, Benny and Anni-Frid enjoyed themselves and gave permission for the numerous reporters present to take photographs.

15 February ABBA mixed business and pleasure during the day's filming at the Les Diablerettes ski slopes. The group took a break for lunch and gave several interviews while sitting on the terrace of a small local café. During the afternoon, the BBC filmed them singing 'Chiquitita' in front of a snowman. This would become the official video for the song. A second version was later filmed inside the hotel and this was screened in Germany during a 1979 Christmas show.

16 February The *Abba In Switzerland* show was filmed in a big top with an audience of 2000. Even though ABBA mimed to playback tapes, they were accompanied on stage by Rutger Gunnarsson (bass), Ola Brunkert (drums) and Lasse Wellander (guitar). The group performed some of their hits and previewed four tracks from their forthcoming album: 'The King Has Lost His Crown', 'Kisses of Fire', 'Lovers (Live a Little Longer)' and 'Does Your Mother Know' (in a rockier version). The other guests on the show were Roxy Music, Ted Gärdestad and Kate Bush. *Abba In Switzerland* was screened in a number of European countries over the Easter holidays.

At this time, the BBC organized several recordings for the *Snowtime Special* series with artists like Leo Sayer, Patrick Juvet, Leif Garrett, Eruption, Bonnie Tyler and Boney M. This led the *Sun* to announce that Björn's 'new love' was none other than Liz Mitchell, one of the singers of the group Boney M. Björn denied this in *Expressen*: 'It's only a rumour. We are just friends and we talked a lot during our stay in Leysin. That's all!'

On their return to Sweden, Stig announced that this time their tour wouldn't include Australia but would concentrate on North America and Europe. 'Chiquitita' slowly climbed up the French charts, reaching No. 39 on the RTL Hit Parade. The single was breaking records in other countries: No. 1 in Belgium, No. 1 in Holland, No. 3 in Germany, No. 1 in Denmark, No. 2 in Sweden, No. 1 in Ireland, No. 1 in Spain, No. 48 in Italy, No. 3 in Japan and No. 4 in Australia.

8 March Agnetha and Anni-Frid recorded the Spanish version of 'Chiquitita'. The lyrics had been written by Buddy and Mary McCluskey, who worked for RCA in Argentina. Buddy later said: 'ABBA had been gaining popularity [here] for a long time but "Chiquitita" is what really made the break for them. The strange thing is that both versions, Spanish and English, were hits, although the Spanish one really was the biggest smash. I started helping Agnetha and Frida with their Spanish pronunciation. I went over to Stockholm and they are really very good at languages already – now their Spanish pronunciation is perfect.'

On the same evening, Agnetha, Björn, Benny, Anni-Frid, Stig Anderson and his wife Gudrun were present for the first time at the annual dinner organized by King Carl Gustav at the Royal Palace of Stockholm. Among the 160 ministers, ambassadors and other distinguished guests present was the future Swedish Prime Minister, Olof Palme.

During March, 'Chiquitita' was released in Japan. It was an almost instant hit and reached No. 3 on the charts. Since the group's visit to Japan six months earlier, the group had sold 1.5 million records there.

'I USED TO SING ONE OR TWO TRACKS ON EACH ALBUM JUST FOR VARIETY, I SUPPOSE, AND "DOES YOUR MOTHER KNOW" HAPPENED TO BE ONE OF THOSE SONGS AND IT HAPPENED TO BE A STRONG NUMBER, SO IT WAS RELEASED AS A SINGLE.' BJÖRN

Voulez-Vous was chosen as the title for the new album, after a track on side one of the album. For the sleeve, Rune Söderqvist organized a photo shoot with photographer Ola Lager. 'I haven't got good memories of this period,' says Rune. 'I had to work in a hurry. Since the album had a disco sound, we decided to take the photos inside the Alexandra discotheque in Stockholm. I then went to London to work on the artwork for the sleeve and to add some star effects and some brightness on the neon light.'

During the second half of March, Björn and Benny went back to work on the recording and mixing of the album. Two new tracks took shape: 'As Good As New' and 'I Have a Dream'. 'I remember that I was at home working on the lyrics for "I Have a Dream", and when I had finished them I rang Benny up,' says Björn. 'He and Frida were having a party, and he told me to come on over. When I got there, we ran the song through on the piano in front of the other guests, and after a while they were all singing along, because it was so easy to learn.' (*The Complete Recording Sessions*, 1994.)

24 March   Anni-Frid's evening was disturbed by an unpleasant incident. While she was at home with her two children, an intruder tried to get in. She told *Expressen*: 'The man knocked at the door and when I opened it he tried to come in. He was shouting "Can I use the phone?" I quickly slammed the door and called the police. As soon as they arrived, they took the man away for questioning.' Since no crime had been committed, he was released several hours later. The police sent someone to guard the property day and night. 'He'll keep a watch on the house until we feel safe again,' explained Anni-Frid.

5–6 April   Lasse Hallström filmed the promotional videos for the songs 'Does Your Mother Know' and 'Voulez-Vous'. A discotheque atmosphere was recreated in the Europa Films studios in Stockholm and a group of teenagers were invited along to dance around the group. Photographer Torbjörn Calvero took several hundred shots of the group during the two days of filming.

23 April   Polar Music released the *Voulez-Vous* album and the 'Does Your Mother Know' single simultaneously, with the other European record companies planning the releases at around the same time. In Scandinavia, 450,000 advance copies had already been ordered. Five pressing plants worked day and night to reach the album's deadline.

The lyrics of the ten songs had matured compared with those in previous albums. Stig, who had been preoccupied with business matters, had not collaborated in the writing. And if *Voulez-Vous* is an album with a disco feel, the famous ABBA sound was still recognizable. Björn and Benny just added a few disco ingredients (like brass and rhythm) to their arrangements. The violin sound, omnipresent in other European disco productions, especially those from Germany with Donna Summer, Boney M, Silver Convention and Penny McLean, was not to be found here. However, with the *Voulez-Vous* album, journalists and other music professionals still often made the mistake of referring to ABBA as a disco group. Benny explains: 'We found that disco-based rhythms suited and enhanced our music, so naturally we used them.'

Mats Olsson wrote in *Expressen*: 'This ABBA album is real quality. Is it better or worse than the earlier ones? I don't know. Their music is sophisticated and quite complex and a lot of the tracks need to be heard a few times before you get hooked. If you listen to "Voulez-Vous" with the volume turned right up, you realize that it's an ideal disco track. "Voulez-Vous" and "The King Has Lost His Crown" are, together with "Dancing Queen" and "Eagle", what ABBA do best.' In *Vecko-Revyn*, Christer Olsson wrote: 'Every song on the album could be a hit, which strikes a happy balance against the syrupy, cheap disco-sounding ballads and tasteless schmaltz which is dominating the charts around the world. ABBA are on the attack with their

fists full of simple, effective melodies, including disco, funk, rock and even a ballad from time to time. The songs are excellent and really catchy, full of *joie de vivre*.' And Lars Weck wrote in *Aftonbladet*: 'The track which is the best disco number, "Lovers", is, in my opinion the best one on the album, with a great heartfelt bluesy feel. After hearing a song like that and the great segments in some of the other songs, it makes you wonder what the team would come up with without the pressure and commercial constraints.' In Sweden, *Voulez-Vous* went straight into the album charts at No. 1 on 4 May. During its six months on the Swedish charts, it remained at the top spot for ten weeks.

The *Voulez-Vous* album was released on the same day in France and Belgium. To commemorate the event, Vogue decided to release a limited edition in red vinyl, as well as a picture disc. The 'Does Your Mother Know' single was No. 1 in Belgium and stayed in the charts for eleven weeks. In France, it reached No. 3 on 5 August and remained in the charts for twelve weeks.

With 'Does Your Mother Know', ABBA proved, once again, that they were always looking for new ideas for each song. The track was rockier than usual, and for the first time, Björn sang lead vocal on the A-side, with Agnetha and Frida on backing vocals. This change did not affect the record's success at all: it reached No. 4 in Britain, No. 1 in Belgium, No. 4 in Holland, No. 10 in

Germany, No. 1 in Austria, No. 1 in Finland, No. 7 in Australia, No. 27 in New Zealand and No. 9 in Zimbabwe.

3 May Agnetha, Björn, Benny and Anni-Frid took part in a demonstration in the centre of Stockholm. More than 500 artists and musicians gathered together at the Hamburger Börs to protest against the government's attempts to block the creation of an agency aimed at finding work especially for artists. At the end of this day of protest, a petition was sent to the Minister of Employment.

4 May Epic-CBS released the *Voulez-Vous* album in Britain. It was an instant hit, with advance orders of more than 400,000 copies, and had already achieved platinum-disc status. In just five weeks of sales, it would pass the million mark. Going straight in at No. 1, it stayed in the British charts for almost a year. David McCullough wrote in *Sounds* magazine: 'For ten years, the critics have been unanimous in saying that each member of ABBA is a genius.'

7 May Benny began production on the *Kom Ut, Kom Fram* album for the young Norwegian singer Finn Kalvik. Anni-Frid sang backing vocals on most of the tracks, and Agnetha and Tomas Ledin took part on the album's title track.

'Chiquitita', *Musikladen, Germany*

'OURS WAS WHAT YOU MIGHT DESCRIBE AS A HAPPY DIVORCE IN SO FAR AS WE BOTH AGREED THAT THIS WAS THE BEST THING TO DO. IT WAS NOT LIKE, YOU KNOW, ONE OF US HAD FOUND SOMEONE ELSE. SO, IT WASN'T AS BAD AS IT MIGHT HAVE SEEMED. THE BAD THING WAS THE KID, OF COURSE, THAT WAS THE UNHAPPY THING ABOUT IT.' BJÖRN

'WHEN AGNETHA AND I SEPARATED AND EVENTUALLY DIVORCED, I THINK PEOPLE ASSUMED THAT IT WAS BECAUSE OF THE PRESSURES OF THE BAND, BUT REALLY WE HAD DRIFTED APART AND IT WOULD HAVE HAPPENED NO MATTER WHAT OUR JOBS WERE.' BJÖRN

In the middle of May, the Swedish press announced that Björn was in love with Lena Källersjö, a twenty-nine-year-old publicist. The couple had met at a party in March. Lena, a friend of Benny and Frida, told *Expressen*: 'We are always being followed by photographers. It's quite tough. I don't want to be in the papers because I live with Björn. It makes me scared and a bit hysterical. Björn takes it all in his stride. He's used to public life. If I run away they follow me. The worst thing is when we have Björn and Agnetha's children with us. We want to protect them from the photographers.'

The following day, it was Agnetha's turn to be on the front pages of the papers. According to them, she was caught up in a passionate love affair with ice-hockey player Lars-Erik Ericsson. 'I cannot deny that we are seeing each other regularly,' Agnetha declared in *Aftonbladet*. 'Our relationship is serious and we like being together. But I don't want to discuss our private life in the press.' Agnetha and Lars-Erik met at the Atlantic discotheque, at a birthday party for Hasse Blomgren, one of Thomas Johansson's colleagues.

The press also published some other good news. A fifteen-year-old Swedish fan, Beatrice Hansson, had written to ABBA: 'I belong to an equestrian club in Ljusdal which has about two hundred members. Unfortunately, we only have six horses and five ponies. We would be over the moon if you could help us to buy another horse.' A short time afterwards, the club received 5000 Swedish kronor and Beatrice received a photo signed by the four members of the group with a message on the back, saying: 'Thank you for your nice letter. It's obvious that you need an extra horse. So we have put 5000 Swedish kronor into your bank account. We hope that's enough. Good luck! ABBA.'

16 May Agnetha, Björn, Benny and Anni-Frid began rehearsals for the forthcoming tour at the Grünewaldsalen concert hall, in the Konserthuset building in Stockholm.

18 May The 650 customers of the Diskoland nightclub in Landskrona were in for a big surprise. ABBA gave a test concert on the stage of the club, as part of the preparations for the tour. To prevent a riot, it had been kept a closely guarded secret. The following day, the same surprise was in store for the customers of a discotheque in Norrköping. ABBA were joined on stage by the musicians who would be with them on the tour.

21 May A Swedish publicity campaign began, aimed at encouraging the young unemployed to look for work or enrol on vocational courses. A superb photo of Anni-Frid Lyngstad (left) was seen in the press, on posters and on the cover of brochures, alongside the slogan: 'You've got to fight!' Gunnar Sjögren, who was responsible for the campaign, explained: 'This is the first time that a member of ABBA has publicized something which has nothing to do with the group. Frida accepted immediately and also agreed to do it free of charge! She's got children of her own and thinks that the campaign is important.'

27–28 May Agnetha, Björn, Benny and Anni-Frid were in Madrid to record two TV shows. On the programme *300 Millones*, ABBA performed four tracks from the new album: 'I Have a Dream', 'Does Your Mother Know', 'Voulez-Vous' and 'Chiquitita' (in Spanish). On the programme *Aplauso*, they sang 'Does Your Mother Know', 'Voulez-Vous' and 'Chiquitita'. The show's host presented the group with a gold disc for sales of the 'Chiquitita' single. These two programmes were televised in Spain and also in most Spanish-speaking countries, where the *Voulez-Vous* album had included this new version of 'Chiquitita'.

7 June ABBA and Stig were in the Polar Music studios to record a song to commemorate the birthday of Görel Johnsen, assistant to Stig and the group. 'Sång Till Görel' (Song For Görel) was a tribute to their closest colleague. The amusing lyrics by Stig referred to her incredible organizational skills and her constant efficiency. On this recording, with vocals by Agnetha, Frida and Stig, Björn played banjo and Benny keyboards.

'IN SOUTH AMERICA, THEY SAID: "WE KNOW ABOUT THE SUCCESS IN EUROPE, IN AUSTRALIA, IN JAPAN, BUT THIS WOULD NEVER HAPPEN IN LATIN AMERICA!" SO I SAID, "LET'S PROVE IT!" WE MADE A SPANISH VERSION OF "CHIQUITITA" WHICH BECAME A HIT ACROSS THE LATIN AMERICAN CONTINENT. WE SOLD NEARLY ONE MILLION SINGLES IN MEXICO ALONE. WE HAD TO PROVE IT ALL THE TIME.' **STIG**

ABBA make prints of their hands at the Europa Films studios

A limited edition of fifty copies (a 12-inch single in blue vinyl) was issued on 21 June (Görel's thirtieth birthday), but was never released commercially. Only the group's colleagues and friends of Görel Johnsen were given copies as gifts.

12 June Vogue released the Spanish version of 'Chiquitita' as a single. Issued in a number of countries, the record was much appreciated by the fans. In Spanish-speaking territories, the single's success was colossal: No. 1 in Spain, No. 1 in Mexico, and No. 1 in Argentina and the majority of other South American countries.

13 June Atlantic USA released the *Voulez-Vous* album. It stayed in the charts for twenty-seven weeks, peaking at No. 19. The record company chose to release 'Does Your Mother Know' as a single instead of 'Chiquitita', which had been programmed for release in the autumn. In May, Stig and Thomas Johansson travelled to the United States to finalize details for the forthcoming tour.

During the middle of June, Polydor released the album *The Music For Unicef Concert*, recorded on 9 January in New York. Among the numerous international superstars who had sung that evening, ABBA were featured with a shortened version of 'Chiquitita' (the instrumental is drowned out by applause). The record company did no promotion, but even so, it is strange that an album featuring such a host of stars went almost unnoticed.

Agnetha and Anni-Frid were turned into perfumes by a perfume manufacturer in New Zealand who had created an eau de toilette in the style of each of the ABBA singers. The 'Anna' scent was described as being 'light, fresh and flowery' and for daytime use, while 'Frida' was more suitable for evening use and was 'warm and spicy'.

The group took a break during the month of July. Benny and Anni-Frid spent their time travelling up and down the Swedish coastline and around the island of Gotland in their boat, together with their children. Björn and Lena Källersjö stayed on the Swedish archipelago, whilst Agnetha spent her holidays with Linda and Christian.

2 July Benny and Anni-Frid were on their way to Västervik, on the east coast. In the evening, they dropped anchor off Arkösund. During the night, the anchor freed itself and the boat began drifting. The couple did not realize what had happened until the morning, when Benny discovered that the boat was caught up in a perch net. Two men from Arkö heard their cries for help and helped to free the boat and return it to port. No damage was done, and after several hours, Benny, Frida and their children set out to sea once more.

6 July Epic-CBS released 'Angeleyes'/'Voulez-Vous' in Britain, deciding to promote it as a double A-side, which caused some confusion in the beginning but didn't prevent the single from reaching No. 3 on the British charts. Elsewhere, 'Voulez-Vous' reached No. 14 in Germany, No. 4 in Holland, No. 4 in Spain, No. 2 in Japan and No. 79 in Australia. In the United States, 'Voulez-Vous' reached No. 80 and 'Angeleyes' No. 64.

9 July Benny and Anni-Frid went to the Visfestival in Västervik especially to see Swedish rock group Boppers, Maritza Horn and bassist Rutger Gunnarsson, who appeared on stage with ex-Hootenanny Singers, Tony Rooth and Hansi Schwarz.

17 July Vogue released 'Voulez-Vous' as a single, and gave the fans the added bonus of releasing a 12-inch single in green vinyl, with 'Does Your Mother Know' on the B-side. In Belgium, 'Voulez-Vous, reached No. 1 on 21 July. In France, it didn't enter the RTL chart until 23 September, eventually peaking at No. 17. In France, ABBA were finally being acknowledged as one of the major groups of the past decade, and the *Voulez-Vous* album earned a platinum disc.

1 August ABBA continued rehearsals for their tour at the cinema studios of Europa Films in Sundbyberg, near Stockholm.

6 August ABBA made prints of their hands at the Europa Films studios. Agnetha, Björn, Benny, Anni-Frid and Stig, together with other Swedish personalities including Lill-Babs, Siw Malmkvist and Lasse Berghagen, came along to print their right hands in a block of clay. Casts were made in bronze

Agnetha Fältskog

Högt på svensktoppen
med "När du tar mig
i din famn".

Finns på nya LPn
"Tio år med Agnetha"
som innehåller
samtliga hennes
svensktopps-
succéer.

LP/kassett

CBS

and combined to make a massive fresco to decorate the hall of the new studios which were due to be opened on 1 November.

9 August   The group were back in the studio to finish a new track entitled 'Gimme! Gimme! Gimme! (A Man After Midnight)' Originally called 'Been and Gone and Done It', the lyrics had been rewritten several times by Björn.

10 August   Rehearsals continued at the Europa Films studios and were recorded on 24-track tape. Photographer Torbjörn Calvero took a whole session of pictures of the group at work.

27 August   ABBA finished rehearsals for the tour. Björn told the press: 'We wrote some new songs during rehearsals. One of them will be our new single and will feature on a new *Greatest Hits* album. We intend to stop touring after this one, but we've had offers from Japan and South America.'

Buddy McCluskey of RCA Argentina was visiting Stockholm. He had brought with him 'Estoy Soñando', the Spanish lyrics for the song 'I Have A Dream'. ABBA recorded the Spanish-language version before setting off for their tour of North America.

Meanwhile, during the month of September, the London Symphony Orchestra recorded twelve of ABBA's biggest hits. The idea had come from Stig, who had chosen the songs together with Björn and Benny.

5 September   ABBA finished mixing 'Gimme! Gimme! Gimme!' in the Polar Music studios. Lasse Hallström used this session to record videos for this song and for 'Estoy Soñando'.

8 September   Stig Anderson took off for New York, where he would meet the Atlantic team.

10 September   Björn and Agnetha, together with the musicians, backing vocalists and technicians, took off for Canada. After a 16-hour flight, they landed in Edmonton. Benny and Frida arrived a few hours later.

13 September   ABBA kicked off their tour with the first concert at the Edmonton Sports Arena. Between now and 7 October, ABBA would perform in eighteen North American towns. After a break, the group would carry on with a series of concerts in Europe, between 19 October and 15 November. (See '1979 Tour' chapter.)

17 September   The premiere of the film *Gå På Vattnet Om Du Kan* took place at the Festival cinema in Stockholm, although Anni-Frid didn't attend. The full-length movie, produced by Stig Björkman, was also released in Norway, under the title *Gå På Vannet Hvis Du Kan*.

During September, 'Estoy Soñando' was released in Spain and South America, with 'Kisses of Fire' on the B-side. The song reached No. 9 in Spain and No. 4 in Argentina.

21 September   CBS-Cupol released the compilation album *Tio År Med Agnetha* (Ten Years With Agnetha) in Scandinavia. The album featured fifteen of the singer's biggest hits, as well as the new song 'När Du Tar Mig I Din Famn' (When You Take Me In Your Arms), recorded on 29 January.

30 September   Swedish radio station 88FM broadcast an hour-long programme about ABBA's American tour. Produced and directed by Anders Hanser, the documentary concentrated on their concerts and featured interviews with the group and their entourage, including Stig, Clabbe af Geijerstam, Tomas Ledin and Björn Skifs.

9 October ABBA, Stig and the rest of their team landed at Stockholm's Arlanda airport after a 12-hour flight from Toronto. They looked pale and tired, but were happy to return to Sweden.

10 October Vogue released the 'Gimme! Gimme! Gimme! (A Man After Midnight)' single. As with the *Voulez-Vous* album, Björn and Benny had produced another song in the disco style but with the ABBA touch. The single's success was slower in France in comparison with other European countries, but this didn't prevent the song from staying on the RTL HIt Parade for three months and reaching No. 4. In Belgium, the single entered the charts a week after its release and quickly went up to the top.

12 October Epic-CBS released the 'Gimme! Gimme! Gimme!' single in the UK. It entered the British charts a week later, reaching No. 3 on 10 November and notching up a total of eleven weeks on the chart. It was just as successful in other countries: No. 2 in Ireland, No. 3 in Germany, No. 1 in Austria, No. 2 in Holland, No. 1 in Denmark, No. 16 in Sweden, No. 1 in Finland, No. 1 in Japan, No. 8 in Australia and No. 15 in New Zealand.

17 October Benny and Anni-Frid attended the premiere of Swedish entertainers Hasse and Tage's new show at the Berns music hall. They left for Gothenburg the next day.

19 October The European tour began in Gothenburg. Atlantic USA finally released 'Chiquitita'. Two different singles were available: the English version with 'Lovelight' on the B-side, and the Spanish version with 'Estoy Soñando' on the B-side. 'Chiquitita' reached No. 29 in the United States on 12 January 1980.

26 October Polar Music released the album *Greatest Hits Vol.* 2 simultaneously throughout Europe to coincide with the tour. This new compilation featured fourteen tracks, including 'Gimme! Gimme! Gimme!' and 'Summer Night City', available for the first time on an album. In Britain, 600,000 advance copies had already been sold. *Greatest Hits Vol.* 2 stayed at the No. 1 spot for a whole month and spent a total of sixty-three weeks on the chart. Elsewhere, the album reached No. 4 in Holland, No. 20 in Sweden, No. 3 in Spain, No. 3 in Argentina, No. 1 in Japan, No. 20 in Australia and No. 46 in the United States.

4 November Agnetha made a dramatic return to the Swedish Svensktoppen chart with 'När Du Tar Mig I Din Famn'. CBS-Cupol had decided to release the track as a single with 'Jag Var Så Kär' on the B-side. The single would stay at the top of the charts for six weeks.

15 November ABBA concluded their European tour with a concert in Dublin.

16 November The group returned to Stockholm.

22 November *Expressen* printed an article in which Agnetha talked about her indignation about the numerous rumours which had appeared in the press saying: 'Agnetha is exhausted! She is a nervous wreck! She is leaving ABBA!'. 'Not a single word is true!' she said. 'It's ridiculous, because I've never felt so good. During the tour, we were like one big family. I felt much more confident on stage. I was nervous and inhibited before but now I'm not like that at all. Being in front of an audience again really did me some good. Also, as far as the group is concerned, we have no intention of splitting up – in fact, quite the opposite. On a personal level, I have no plans for a solo career.' Agnetha added: 'You get the impression that the press is going through a crisis at the moment and is licking its wounds by inventing stories about me and other famous people. I hope this behaviour soon comes to an end.'

5 December 'I Have a Dream' was released in many countries. It was the fourth track to be lifted from the *Voulez-Vous* album. ABBA, who had begun the Year of the Child with 'Chiquitita', decided to end it with 'I Have a

Dream', performed together with the children's choir of the International School of Stockholm. A 12-inch single was also released. On the B-side of the single, the group gave their fans a live version of 'Take a Chance On Me', recorded at Wembley. 'I Have a Dream' reached No. 2 in Britain, No. 1 in Ireland, No. 1 in Belgium, No.1 in Holland, No. 4 in Germany, No. 2 in Finland, No. 1 in Switzerland and No. 64 in Australia.

20 December The press published a rumour that Benny and Frida were getting divorced. 'That's the worst rumour I've heard for a long time!' said Benny. 'Frida and myself have only asked for our possessions to be divided for personal reasons. It's just a legal formality. It doesn't mean that we're getting divorced.' Benny and Frida, who had been living together for ten years, had decided to value their possessions so that their respective children wouldn't be landed with any inheritance taxes in the future. The couple owned a villa in Lidingö, plus a second home in Grinda (on the Stockholm archipelago), a boat, part of the company Polar Music International and numerous shares in Swedish companies.

22 December Frida and Benny took part in the radio programme *Uppesittarkväll* in the company of jazz singer Monica Zetterlund, Lars Forssell and the Swedish Minister for Communication, Ulf Adelsohn. The theme was Christmas, and the listeners were surprised to hear Frida sing 'Stilla Natt' ('Silent Night') accompanied by Benny on keyboards.

A year and a decade were drawing to a close. The group were awarded numerous gold and platinum discs. In the United States, where their series of concerts had consolidated ABBA's popularity, more than 140,000 Americans had seen the group and reviews had been encouraging. The *Voulez-Vous* and *Greatest Hits Vol.* 2 albums had achieved gold-disc status. One journalist wrote: 'One thing is for certain – the ABBA explosion is just beginning in the USA.'

In Britain, the *Voulez-Vous* album had sold an astonishing two million copies, while *Greatest Hits Vol.* 2 had earned two platinum discs. ABBA had managed to get five songs into the UK Top 5 that year, and the new edition of the *Guinness Book of Records* said of ABBA: 'The group has sold the most records in the history of music after the Beatles.' Sales had been estimated at 150 million in only six years.

In France and Belgium, the *Voulez-Vous* and *Greatest Hits Vol.* 2 albums had both been awarded platinum discs. The 'Gimme! Gimme! Gimme!' single had just been awarded a gold disc. In Belgium, ABBA had achieved five No. 1s in the same year.

In Spanish-speaking countries, ABBA's success surpassed all expectations thanks to 'Chiquitita' and 'Estoy Soñando'. The countries of South America were now calling for the group to tour their territory.

Stig declared: 'What gives us the most pleasure is that we have proved music can come from anywhere, not just England or North America.'

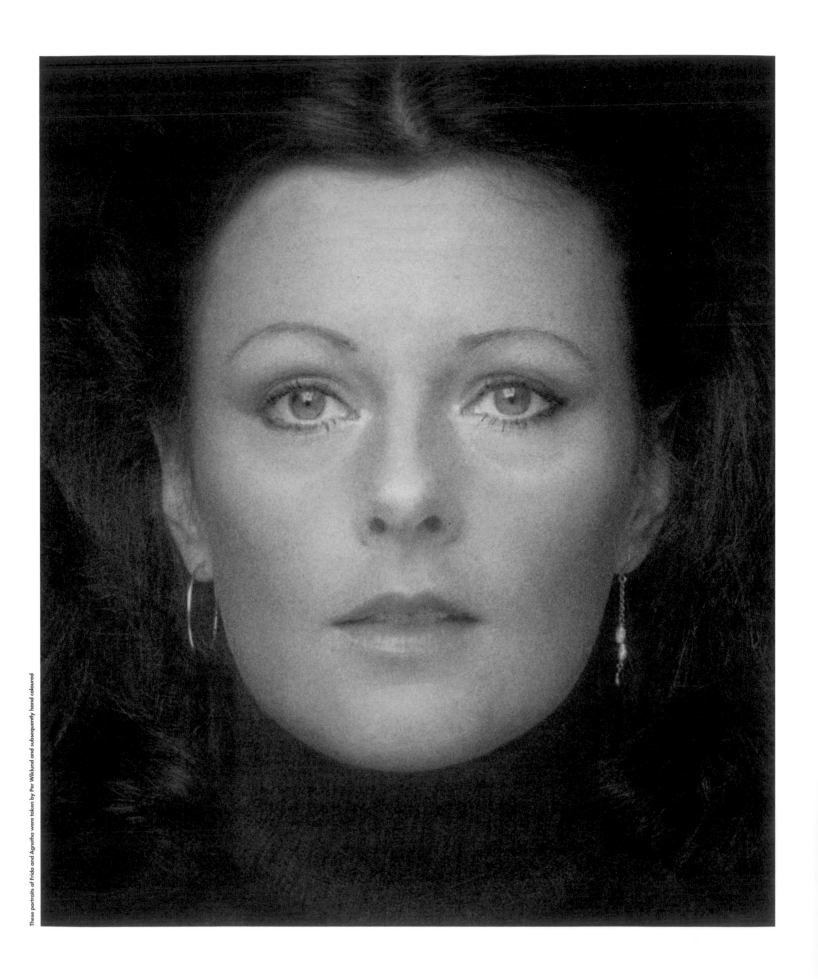

These portraits of Frida and Agnetha were taken by Per Wiklund and subsequently hand coloured

1979 TOUR

Agnetha, Björn, Benny and Anni-Frid were about to embark on the most important tour of their career, with a schedule of forty-one concerts in North America and the main countries of Europe between 13 September and 15 November 1979. ABBA's collaborator on this tour, Thomas Johansson of EMA-Telstar, was a specialist in his field, having worked on tours for many years in close collaboration with Polar Music.

The first rehearsals took place in May 1979 at the Grünewaldsalen concert hall, Stockholm. Meanwhile, ABBA's other colleagues were working hard on the visual part of the tour. Rune Söderqvist, who created the visual concept for the *Voulez-Vous* album, explains: 'I designed the mountains in blue and white for the stage set. They symbolized the Nordic countries. I had made a sketch in paper and I took pictures of it. I realized that I could use it in many ways. The mountains became the tour symbol. They were made of canvas and were removable. Technicians could build them up in different ways according to the size of the stage.' For their part, Owe Sandström and Lars Wigenius (from Artist dressing) created all the costumes to match the set, using the same colours as Rune. Owe says: 'They wanted these colours and these designs to be part of the costumes, even on the crew. I made a military look for the boys, and I made white overalls for the crew.' Rune's blue-and-white mountains became the tour's symbol and would feature on the tour programme, badges, stickers, press packs and merchandising. Stig even decided to make them Polar Music's official logo.

Rehearsals continued between 1 and 27 August at the Europa Films studios in Sundbyberg, near Stockholm. As well as the musicians, backing vocalists and technicians, photographer Torbjörn Calvero was also present, along with the group's children and some of the group's friends. The sun shone brightly and the atmosphere was very laid-back. During breaks in rehearsals, everyone had a great time, joking around or sunbathing. ABBA rehearsed a total of about thirty songs, including some new numbers like 'Gimme! Gimme! Gimme!' and 'Under My Sun' (previously recorded as 'Rubber Ball Man'). Michael B. Tretow recorded some of the rehearsals on 24-track tapes. One of the big surprises on the tour was 'I Have a Dream', which would feature a different children's choir in each town. Another was 'I'm Still Alive', a song written and performed by Agnetha on the piano, as well as 'The Way Old Friends Do', a very emotional farewell hymn, with Benny playing the accordion. 'We wrote that number especially for the tour,' says Björn. 'We felt things needed cooling down if we did an encore. It is a number we all love singing and it gives Benny a chance to play his favourite instrument.' In the middle of the show, singer and backing vocalist Tomas Ledin would be performing one of his songs: 'Not Bad At All.'

ABBA performed a total of twenty-five songs without an interval: 'Gammal Fäbodpsalm' – 'Voulez-Vous' – 'If It Wasn't For the Nights' – 'As Good As New' – 'Knowing Me, Knowing You' – 'Rock Me' – 'Not Bad At All' – 'Chiquitita' – 'Money, Money, Money' – 'I Have a Dream' – 'Gimme! Gimme! Gimme!' – 'S.O.S.' – 'Fernando' – 'The Name of the Game' – 'Eagle' – 'Thank You For the Music' – 'Why Did It Have To Be Me' – 'Intermezzo No. 1' – 'I'm Still Alive' – 'Take a Chance On Me' – 'Summer Night City' – 'Does Your Mother Know' – 'Hole In Your Soul' – 'The Way Old Friends Do'.
Encore: 'Dancing Queen' – 'Waterloo'

Keyboards: Anders Eljas.
Guitars: Mats Ronander, Lasse Wellander. Bass: Rutger Gunnarsson.
Drums: Ola Brunkert. Percussion: Åke Sundqvist.
Backing vocals: Tomas Ledin, Birgitta Wollgård, Liza Öhman.
Sound engineer: Claes af Geijerstam.

The tour involved fifty people, 40–50 tons of equipment, three articulated lorries for the equipment, and two buses for the musicians and technicians. To make travelling easier in North America, the group hired a Lear jet.

Press conference

'THE FIRST TWO WEEKS IT WAS REALLY EXCITING, OF COURSE, BUT THEN AFTER A WHILE IT BECAME VERY MUCH THE SAME, THE SAME WONDERFUL REACTIONS FROM THE FANS, FROM THE AUDIENCE … AFTER A WHILE, YOU WANT TO DO SOMETHING NEW. WE DIDN'T ENJOY THE TOURS THAT MUCH. WE DID THEM MORE BECAUSE I GUESS THE FANS AND PEOPLE DEMANDED IT.' BJÖRN

NORTH AMERICA

A week before the first concert, part of the team arrived in Edmonton. Bad news awaited the technicians. Firstly, there was no stage in the hall, and secondly, the stage set, built in a studio in London, hadn't arrived. Somebody discovered quite by chance that it was being flown to Nairobi, Kenya! Rune remembers: 'At each venue, I helped with the construction of the set and with any adjustments that needed to be made, together with the chief electrical engineer. A week before the first concert in Canada, we had to build the stage at the Sports Arena in record time as the set, which had been sent to Africa by mistake, arrived at the last minute in Edmonton. After the concert, journalists wrote a lot about the stage design. They thought we were so polite that we had made Indian tents especially for Canada.'

7 September

Benny and Anni-Frid left Sweden ahead of the others to relax for a few days in Seattle and to attend the world sailing championships.

10 September

Agnetha and Björn flew to Vancouver via London.

12 September

Dress rehearsal at the Edmonton Sports Arena. ABBA met the Swedish ice-hockey player Bengt-Åke Gustafsson, who played for the Edmonton team. Everyone was on good form apart from guitarist Mats Ronander, who had stomach pains. The rehearsal finished at 11.30 p.m. The day had been marred by technical problems.

13 September – Edmonton, Sports Arena

Agnetha, Björn, Benny and Anni-Frid had all slept badly; they were nervous. After a final rehearsal late that morning, Björn and Rutger Gunnarsson went for a jog in town. Everyone rested during the afternoon. At 6 p.m., the group left the hotel. Many fans were already waiting outside the venue. At 8 p.m., Benny struck up the first few notes of 'Gammal Fäbodpsalm' (a traditional Swedish folk song) on his piano. As he finished playing, Agnetha and Anni-Frid, dressed in giant capes, appeared like butterflies in a swirl of colour, and launched straight into 'Voulez-Vous'. It was a strong sound and their voices were powerful.

The 2-hour show was a resounding success. The concert had been a blaze of sound and light, and the 14,700-strong audience gave ABBA a standing ovation. The twenty children from the the Knights of Columbus Columbian Choir from Edmonton had been given a great reception by the crowd.

On their return to the hotel, the group gave a press conference. Atlantic presented ABBA with a number of gold and platinum discs, enough to cover an entire wall. After the interview, the whole team threw a big party. The centrepiece was a giant cake in the shape of North America showing the towns where ABBA were to perform, into which Tomas Ledin and Thomas Johansson plunged John Spalding's head!

14 September

A lie-in for ABBA. The reviews were quite positive. Graham Hicks of the *Edmonton Journal* wrote: 'Musically it was very good, but the beginning of the show was much too cold and too cautious. It got better towards the end. In future, ABBA should take more risks and be more spontaneous.' The *Sun* wrote: 'ABBA have concocted a brilliant show and give a great performance.'

15 September – Vancouver, P.N.E. (Pacific National Exhibition)

At 8 p.m., the 17,000-strong audience at the P.N.E. began to chant: 'ABBA! ABBA!' The atmosphere was electric, with the audience singing and dancing throughout the concert. At the beginning of 'Why Did It Have To Be Me', Anni-Frid received a standing ovation when she came on stage wearing a jersey belonging to the local football team, the Whitecaps. The concert was a triumph, despite a few small technical problems which had been bothering Björn and Benny. After the show, there was a party to celebrate drummer Ola Brunkert's thirty-third birthday.

16 September

The group were enjoying themselves in Vancouver and decided to postpone their departure for Seattle by a day. Björn and Benny gave a few radio and TV interviews; the others spent the day by the pool.

17 September – Seattle, Seattle Arena

Björn, Benny, Anni-Frid, Stig and the others took off for Seattle in the private jet, while Agnetha decided to travel by car. The musicians who had already arrived made the most of their free time and went on a fishing expedition. This was their first concert in the United States and even though the hall wasn't full, the concert was still a great success. There were a lot of Scandinavians in the 5000-strong audience. Patrick MacDonald, who didn't enjoy the show, wrote in the *Seattle Times*: 'ABBA's début is a disappointment. Their performance was almost passive. Agnetha sang a song about staying alive which was so banal it was laughable. When she and Anni-Frid Lyngstad harmonized, however, it was a different story. Their combined voices are ABBA's saving grace.'

18 September – Portland, Portland Opera House

After lunch, Agnetha left Seattle for Portland by car. The others took the plane. During the afternoon, the team relaxed by the hotel pool. ABBA were a triumph that evening. The Portland Opera House is a small venue with only 3000 seats, but the audience gave them a warm reception. At the end of the concert, the equipment was loaded into the three articulated lorries and transported overnight to ensure that it would reach San Francisco as quickly as possible.

19 September – San Francisco, Concord Pavilion

The whole team took the plane in the morning, including Agnetha. The Concord Pavilion is an open-air stadium and many of the 8000 people who had come to see ABBA were sitting on the grass. After the concert, Björn and Benny met journalists before boarding the private jet taking them to Los Angeles.

20 September
ABBA spent six days in Los Angeles and the whole team had adjacent bungalows at the hotel. The group's children had come over to join their parents – Linda and Lise-Lotte (Anni-Frid's daughter), along with Benny's children, Peter and Helen. Lena Källersjö had arrived from Stockholm as well to spend a few days with Björn. During the afternoon, the group gave a press conference which was attended by about twenty journalists and photographers who had come over especially from Japan.

21 September – Los Angeles / Anaheim, Anaheim Convention Center
A day at Disneyland for everyone. ABBA gave one of their best concerts that evening to an adoring crowd. In the audience were Swedish actress Britt Ekland, Donna Summer and Ronnie Wood, guitarist with the Rolling Stones. After the show, there was a party for the press and the group's friends. Robert Hilburn wrote in the *Los Angeles Times*: 'ABBA is a charming group in concert. Even if they lack experience, and if things could be improved, the show is good on the whole.'

22 September – San Diego, San Diego Sports Arena
The morning was spent by the pool. After lunch, Agnetha and the musicians left by bus for San Diego, while everyone else took the plane. Although the hall in San Diego wasn't full (with an audience of only 3000), they received a warm reception. The group returned to Los Angeles after the concert.

23 September – Phoenix / Temp, The Active Center

24 September – Las Vegas, Aladdin Hotel Performing Arts Theatre
ABBA landed in Las Vegas at 5 p.m. It was 35 degrees Centigrade. Despite tough competition – Diana Ross was performing at Caesar's Palace and Engelbert Humperdinck was at the MGM – ABBA played to a full house. The 5000-strong audience seemed subdued at first, but they soon woke up when the children's choir began singing 'I Have a Dream'. How many of them noticed Linda (Björn and Agnetha's daughter) in the choir? She later fell asleep in her father's arms, in the plane bringing the group back to the hotel.

25 September
The technical crew and musicians left Los Angeles for Omaha. The four members of ABBA spent the day in the hotel with their close friends and family. After lunch, Lise-Lotte, Lena Källersjö and a few others returned to Sweden. Linda, together with Benny's children, would stay with the tour as far as New York.

26 September – Omaha, Civic Auditorium
Departure for Omaha at 9 a.m. In the evening, ABBA were a big success before a capacity audience.

27 September – Minneapolis/St. Paul, St. Paul Civic
Swedish Television were filming a documentary entitled *ABBA In Concert*. In the United States, the crew, directed by Urban Lasson and Jack Churchill, had decided to film the group backstage and away from the concerts. Some of the shows would later be filmed in Europe.

29 September – Milwaukee, Auditorium

30 September – Chicago, Auditorium Theatre

'TO BE ON STAGE WAS GREAT, BUT ALL THAT TRAVEL MAYBE WASN'T THAT PLEASANT ALL THE TIME. IT WAS A KIND OF HYSTERICAL TIME WHERE WE HAD DIFFICULTIES JUST GOING OUTSIDE THE HOTEL.' FRIDA

2 October – New York, Radio City Music Hall

There was another 'star' in town: Pope John-Paul II celebrated a mass at the Yankee Stadium before a congregation of 75,000. ABBA filled the Radio City Music Hall with 6000 of their faithful fans. The street vendors were doing a roaring trade – they were selling T-shirts for both the Pope and ABBA. Anni-Frid was a sensation, wearing the jersey of the New York Rangers ice-hockey team. The *New York Post* wrote: 'The stars of Swedish pop provide a family show which is melodious and lively… with lots of energy, rich in colour and nice to watch.'

3 October – Boston, Music Hall

Because of bad weather, the musicians and equipment made the journey between New York and Boston by road. Despite this, ABBA and the TV crew chose to take the plane. Unfortunately, the aircraft found itself in the midst of a raging storm and the plane was tossed around violently. Agnetha was terrified. To make matters worse, Boston Airport had been closed and the plane had to turn back, finally landing in Manchester, 100 miles away. ABBA were driven to the Boston Music Hall by van. Although Agnetha was feeling weak and ill, she still managed to sing. The show began 2 hours late. Because Agnetha was unable to take the plane at the end of the concert, the group decided to stay in Boston.

'AGNETHA HATED ALMOST EVERYTHING TO DO WITH BEING THE BAND'S PIN-UP GIRL. SHE WAS A SIMPLE COUNTRY GIRL AND WANTED TO STAY AT HOME WITH THE KIDS.' **JOHN SPALDING** ABBA'S UK MUSIC PUBLISH

4 October – Washington DC, Constitution Hall

During the night, Agnetha's state of health worsened – she had a temperature, had suddenly started vomiting and was suffering from violent stomach pains. The doctor diagnosed the onset of a virus, caused by stress and recent gastric problems. He prescribed strong antibiotics. Agnetha was unable to sing and the concert had to be cancelled. Stig prepared a radio announcement. The 6000 ticket holders were reimbursed.

5 October

Agnetha was slowly recovering but had to stay in bed for another 24 hours. During this time, Anni-Frid, Benny and Björn visited Amy Carter at the White House. The daughter of Jimmy Carter, the President of the United States, was disappointed that she had missed her idols in concert but was lucky enough to be able to meet them at home. To console her, the three members of the group signed records for her and gave her an ABBA pendant.

6 October – Montreal, Forum

In the middle of the day, the team took off for Montreal. Agnetha was feeling better and announced that she would be able to sing that night. After the concert she said: 'When I walked out on stage I wasn't sure if I'd be able to last until the end of the show. My legs were trembling. And then we had the best audience of this tour. So everything became easier for me.' In the daily newspaper *La Presse*, Denis Lavoie wrote: 'ABBA on stage is a phenomenon which is, strangely enough, both simple and grand at the same time. A show of class which they make seem quite straightforward, especially where the lighting and the set are concerned. There is nothing provocative here. With the cleverly orchestrated music, the girls' sublime voices and "sex appeal", ABBA manage to reach the real general public.'

7 October – Toronto, Maple Leaf Gardens

The last concert in North America was, once again, a success. Anni-Frid, wearing Swedish hockey player Börje Salming's Toronto Maple Leaf jersey, was given a standing ovation.

EUROPE

19 October – Gothenburg, Scandinavium
A 12,400-strong audience welcomed ABBA. Thirty children from the International School of Stockholm (based in the Vasastan district of Stockholm) accompanied ABBA on 'I Have a Dream'. They also sang with the group at the Stockholm concert. Stig invited the team out for dinner after the show to one of the town's restaurants. Anni-Frid's aunt, Lollo Lyngstad, travelled from Norway for the show. Jan-Olov Andersson wrote in *Aftonbladet*: 'Despite a rather clumsy beginning (the first two or three songs didn't sound very good), I can certify that ABBA give a remarkable show. Which other pop group can give a concert lasting almost 2 hours made up totally of hits?'

20 October – Stockholm, Isstadion
More than 6000 people gave ABBA a fantastic welcome at that night's show. After the concert, Queen Silvia went backstage to congratulate the group and spent some time chatting with Anni-Frid. Anders Björkman wrote in *Expressen*: 'I think that it's time for us in Sweden to admit that ABBA are an international group. It's great that a Swedish group is topping the charts all over the world. Of course you can criticize their music, their records and their production. You don't have to like everything they do just because it's ABBA.'

'EVEN IF WE ARE, BY NOW, PRETTY WELL KNOWN IN THE STATES, IT'S NOT UP TO THE SAME STANDARD AS IT IS IN THE REST OF THE WORLD. WE'RE NOT PREPARED TO STAY FOR MONTHS AND MONTHS LIKE ALL OTHER FOREIGN GROUPS HAVE TO DO IF THEY WANT TO MAKE IT BIG IN THE STATES. WE DON'T LIKE TOURING; WE HAD OUR SHARE OF TOURING BEFORE WE STARTED ABBA.' BJÖRN

21 October – Copenhagen, Falkoner Theatre

23 October – Paris, Pavillon de Paris
This was ABBA's first concert in France and they were an enormous success, with the 7000-strong audience singing along to every one of the group's hits. Björn spoke to the audience in French. *Salut* magazine wrote: 'ABBA have just triumphed in France. Everything was meticulously planned, and there wasn't a single mistake during this unforgettable evening. Everyone was standing on their seats, shouting and clapping.'

24 October – Rotterdam, Ahoy Sportpaleis

25 October – Dortmund, Westfalenhalle
The Dortmund audience adored ABBA. Björn declared in *Bravo* magazine: 'We knew that we had our most faithful fans in Germany. But you can never estimate how the audience will react. We were bowled over by the reception. Even in our wildest dreams, we could never have imagined that the show would have been such a success!' After the show, the group and their musicians were invited to a Dortmund bar. The party went on until 4 o'clock in the morning.

26 October
ABBA's private jet landed at Munich's Riem airport at 1.45 p.m. Two cars drove the group to the BMW car factory in the Milbertshofen district of town. Björn was very excited because he got to drive the car of his dreams, a dark-blue M1. However, after much deliberation he finally decided not to buy the car.

27 October – Munich, Olympiahalle
Between 12 and 1 p.m., *Bild* newspaper had arranged a direct line so that fans could speak with members of the group. Lena arrived from Stockholm and would stay with Björn until the end of the tour. At 5.30 p.m. the group arrived at the concert hall for the sound check. At 8 p.m. there wasn't an empty seat in the hall. During the 2-hour show, the audience went wild, singing along and dancing. It was a great success. The evening came to a close in an Italian restaurant for everyone except Björn and Lena, who decided to spend some time together in private.

28 October – Zurich, Hallenstadion

29 October – Vienna, Stadthalle
Each evening, while Anni-Frid was a resounding success with her duet with Björn, 'Why Did It Have To Be Me', and her very personal version of 'Money, Money, Money', it was Agnetha who stirred up the audience's feelings, sitting alone at the piano to perform her song 'I'm Still Alive'. She said: 'There is no real story behind it. I am writing all the time now. This number is probably one of my best so far and I hope some more will come. Actually, I only wrote the melody, Björn thought it was so strong that he wrote the lyrics.'

30 October – Stuttgart, Sporthalle Boeblingen
Anni-Frid's father attended the concert.

1 November – Bremen, Stadthalle

2 November – Frankfurt, Festhalle

3 November – Brussels, Forest National
The concert hall was full and the audience were very enthusiastic. Frida wore the Anderlecht Sportsclub's mauve-and-white jersey for 'Why Did It Have To Be Me'. Gifts showered onto the stage during the concert: Björn and Benny were given two fluffy monkeys, while Agnetha and Anni-Frid shared dozens of bouquets. Eddy Przybylski wrote in *La Dernière Heure*: 'A great production with an absolutely precise technical side and non-stop hits one after the other. The set completes this spectacular ensemble which suits ABBA's music. ABBA found the audience very warm in Brussels.' Erik Machielsen wrote in magazine *Plaisirs*: 'Two hours of non-stop songs, dancing and colour. One of the major revelations at an ABBA concert is the notable participation of the two male members of the group, whereas on television, record and photos, all the attention is concentrated on the girls.'

4 November
ABBA took off for London during the day. Linda and Christian had arrived to spend a few days with their parents. The Swedish Television crew, directed by Urban Lasson, was all set. All the London concerts, as well as some backstage footage, were filmed for the TV programme *Abba – In Concert*.

5 November – London, Wembley Arena
As the show came to a close with the last notes of 'Waterloo', the 8000-strong audience clapped and screamed with joy. ABBA had triumphed in the capital city of pop.

6 November – London, Wembley Arena
The press gave ABBA a rough ride. The majority of the journalists clearly expected something else from the show. Garth Pearce wrote in the *Daily Express*: 'The group failed to transfer their special hit quality of the recording studio to the stage. Much of the group's magic seemed locked into a Swedish iceberg, and it struggled to get out. What we had was efficiency without excitement, clinical precision with little passion, and cold professionalism rather than pace and abandon.'

7 November – London, Wembley Arena
While the press ripped ABBA's show to shreds, the audiences were ecstatic, calling for more every night. Simon Kinnersley wrote in the *Daily Mail*: 'Despite colourful scenery, lavish costumes and a large backing band, it was one of the most dull and turgid concerts I've attended in months.'

8 November – London, Wembley Arena
There had been lots of talk in ABBA circles about a future live album. Mobile recording equipment had been hired especially for the occasion and Michael B. Tretow had come over from Stockholm to record all the group's concerts in London.

9 November – London, Wembley Arena
Each afternoon, after the sound check, Agnetha and Frida spent 2 hours on their make-up and hair. Agnetha said: 'We have been here since 6 o'clock and later in the week we shall arrive around 4.30 to do some filming. But we do need at least 2 clear hours to make up because of the various layers that need to go on.'

10 November – London, Wembley Arena

11–12 November – Stafford, Bingley Hall

13 November – Glasgow, Apollo Theatre
ABBA were pleased not to be staying in a luxurious hotel for once, which they often found cold and inhuman. The team decided to stay in the idyllic setting of the Turnberry Hotel, 90 miles from Glasgow on the east coast of Scotland.

15 November – Dublin, R.D.S. Main Hall
The Irish were overjoyed to welcome ABBA. The previous June, tickets had sold out in just 2 hours. This was the group's first concert in Ireland and the last one of the tour. The event was heavily covered by the media. Every record store in town had a special ABBA window display. Throughout the entire week, RTE Radio 2 devoted an hour each day to the Swedish group. On top of all this, *Abba – The Movie* was showing again at the Odeon cinema.

Agnetha had arrived by plane the previous day, along with the musicians. Björn, Benny, Anni-Frid and John Spalding travelled from Glasgow to Dublin by helicopter, flying over the magnificent Scottish mountain tops which were covered in snow. After the traditional sound check, Björn and Benny met the press.

That evening, at the beginning of the concert, Benny played 'Danny Boy', a traditional Irish song, which was much appreciated by the audience. It was Frida's birthday and she had a very emotional moment when, in the middle of the show, the musicians presented her with a bouquet of red roses and played 'Happy Birthday Frida', with the audience joining in. After the concert, there was a big party at the hotel to celebrate the end of the tour. ABBA gave each member of the team and all the technicians a silver medallion engraved with 'ABBA' on one side and 'Thank you' and the person's name on the other.

16 November
The press gave the concert rave reviews. The *Independent* wrote: 'The Swedish superstars gave us a whirlwind show which was well worth the wait. "I Have a Dream" literally raised the roof in Dublin.' And for the *Irish Times*, the highlight of the evening was 'Agnetha and her aggressive rendition of "Gimme! Gimme! Gimme!".'

'I FEEL THAT ONE OF THE BIGGEST PROBLEMS IN THE WESTERN WORLD TODAY IS THE LACK OF CONFIDENCE, AND THE WAY OF LOOKING NEGATIVELY AT THE FUTURE. SO, "HAPPY NEW YEAR" IS ABOUT TRYING TO SET UP POSITIVE GOALS FOR THE FUTURE. THAT'S A POLITICAL MESSAGE IN ITSELF.' BJÖRN

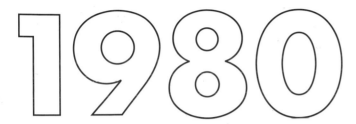

At the beginning of the year, Björn and Benny were lacking inspiration and decided to visit Barbados to compose songs for the next album. They came back with several new songs: 'Hold Me Close' (working title for 'Andante, Andante'), 'Elaine', 'Ten Tin Soldiers' (which would later become 'The Piper') and 'Happy New Year'.

On stage at Tokyo Budokan, Japan

On the plane to Barbados, Björn and Benny had the idea of writing a musical based on New Year celebrations. 'We thought it would be a good framework: a few people in a room, looking back on what has been, thinking about the future, that sort of thing,' remembers Benny (*The Complete Recording Sessions*, 1994). While staying in Barbados, they met British comedian John Cleese, and over dinner, they asked him if he would be interested in writing the story for the musical. He wasn't very enthusiastic about the idea and declined the offer. The two musicians finished writing 'Happy New Year' anyway, but abandoned the idea of the musical.

4 January Polar Music announced that ABBA would be doing a series of eleven concerts in Japan the following March. Demand for tickets was so great that they sold out within two days of going on sale on December 16. The *Greatest Hits Vol. 2* album was currently No. 4 in the Japanese charts.

7 January Agnetha and Anni-Frid began recording some of ABBA's hits in Spanish at the Polar Music studios. After the huge success of 'Chiquitita' and 'Estoy Soñando', the idea of recording a whole album in Spanish had been suggested, although at first Björn and Benny hadn't been too enthusiastic about the idea. Among the ten tracks which had been chosen were the obviously Spanish-sounding songs like 'Hasta Mañana', 'Fernando' and 'Move On'. Buddy McCluskey and his wife Mary had written new lyrics, and, to ensure that they pronounced the words perfectly, Agnetha and Anni-Frid called in journalist Ana Martinez del Valle to assist them. Michael B. Tretow later mixed the songs in his own studio in Sollentuna, north of Stockholm. On the new mix of 'Reina Danzante' ('Dancing Queen'), Janne Schaffer's funky guitar riffs would be more prominent than on the English-language version, where they had virtually disappeared.

At the beginning of February, on their return from Barbados, Björn and Benny immediately began recording sessions for the forthcoming album. The first few songs they worked on included 'Andante, Andante,' 'Elaine', 'The Piper', 'Happy New Year' and 'On and On and On'.

During February, the single 'Dame! Dame! Dame!' ('Gimme! Gimme! Gimme!') was released in Spanish-speaking countries. The song would stay in the Spanish charts for four weeks, peaking at No. 28.

7 February A reception was held at the Polar Music studios to celebrate Swedish skiing-champion Ingemar Stenmark's departure for the Winter Olympic Games in Lake Placid, USA. Numerous well-known politicians and artists were present. The party continued at the Shazam nightclub with the launch of a special album entitled *Olympic Games*, featuring thirteen different Swedish artists including ABBA, Björn Skifs, Ted Gärdestad, Ann Louise Hanson, Lill Lindfors and Tomas Ledin.

24 February The Swedish press announced that ABBA's next album would be released in October. Meanwhile, following the success of Agnetha's song 'När Du Tar Mig I Din Famn' in Sweden, an English version entitled 'Take Me In Your Arms' was planned for release in Britain, France, Germany and Holland. For some reason, however, this English version was never released.

The Japanese fans welcome ABBA

'MY DREAM WAS TO MAKE A WORLDWIDE TELEVISION PROGRAMME WITH ABBA LIVE FROM CHINA. THE PROBLEM WAS THAT THE TIME WAS NOT THE SAME IN DIFFERENT PARTS OF THE WORLD. SO, WE NEVER DID IT.' STIG

After a break of a few months, ABBA returned to the stage for a series of eleven concerts in Japan. Rehearsals took place between 28 February and 6 March. Agnetha, Björn, Benny and Anni-Frid used the same team as they had for the 1979 tour, with the exception of backing vocalist Birgitta Wollgård, who was replaced by Lena Eriksson.

8 March
ABBA took off for Tokyo, via London, Anchorage and Canada. At London's Heathrow Airport, the group had a 2-hour stop and several reporters took advantage of the opportunity to interview Björn.

9 March
After a 22-hour flight, the group arrived at Tokyo's Narita Airport. There was a riotous welcome awaiting them, with 200 police officers being called in as reinforcements to contain the hundreds of fans and dozens of photographers. The 'Gimme! Gimme! Gimme!' single was currently at No. 2 in the Japanese charts and the ABBA fan club had more than 30,000 members.

10 March
ABBA met 500 journalists and photographers at a press conference, as well as three television crews. Meanwhile, the technicians were building the stage and set at the Budokan concert hall. The day ended with a party in honour of Tomas Ledin, who had just arrived from Stockholm after having won the Melodifestivalen 80. He would be representing Sweden at the forthcoming Eurovision Song Contest with his song 'Just Nu'.

12 March – Tokyo, Budokan
Although the 12,000 spectators were quite reserved for the first hour, they went crazy when they heard the first few notes of 'Dancing Queen'. The children's choir sang a Japanese version of 'I Have a Dream' and Björn

addressed the audience in Japanese – two factors which were really appreciated.

MARCH

Wednesday	12	Tokyo	Budokan
Thursday	13	Tokyo	Budokan
Friday	14	Koriyama	
Monday	17	Tokyo	Budokan
Tuesday	18	Tokyo	Budokan
Thursday	20	Fukuoka	
Friday	21	Osaka	
Saturday	22	Osaka	
Monday	24	Nagoya	
Wednesday	26	Tokyo	Budokan
Thursday	27	Tokyo	Budokan

'YOU ARE ALWAYS A LOSER AFTER A DIVORCE, ESPECIALLY WHEN YOU HAVE CHILDREN. THAT'S WHY "THE WINNER TAKES IT ALL" IS ONLY HALF PERSONAL.' BJÖRN

Even if they sometimes mentioned the qualities of ABBA's show, the journalists seemed to have noticed only one thing: Agnetha's bottom. While daily newspaper *Sports Nippon* ran the headline: 'Lovely buttocks', the *Tokyo Chunichi Sport* wrote: '20 melodies and swinging bottoms'. Agnetha no longer found it funny: 'It's stupid! Aren't there more important things to write about ABBA?'

Fortunately, some newspapers were more objective. The *Nikkan Sports* wrote: 'The concert is visually attractive as well as musically good. From the jewellery box of melody and harmony, such hit songs as "Chiquitita" and "Fernando" popped out.' *Tauki Sport* concluded: 'The 12,000 spectators were fascinated by this perfect harmony.'

Although ABBA gave only eleven concerts, they were seen by more than 100,000 Japanese fans.

☆ ☆ ☆ ☆

29 March   ABBA returned to Stockholm from Japan.

7 April   Swedish Television screened the *Abba In Concert* documentary which had been filmed by Urban Lasson on the group's American and European tour. The programme had been selected to represent Sweden at the Montreux television festival. Journalist Hemming Sten wrote in *Expressen*: 'The show will be loved by shoe fetishists. We get to see high-heeled shoes, jogging shoes and roller skates. You never see ABBA arriving at the hotel but we are shown the porter putting the key in the lock. However, the programme is good enough that it could win in Montreux. I've never seen a pop group filmed with such imagination and ingenuity.' Whatever its chances at Montreux, *Abba In Concert* had already been sold to numerous other countries including Australia, Japan, Germany, Ireland, Canada and Britain.

22 April   Stig and the group announced that there would be no live album released. They had decided that a record of ABBA in concert would not be sufficiently different to the two existing greatest-hits albums.

Swedish Radio were in the process of making five 40-minute programmes retracing the life of Stig Anderson. The series, entitled *The Stikkan Anderson Story*, would feature ABBA, together with other artists, including Jan Malmsjö, Lill-Babs, Anna-Lena Löfgren, Siw Malmkvist and Bosse Larsson, performing Stig's songs. Anni-Frid recorded 'Tango I Det Gröna (Pettersson)' for the occasion at the Polar Music studios, while Agnetha did a cover of 'Ljuva Sextital', which had been a hit for Brita Borg in 1969. The series was broadcast at the beginning of the summer.

Linda with Daddy

'IT'S BECOMING MORE IMPORTANT [IN OUR SONGS] TO INTEGRATE PERSONAL FEELINGS. THINGS HAPPEN TO YOU, THE OLDER YOU GET, AND MAYBE YOU WISH TO TRY TO EXPLAIN A LITTLE.' BENNY

4 May   Anni-Frid attended a show for young people at Skansen park. She had come along especially to support her thirteen-year-old daughter Lise-Lotte, who was appearing on stage. Among the other new artists appearing for the first time were Malin and Christine (Lill Babs' daughters) and Petronella (Lill Lindfors' daughter).

During May, the *Gracias Por La Musica* album was released in Spain and South America. For the occasion, a Spanish television crew came to Stockholm to film the show *Aplauso*. ABBA performed 'Conociéndome, Conociéndote' ('Knowing Me, Knowing You'), 'Gracias Por La Musica' and 'Dame! Dame! Dame!' For the last of these tracks, the group mimed to the song while reading the text. During the interview, Björn spoke in Spanish.

The *Gracias Por La Musica* album was an instant hit. It stayed in the Spanish charts for four-and-a-half months, peaking at No. 5. The single 'Fernando'/'Gracias Por La Musica' reached No. 9 in Spain, while both album and single reached No. 4 in Argentina.

16 May   Björn Skifs, together with his new group Zkiffz, gave a concert at the Atlantic nightclub in Stockholm. Agnetha was in the audience, accompanied by Dick Håkansson, and Benny, Anni-Frid and Claes af Geijerstam were also there. The press had revealed Agnetha's relationship with Dick Håkansson several weeks earlier. He was a thirty-four-year-old businessman and director of ladies' clothes manufacturers Dots Design AB.

19 May   Görel Johnsen – Stig's right-hand woman and the recently appointed vice-president of Polar Music – married photographer Anders Hanser.

' "SUPER TROUPER" SOUNDS LIKE A SIMPLE POP SONG, BUT IT PAINTS A GOOD PICTURE OF A POP STAR WHO HAS THE CONFIDENCE TO SAY, "I'M AT THE TOP OF THE TREE AND I'M NOT HAPPY." BJÖRN'S LIFE IS IN THOSE LYRICS.'   TIM RICE

The ceremony took place in the chapel of Ulriksdal Castle, near Stockholm. Agnetha was at the wedding with Dick Håkansson, but Björn was unaccompanied – his fiancée Lena was unwell.

2 June   After a month of composing new songs, Björn and Benny began recording the next album. Two new tracks emerged: 'Our Last Summer' and 'The Story of My Life' (which would later become 'The Winner Takes It All'). Benny says of this song: 'We were sitting in our small cottage on Viggsö, in the Stockholm archipelago. And all of a sudden, it came up from old ideas, from our small musical pictures we had. The music came first, as usual.'

23 June   Polar Music released the *Gracias Por La Musica* album. In most countries, the album was released as an import by the label Septima Records (Polar Music). In Japan, the album reached No. 3 in the charts and sold more than 80,000 copies.

At the beginning of July, ABBA took a few weeks off. Björn and Lena went to the island of Viggsö, while Agnetha spent her holidays in her new summer house in Roslagen, in the Swedish archipelago, together with her children and Dick Håkansson. Meanwhile, Benny and Anni-Frid decided to sail along the west coast of Sweden, travelling up as far as Norway aboard their boat. They had invited their Norwegian friends, Alfred Jansson and his wife, singer Grynet Molvig, to join them. The group's holidays were interrupted by just one day of filming.

12 July   Agnetha, Björn, Benny and Anni-Frid joined director Lasse Hallström about 50 kilometres to the north of Gothenburg. Lasse, who was in the middle of filming his full-length movie *Tuppen* (The Rooster) in Marstrand, had the idea of filming the video for the song 'The Winner Takes It All' on this beautiful island off the west coast. The atmosphere was very relaxed. Agnetha travelled from Stockholm with Linda and Dick Håkansson, while Björn was accompanied by Lena.

17 July   Vogue released 'The Winner Takes It All' as a single in France and Belgium. On the B-side was a track entitled 'Elaine', a song which never featured on an album. The single's success was almost immediate. It went straight into the RTL chart at No. 10, the highest position it would reach. In Belgium, it made it to No. 1 after two weeks.

'The Winner Takes It All' is a classic. From the very first hearing, it is clear that this is a great, timeless song which cannot be categorized. Even if there is no real chorus, the listener is hooked by the four magical notes which fade into infinity. Agnetha, singing with great emotion in her voice, gives one of her best vocal performances ever.

21 July   Polar Music released 'The Winner Takes It All'. 300,000 copies of the single were pressed for the Scandinavian market. Erik Hörnfeldt wrote in *Expressen*: 'I don't think that ABBA's fans will be disappointed. "The Winner Takes It All" is a sad little disco ballad, dominated by Agnetha's vocals and Benny on piano. "Elaine" is much nicer – a little rock symphony for teenagers in the same vein as "Summer Night City". As usual, ABBA's strength is in their melodies. There are more melodies in an ABBA single than in the whole of the chart put together.' In Sweden, 'The Winner Takes It All' reached No. 2 in the charts.

25 July   Epic released the single in Britain, where it was an instant hit, reaching No. 1 two weeks later. This was the first time that this had happened since 'Take a Chance On Me'. This time, the record company also decided to release a special 12-inch single as a collector's item. The video had its premiere on 6 August on *Top of the Pops*.

'The Winner Takes It All' also did well in other countries: it got to No. 4 in Germany, No. 1 in Austria, No. 1 in Holland, No. 4 in Denmark, No. 10 in Spain, No. 7 in Italy, No. 4 in Japan, No. 4 in Zimbabwe, No. 7 in Australia and No. 16 in New Zealand.

8 August   Björn, Benny and Frida flew to London. Agnetha stayed behind in Stockholm. They were accompanied by Claes af Geijerstam and Stig's children, Marie and Lasse. That evening, they attended Pink Floyd's *The Wall* concert. The following day the three members of ABBA met with Judd Lander, head of record-label Epic, who had arranged this whistle-stop trip to London. After meeting with the *Sun* and the *Daily Mail*, they were interviewed by Radio One. During the evening, the three of them had dinner at La Nassa restaurant in Chelsea. Everyone cheered when Judd Lander announced that 'The Winner Takes It All' had reached No. 1. The party continued at Wedgies nightclub, with champagne flowing until 4 o'clock in the morning.

12 August   Polar Music sent the following message to the Swedish press: 'Following an article in *Aftonbladet* concerning the relationship between Agnetha Fältskog and Dick Håkansson, the couple have asked us to communicate the following message: "We have decided not to see each other as much as previously but to let things take their course." No comparison should be made

'BENNY AND BJÖRN
KNEW PERFECTLY
WELL OUR RANGES
AND WHICH KIND
OF VOICE THEY
WANTED ON A
SPECIFIC SONG.
AND SOMETIMES,
I ENVIED
THE CHOICE
OF AGNETHA,
I MUST ADMIT.'
FRIDA

Photo shoot near the Champs-Elysées, Paris

'I'VE BEEN VERY CAREFUL TO TREAT WOMEN AND MEN EQUALLY. I WAS ONE OF THE FIRST IN THE 1970s TO MAKE MY SECRETARY A MANAGING DIRECTOR. THAT WAS BECAUSE OFTEN SHE WAS TREATED AS A PRETTY YOUNG THING, ESPECIALLY BY INTERNATIONAL BUSINESS COLLEAGUES, EVEN THOUGH SHE WAS VERY KNOWLEDGEABLE. SO WHEN THOSE MALE-CHAUVINIST PIGS CALLED, SHE COULD PUT THEM IN THEIR PLACE.' STIG

with the events following Agnetha's divorce from Björn Ulvaeus.' Obviously, this announcement made many journalists curious.

23 August Björn took part in the Stockholm Marathon. Jeff Wells, from Dallas, was the first to finish in 2 hours 15 minutes and 49 seconds. Björn passed the finishing line after 3 hours 22 minutes. It was the first time that he'd taken part in the competition. Björn, a real jogging fanatic, said: 'Sometimes, I wonder why we make ourselves suffer so much. But in a way it's become a drug and it clears all your excesses. In Brighton, I realized how overweight I'd become – I couldn't even sit down in my stage clothes. Since then I've been running regularly. I started by doing a few kilometres in the forest and now I run 50–60 kilometres every week. It's great fun. When we're on tour, I train in every town that we visit.'

26 August Anni-Frid went back to school, or in fact to the Norra Real training college for adults. The ABBA singer had enrolled for a French course. Lillemor Silfverhielm, her teacher, explained: 'These intensive courses for beginners last for a term, with classes three times a week. They are designed for people who couldn't learn French at school.'

5 September Anni-Frid and Benny attended the premiere of *All That Jazz* at the Sandrew cinema in Stockholm. Afterwards, a party was held at the Alexandra discotheque in honour of the film's leading man, Roy Schneider.

From 8 September onwards, Björn and Benny continued recording sessions at the Polar Music studios. They recorded several titles which had been composed during August: 'Me and I', 'Lay All Your Love On Me', 'Put On Your White Sombrero' and 'Super Trouper'. Michael B. Tretow later explained: 'It took one or two years before I got accustomed to that studio. When we made the *Super Trouper* album, I felt that I had really mastered the console. It was the best-sounding album because everything had come together.'

3 October All the group's friends and work colleagues gathered in the Europa Films studios, where the photos for the sleeve of the new album were to be taken, as well as some of the footage for the 'Super Trouper' and 'Happy New Year' videos. Rune Söderqvist, who organized the event, explains: 'First, we had the idea to shoot on Piccadilly Circus with a real circus around, with animals and artists. We had arranged that but we had to stop because the police said "This is not the centre of London, this is the centre of the universe. You are not allowed to use animals and wear funny clothes!" So we had to stop the project and we decided to shoot in Stockholm.' To create a circus atmosphere in the large studio, Rune Söderqvist called in a Swede who was a professional in his field, François Bronett. He arrived with about twenty artists, including clowns, jugglers, acrobats and fire-eaters. He also brought along two white horses, a donkey and two poodles. As extras, Rune had the idea of bringing together all ABBA's friends and colleagues, including Görel Hanser, Tomas Ledin, Björn Skifs and Marie Anderson.

Photographer Lars Larsson took the photos for the new album while Lasse Hallström filmed footage for the 'Super Trouper' and 'Happy New Year' videos. The director would complete filming on 4, 5 and 8 October.

6–15 October Björn and Benny finished mixing the album. It had been decided that the album would close with 'The Way Old Friends Do', recorded at London's Wembley Arena during the 1979 tour.

21 October Agnetha, Björn, Benny and Anni-Frid arrived in Paris for two days of promotion. The high point of their visit was the recording of the television programme *Stars*, presented by Michel Drucker, at the Pavillon Baltard in Nogent. The group performed 'The Winner Takes It All' on the show and premiered their new single, 'Super Trouper'. Beforehand, ABBA had been interviewed by the French press at the George V Hotel and had undertaken several photo shoots, including one along the Champs-Elysées.

28 October Benny and Frida attended an auction at the famous Bukowski auction house in Stockholm. The couple, who were lovers of art, had come along to buy the famous painting *Reflexer* (Reflections) by Swedish artist Anders Zorn for ABBA's gallery, AH-Grafik. They managed to purchase the canvas for 860,000 Swedish kronor.

At the beginning of November, Björn travelled to Madrid to do some promotion for the TV show *Abba In Concert* which was about to be screened on Spanish TV. In Spain and South America, there was a lot of excitement about the new album because ABBA had recorded two songs in Spanish for these countries: 'Andante, Andante' and 'Felicidad' ('Happy New Year').

3 November Polar Music released the *Super Trouper* album and the single of the same name. By this point, the song 'Put On Your White Sombrero' had been omitted in favour of the title track, 'Super Trouper'.

Super Trouper is one of ABBA's most successful albums; once again the group surprised everyone with the richness of their arrangements and the diversity of their melodies. Vocally, Agnetha and Anni-Frid were on top form, and as for the technical side of things, it is clear from such musical gems as 'Me and I' and 'The Piper' that Michael B. Tretow had perfectly mastered the new recording studio. The last of these tracks was another surprise: ABBA covered new ground with a medieval sound and vocals sung in Latin: *'sub luna saltamus'*, which means 'dance beneath the moon'. The theme of the song is often compared to The *Pied Piper of Hamlyn*, but the subject of the lyrics is more profound, with undercurrents of dictatorship. Björn admitted it had been inspired by a novel by Stephen King.

Erik Hörnfeldt wrote in *Expressen*: 'Yet again the group have a lot of vitality. Benny Andersson is using more and more synthesizers which makes the music more powerful. The melodies are fantasy-like and the lyrics are disastrous. But there is also "Me and I", which is one of the best and most intelligent tracks the group has produced.' In *Aftonbladet*, Arne Norlin wrote: '*Super Trouper* is ABBA's best album. It's a dynamic, happy album which shows that the group is progressing. The curious thing is that it doesn't sound very much like ABBA this time.'

In France, the *Super Trouper* album and single were released at the same time as in Scandinavia. The group's appearance on the programme *Stars* and several articles in the press gave the record a good start. The single stayed on the RTL chart for thirteen weeks and peaked at No. 1 on 11 January 1981. Like some other countries, France now had an ABBA fan club which had been set up by a group of fans led by Guy Bodescot.

4–5 November Agnetha was in the Polar Music studios to record an album of traditional Christmas songs with her daughter Linda. The record, entitled *Nu Tändas Tusen Juleljus* (A Thousand Christmas Candles Are Now Being Lit)

'Super Trouper', *Stars 80* TV show, Paris

' "OUR LAST SUMMER" WAS WRITTEN WITH A CERTAIN GIRL IN MIND THAT I HAD A ROMANCE WITH IN PARIS AS A TEENAGER.' BJÖRN

Polar Music press advertisement

was co-produced by Michael B. Tretow and Agnetha. Its release was planned for 1 December, but for technical reasons it was delayed by a year.

In the Swedish press, Görel Hanser denied a rumour that had swept across Europe and had now reached the United States. 'No – ABBA are definitely not leaving Sweden to move to England,' she stressed. 'This rumour has been around for three months and we don't seem to be able to stop it. It began at the end of the summer when a journalist from the *New Musical Express* misinterpreted remarks made by Björn and Benny. This time the *New York Post* have said that ABBA have had enough of paying 50 per cent taxes and that they're going to leave. It's not true!'

7 November The *Super Trouper* album established a new record for advance sales in Britain. More than a million copies of the album had already been sold. At the end of October, Stig had invited the ten most important British retailers to dinner and played them the new album in its entirety.

8 November Lasse Hallström filmed the rest of the 'Happy New Year' and 'Felicidad' videos in his own flat at Karlavägen, Stockholm.

15 November Benny, Frida, Björn and Lena Källersjö attended Rod Stewart's concert at the Isstadion in Stockholm. Benny and Frida had just bought an enormous property in Philipstad, south of Trosa. Situated in the archipelago, the estate consisted of several islands and chalets, as well as a beach and a small harbour.

17 November ABBA were invited onto the TV show *Måndagsbörsen*. The group were interviewed and the videos for 'Super Trouper' and 'Happy New Year' were shown. Before the show began, during a conversation with the TV crew, Anni-Frid and Björn admitted that they couldn't understand why the new album was only at No. 2 in the Swedish charts. Björn announced: 'Only No. 2? Is there a mistake on the chart? This position doesn't match my statistics at all.' These remarks were reported in the press the following day.

18 November ABBA welcomed journalist Jürgen Tiedt and photographer Wolfgang Heilemann from German magazine *Bravo* to Stockholm. They were accompanied by Manfred Weichel, a fan who had been invited to spend a few hours with his idols. Wolfgang arranged a long photo shoot in one of the studios in town. Agnetha and Anni-Frid had chosen several different costumes for the occasion, including red, white and blue can-can dresses. At the end of the shoot, Manfred presented the group with the silver Otto-*Bravo* 79 award, which had been voted for by readers of the magazine.

21 November Epic released the new album in Britain. With more than a million advance orders, the record went straight into the charts at No. 1 and stayed there for nine weeks. Compared to the previous albums, critics seemed to be unanimous about *Super Trouper*. James Johnson wrote in the *Evening Standard*: 'Their music is coldly efficient and streamlined if sometimes lacking in passion and colour. At their best however, there is still no doubt they possess a chilly magic. In terms of producing straightforward pop they are almost unbeatable.' In *Melody Maker*, Lynden Barber wrote: 'For unlike some of their contemporaries, ABBA make great pop songs that have magic – that ethereal quality which no critic can define, analyse or rationalize. The final tracks, "Lay All Your Love On Me" and "The Way Old Friends Do", are more than just songs, they are hymns, uplifting in the same way as their earlier *Arrival*.' And Mike Gardner of *Record Mirror* wrote: 'The secret of ABBA is never to hear them on an album where the highs become a level; each track needs to be savoured amid the dross that most other musicians Xerox out in the name of rock 'n' roll on the radio.'

To promote the album, Polar Music produced a TV documentary entitled *Words and Music*. In this 25-minute programme, filmed by a British crew, ABBA talked about their way of life and their work, particularly *Super Trouper*.

25 November The Swedish press announced that Agnetha, Björn, Benny, Anni-Frid and their children were currently under police protection. In an anonymous letter addressed to Polar Music two weeks earlier, it had been made clear that a member of the group would be kidnapped sooner or later. The police, who took these threats very seriously, advised ABBA to avoid travelling abroad for a few weeks. Bodyguards with guard dogs were appointed to keep an eye on the four Swedes and the promotional trip to Germany had to be cancelled, although ABBA's appearance on the TV programme *Show Express* would still go ahead.

27 November ABBA arrived at 3 o'clock in the afternoon at the SVT television studios. Rehearsals were to begin immediately. The building was being watched by about a dozen policemen and the live link with Germany had been kept secret. At 8.40 p.m., the link-up with *Show Express* began and presenter Michael Schanze interviewed Björn in German. The group then performed 'The Winner Takes It All', 'Super Trouper' and 'On and On and On'. Twenty minutes later, the show was over and the German audience went wild. As a special thank-you to everyone involved, ABBA performed the song 'Happy New Year'. This clip would be sold to numerous other countries and it became the official TV version of this track. In party mood with a white piano, long dresses, suits, a candelabra and champagne, Agnetha, Björn, Benny and Anni-Frid wish viewers a Happy New Year in several languages and then perform their New Year hymn. Producer Leif Göthlund said: 'It was great to produce a programme with ABBA – they were really nice to work with. Despite the fact that they were under close protection, they took things very calmly. They were all very happy and relaxed.'

French viewers got to see 'Happy New Year' on a special New Year's Eve show introduced by Guy Lux, *Tous Sur Votre 31*, on Antenne 2. Before performing the song, Anni-Frid delivered a New Year's greeting in French.

At the end of November, Polar Music released the video cassette ABBA *Music Show 2*. Following the success of the first video collection, Stig had had no hesitation in releasing a second one, which featured seven more of ABBA's promotional videos, produced by Lasse Hallström. With video recorders in the majority of homes now, the video market was rapidly growing. Artists were realizing that videos could have a great effect on the success of a song. ABBA had been among the first to record promotional 16mm films for their songs, in 1974.

4 December Benny began production on Norwegian singer Finn Kalvik's second album, *Natt Og Dag* (Night and Day). For the duration of the recording sessions, Finn and his wife Britt stayed with Benny and Anni-Frid in Lidingö. Finn later commented: 'Benny always advised me. He knows exactly what is good or not. One day, I told him I needed some background vocals. He said that he knew two girls who could sing very well. Then, he came up to the Polar studios with Frida and Agnetha. They are great singers. They could sing everything Benny asked for.'

10 – 11 December ABBA were joined by Mireille Mathieu at the Polar Music studios. The French singer had decided to record 'The Winner Takes It All' under the title 'Bravo, Tu As Gagné'. Björn and Benny produced the song and, together with Anni-Frid, sang backing vocals in French. Even if Charles Level's lyrics aren't very convincing, great effort was put into this ABBA cover. One of the least successful examples of this genre is by singer Sylvie Vartan with 'Ca Va Mal (Oh la la la la!)', an unconvincing version of 'On and On and On'.

☆ ☆ ☆ ☆

Having triumphed over the past decade, would ABBA's success continue in the 1980s? The excellent results of the last twelve months would suggest this would be so.

Polar Music had just announced that worldwide sales of the *Super Trouper* album had exceeded seven million. This was a record in itself, as the album had only been on sale for four weeks. In Britain, with 1,700,000 copies sold, ABBA had beaten all records. *Look-In* magazine wrote: 'The key to their success must be in their ability to change with the times, without altering their basic style. Whether you love the group or hate them, you must admit that they have never made a record that has been less than technically superb.'

Elsewhere, Germany had recorded sales of 800,000 copies of *Super Trouper*, Sweden 360,000, France and Belgium 450,000, Japan 180,000, Canada 400,000 and USA 550,000. The 'Super Trouper' single achieved impressive chart positions too: No. 1 in Britain, No. 1 in Belgium, No. 1 in Germany, No. 1 in Austria, No. 8 in Spain, No. 2 in Argentina, No. 1 in Holland, No.1 in Denmark, No. 11 in Sweden and No. 1 in Finland. In Australia, the *Super Trouper* album had been given a good reception and was at No. 5 on the chart. RCA had chosen the rock track 'On and On and On' as a single (it reached No. 9 on the Australian chart) instead of the album's title track.

'I SPEND A LOT OF TIME ALONE PLAYING THE PIANO OR SYNTHESIZERS, AND IT'S MORE LIKE THERAPY: JUST TO BE PREPARED FOR WHEN IT'S REALLY ORGANIZED WORKING.' BENNY

Since 1974, sales of ABBA's singles and albums had been in the millions in the United States, Europe, Japan and Australia. They had become a pop-music phenomenon and their media coverage rivalled that of the Beatles, especially in Europe. However, in France, despite having sold more than ten million records since 1974, the group did not receive the coverage in the media that one would have expected. There was a significant reason behind this – Vogue completely lacked the desire to do any promotion. The French company relied on the success of certain records and had a tendency not to make very much effort as far as radio, TV and the press were concerned. For example, after the group's Eurovision victory, Vogue did nothing to promote ABBA in France. It wasn't until 1976 that the first articles appeared in the French press. In comparison, groups like Boney M and the Rubettes saw themselves becoming very popular in France due to the promotional efforts of their respective record companies. On the other hand, the dynamic team of Gigi Bastin and Bob Navez at Vogue Belgium worked tremendously hard to promote ABBA in Belgium. The results speak for themselves: ABBA had so far had thirteen No. 1s in the Belgian charts.

'SUCCESS REALLY CHANGES YOUR LIFE. YOU'D BE A HYPOCRITE NOT TO ADMIT THAT. THE MONEY GIVES YOU TREMENDOUS FREEDOM. I THINK THAT'S THE MOST IMPORTANT THING ABOUT MONEY.' BJÖRN

1981

6 January Björn married Lena Källersjö in the strictest privacy, with only twelve people present. The ceremony took place in the little church at Grythyttan, in the Swedish province of Västmanland. Nobody knew about the wedding except for the couple's two families.

There were no photographers or journalists present, and it was a complete contrast to the hustle surrounding Björn's marriage to Agnetha in 1971. It was a double celebration: Eva Ulvaeus, Björn's sister, had decided to marry her fiancé Alf Alsterberg at the same time. After Nils-Gustaf Sandbeck, the minister, had given the blessing, the guests were invited to a local restaurant. On the menu were soup marinière, ham and parsley with potato mousse, fillet of venison with celery purée, and French cheeses to finish. Agnetha was not present at the event. She was attending the annual ball in the winter garden of Stockholm's Grand Hotel.

On 18 and 20 January, ABBA were in the Polar Music studios to complete the recording of a song by Björn, Benny, Michael B. Tretow and Rune Söderqvist, entitled 'Hovas Vittne' (Hova's Witness). The song had been written especially for Stig Anderson, who would be celebrating his fiftieth birthday in the next few days. The group had decided to pay tribute to 'the fifth member of ABBA' with a tongue-in-cheek song. Their fans would be disappointed, because the record wouldn't be released commercially – only two hundred copies of the red-vinyl 12-inch single would be pressed. Björn and Benny recorded an instrumental version of Stig's first hit, 'Tivedshambo', for the B-side.

19 January Benny continued production on Norwegian singer Finn Kalvik's album *Natt Og Dag*, at the Polar Music studios. Agnetha, Anni-Frid, Inger Öst, Maritza Horn and Tomas Ledin sang backing vocals on some of the tracks.

24 January A TV crew filmed ABBA on stage at the Berns theatre. The group, wearing their Brighton stage clothes, performed 'Hovas Vittne'. The clip, directed by Kurt Hjelte, would be screened on 3 May 1982 on Swedish Television, on a programme entitled O.S.A. (Om Svar Anhålles – the Swedish equivalent of R.S.V.P.).

25 January Stig celebrated his fiftieth birthday. To mark the occasion, ABBA's producer had invited all his friends to his house in Djurgården. He had planned everything – apart from the many surprises which had been organized by his close friends and family. At 7 a.m., Björn and Benny climbed into his bedroom via a fire-escape ladder and began playing 'Happy Birthday Stig' on the accordion while humming along. They had just finished when a group of seven young women, dressed in cabaret costumes, came into the room and performed a special song for the occasion to the tune of 'Ljuva Sextital'. Among the dancers were Görel Hanser, Agnetha, Anni-Frid and Lillebil Ankarcrona (Rune Söderqvist's wife). An enormous buffet was waiting in the lounge later. An orchestra of fifteen musicians played at the party, welcoming guests as they arrived. More than four hundred people came to pay homage to the king of Swedish showbusiness. The event was recorded by photographers and a TV crew. After dinner, which was exclusively for Stig's close friends and family, there was a video show on a massive screen.

ABBA at Stig's fiftieth birthday party.

'WE ARE IN AN EXTREMELY PRIVILEGED POSITION BECAUSE WE CAN CHOOSE. WE ARE THE ONLY MUSICIANS IN THIS COUNTRY, AND ONE OF THE FEW GROUPS IN THE WHOLE WORLD, WHO CAN AFFORD TO DO EXACTLY WHAT WE WANT TO DO.' BENNY

'THIS WAS A VERY SAD TIME PERSONALLY, BECAUSE I SPLIT UP WITH BENNY ... WE STILL WENT ON BECAUSE WE WANTED TO FINISH *THE VISITORS* ALBUM ... WE NEVER MENTIONED IT, BUT THERE WAS A CERTAIN ATMOSPHERE BETWEEN THE FOUR OF US.' FRIDA

The guests had the opportunity to relive the best moments of the day and to see ABBA singing 'Hovas Vittne'. Stig was overcome when Björn and Benny presented him with the record, together with a contract signed 'Personally to Stig, for the world, for ever!'

The party was far from over, with more presents arriving and songs being sung. Before the dancing began in the evening, a mini-concert was given featuring Benny on the piano, Stig on guitar and John Spalding on drums. As a grand finale, there were fireworks lighting up the sky, spelling out the words 'Long Live Stikkan!' John Spalding remembers: 'When I decided to take Stig's dog Lucas for a walk, I found Stig, flopped out on a chair, surrounded by presents. Apparently he had just sat down, as the last guests didn't leave until 6 a.m. He had been awake for 24 hours!' A few days later, Stig thanked his friends through a mini-newspaper entitled *Stikkan-Expressen*.

During the first week of February, Björn and Benny travelled to New York. On Monday 2 February they took part in the *Tonight* show on NBC. They also met people from Atlantic, as well as American TV presenter Dick Cavett, with whom they confirmed the prospect of a *Dick Cavett Show* with ABBA. The group would make a programme with him, looking back over the past ten years with a mixture of interviews and video.

In the United States, the *Super Trouper* album had reached No. 17 in the Billboard Top 200 and had already sold more than 550,000 copies. *People* wrote: 'The ABBA sound is nasal and antiseptic. For lots of Americans, it's like marinated herring.' The rest of the trip was for their own amusement. Björn and Benny went to see three musicals: *Evita*, *42nd Street* and *Pirates of Penzance*.

From 10 February onwards, Björn and Benny continued work on the next single and the forthcoming album. During this time, Stig presented his new protégée, Kicki Moberg, to the press. Real name Kristina Elisabeth Moberg, Kicki was a nineteen-year-old girl who had sent a tape to Polar Music, and had been offered a recording contract instantly. She was given the opportunity to record a single and would also be one of the five participants in the forthcoming Melodifestivalen.

12 February The Swedish newspapers carried the headline: 'Benny and Frida divorce'. The Polar Music bulletin simply said: 'Benny Andersson and Anni-Frid Lyngstad have decided to separate. On a business level, the decision has nothing at all to do with ABBA's work.' Refusing to give any interviews, Benny only commented: 'We are conscious of the fact that the newspapers are still going to speculate, but we have to accept that. However, our personal life is our concern and no one else's. We have nothing more to add.' Polar Music made no other comment on the matter apart from

'WE FELT THAT ABBA WAS COMING TO AN END DURING THE RECORDING OF *THE VISITORS* ALBUM. BECAUSE WE WERE RUNNING OUT OF OUR ENERGY. WE WERE NOT AS AMBITIOUS ANYMORE, NOT AS COMMITTED.' BJÖRN

The Visitors photo shoot – Rune Söderqvist with Agnetha, Björn & Anni-Frid

Agnetha Fältskog, artist.

Nu är vi ännu fler som gör oss fria.

En rökfri generation.
I samarbete med bl.a. Dagens Nyheter.

the bulletin. Görel Hanser only said: 'There is no reason to worry about the future of ABBA. The atmosphere within the group is excellent and they have never been more successful.' But this was the second divorce to take place within ABBA – and it probably did affect the atmosphere between them.

13 February The press revealed the main reason for the divorce: Benny had a girlfriend, Mona Nörklit, a thirty-seven-year-old woman who worked on a TV news programme called *Kafé* 18. Some of the people close to ABBA were aware of the relationship. Benny had met Mona the previous December, at a party to celebrate Lillebil Ankarcrona's fortieth birthday. Lillebil was Mona's sister and also the wife of Rune Söderqvist and a friend of Benny and Anni-Frid. While Benny moved into a new apartment on Karlavägen in Stockholm with Mona, Anni-Frid went away to ski in Lech, Austria, where she stayed with her friends Charlotte Klingspoor and Egon Zimmermann.

21 February The annual Melodifestivalen took place at the Cirkus in Stockholm. Among the five participants were Björn Skifs, Anders Glenmark and Kicki Moberg. The young girl performed 'Men Natten Är Vår' (But the Night Is Ours), a song which had been written especially for her by Agnetha. Even though Björn Skifs was chosen to represent Sweden at the forthcoming Eurovision Song Contest, Kicki Moberg performed very well. On the B-side of the 'Men Natten Är Vår' single was another of Agnetha's compositions, 'Här Är Mitt Liv', the Swedish version of her song 'I'm Still Alive'.

8 March Benny and Mona Nörklit went to see the first concert given by the group Rendez-Vous, in Eskilstuna. It was an emotional evening for Benny because two of the musicians were part of his family. His son, Peter Grönvall, was on keyboards and Hans Fredriksson, Anni-Frid's son, was playing drums. Rendez-Vous had four members and described themselves as a jazz-rock symphony group.

During this time, Agnetha was taking part in an anti-tobacco campaign, mainly aimed at the young, entitled 'A Non-Smoking Generation'. Numerous Swedish personalities, including Tomas Ledin, Ted Gärdestad and authors Astrid Lindgren and Jan Guillou, lent their support to the campaign. Agnetha had been chosen as the figurehead for the campaign and featured on posters and brochures as well as in the press – an unusual choice, as she was a heavy smoker!

14 March 'The Winner Takes It All' reached No. 8 on the American charts. Harriet Schock would later make an excellent analysis of the song and its lyrics in the magazine *Songwriter*: 'With "The Winner Takes It All", we have a melody that is more Chopin than Ray Charles, more classical than current. Fight it as we may, we are drawn in by the inevitability of the chord progressions and the irresistibility of the melodic power. The song is sung from the viewpoint of the loser. It is appropriate that the world's most successful musical group should have chosen the universal metaphor of a game.'

16 March Björn and Benny began recording sessions for the forthcoming album. Among the new tracks were 'Slipping Through My Fingers', 'When All Is Said and Done' and 'Two For the Price of One'. Björn didn't conceal the fact that, from now on, the private lives of the four ABBA members would be a source of inspiration for their lyrics.

30 March The 'Super Trouper' single entered the Australian charts. RCA had decided to not release the single at the same time as the album the previous November. The result was that the track didn't reach higher than No. 77 in the charts. There was a noticeable decline in ABBA's popularity in Australia, and after the failure of the singles 'Voulez-Vous' (which reached No. 79) and 'I Have a Dream' (No. 64), it seemed that the Australian public was turning its back on the group they had adored during the 1970s.

Björn and Benny spent most of April recording and mixing the first three songs for the forthcoming album. They had also written a short instrumental piece which would become the official fanfare for the 1981 World Ice Hockey Championships and would also be used as the introduction music for T*he Dick Cavett Show.*

24–26 April   ABBA rehearsed songs for the live concert they would give as part of T*he Dick Cavett Show,* at the Europa Films studios. The interviews/videos concept had been abandoned and instead it had been decided that there would be a long discussion with Dick Cavett, followed by a mini-concert. The atmosphere in rehearsals was excellent. Frida later said: 'Rehearsals were held in the same place we had used on the eve of our 1979 world tour with the same musicians. Suddenly, it felt as if there hadn't been any pause at all, that it was yesterday we last stood together on stage. It felt wonderful.'

27 April   ABBA and Dick Cavett recorded the interview for the first part of *Dick Cavett Meets* ABBA (the title which had been decided upon for the programme). A large set had been built in the Swedish TV studio with tiered seating. The programme was recorded in front of an audience and Dick asked ABBA lots of questions, some quite involved. The presenter, true to form, managed to involve the four Swedes in his many jokes. However, ABBA seemed bored and there was a lack of obvious gusto, which was probably

of fun making this programme, most of all because the four members of ABBA were so co-operative. They gave 100 per cent of themselves.'

5 May   Björn, Benny, Michael B. Tretow and Claes af Geijerstam began mixing songs for *Dick Cavett Meets* ABBA. 'Andante, Andante' was left out of the final edited version of the mini-concert.

14 May   The Swedish press announced that Frida had bought herself a 240-metre^2 apartment on Linnégatan, in the centre of Stockholm. The property was situated on the top floor and would be ready the following autumn, after some essential work had been carried out.

18 May   Björn and Benny returned to their recording sessions. The Polar Music studios were now equipped with a 32-track digital tape machine which made perfect recordings without any hiss or interference.

20 May   Stig quashed a rumour which had been circulating for some time. He told the press: 'ABBA are not going to split! The group have never worked as much as they are doing right now! We have three projects in the pipeline. Björn and Benny are working full-time on the forthcoming record. Frida is going to record a solo album made up entirely of other people's songs. For this project, we will be working with the best writers and composers.

'WE ARE WRITING MORE PERSONALLY. THERE ARE SEVERAL DIFFERENT EXPLANATIONS FOR THAT. I'M MUCH FREER NOW WITH THE ENGLISH LANGUAGE THAN I USED TO BE. ALSO, WE ARE GROWN-UP PEOPLE, NOT SO AFRAID OF SHARING WITH OTHERS WHAT WE FEEL. THE MEANING IS BECOMING MORE IMPORTANT. I WRITE IN ENGLISH, AND I EVEN THINK IN ENGLISH WHEN I WRITE THE LYRICS.'   BJÖRN

due in part to nerves and their recent personal problems. There were some unforgettable moments, however, such as when Frida gave Dick Cavett a lesson in Swedish pronunciation with the number 777, when Benny picked up his accordion to play one of his own compositions entitled 'Lotta' (this clip wasn't shown in some countries), and when Dick asked ABBA to perform an acapella version of 'Don't Fence Me In' in both Swedish and English.

Björn said later: 'We wanted to do something really special, a TV show with both an interview and a live performance. Someone suggested Dick Cavett, one of the world's most famous and skilful interviewers. He accepted and came to Sweden. We didn't talk much beforehand. I think we were much more nervous than he was, but his composure made us relax and open up. We never regretted that we chose Dick Cavett.'

28–29 April   ABBA recorded their mini-concert for the show. Instead of performing to playback, the group were joined by their musicians Lasse Wellander and Mats Ronander on guitar, Ola Brunkert on drums, Rutger Gunnarsson on bass, Anders Eljas on keyboards, Åke Sundqvist on percussion and backing vocalists Tomas Ledin, Lisa Öhman and Lena Ericsson. ABBA performed 'Gimme! Gimme! Gimme!', 'Super Trouper', 'Me and I', 'Knowing Me, Knowing You', 'Summer Night City', 'Thank You For the Music', and 'On and On and On', as well as two new songs, 'Two For the Price of One', performed by Björn, and 'Slipping Through My Fingers'. Gunilla Nilars, the producer and director, said: 'When the recording was finished, we began editing and mixing the sound. We had 20 hours of material for a 1-hour programme. With the aid of the best crew and both Micke Tretow and Claes af Geijerstam, the job was done. We really had a lot

And then there is Agnetha and Linda's album of Christmas songs, which is going to be released at the end of the year.'

26 May   The Together Gallery in Stockholm launched an exhibition of ABBA's costumes. For the first time, Owe Sandström had emptied his cupboards and given access to the group's stage gear. The public now had the chance to see the legendary costumes in close-up and to admire the material, the embroidery, the precious stones and exquisite detail in the work. The exhibition lasted two weeks.

At the beginning of June, Björn and Benny were working in the studio finishing off a new track entitled 'Another Morning Without You', which would later become 'Like an Angel Passing Through My Room'. The arrangement of the song seemed to pose problems for the two musicians, and they spent a lot of time trying to find an original way of dealing with the melody. Journalist Björn Vinberg from E*xpressen* visited ABBA in the Polar Music studios at this time and in his article, published on 8 June, he used 'Opus 10' as the name of the forthcoming album. This title, which would never be used by ABBA on a record, was picked up by many foreign journalists, and therefore created the legend of the 'Opus 10' album.

11 June   Anni-Frid attended the wedding of her friends Charlotte Klingspoor and Egon Zimmermann, in Lidköping, making a spectacular arrival by helicopter.

'BJÖRN ASKED ME IF IT WAS SOMETIMES TOO EMOTIONAL TO SING THOSE LYRICS. BUT THAT WAS ALSO, IN A WAY, A CHALLENGE: TO BE ABLE TO PUT YOUR EMOTIONS INTO THE SONGS AND LYRICS THAT YOU SANG.' **FRIDA** ON THE SONGS WRITTEN AFTER THE DIVORCES

Frida & Claes af Geijerstam

On and On' (from November 1980) had been shown, ABBA were interviewed by satellite, live from the Polar Music studios. Björn thanked the American public and apologized for not being able to attend the event in the States, due to the distance involved and the recording of the new album. Stig Anderson, who had recently been to the USA to renew the group's contract with record company Atlantic, had brought the award back with him in his luggage.

18 August Frida and Claes af Geijerstam gave a press conference in the winter garden of Stockholm's Grand Hotel to launch *Lite Grand i Örat*. In the series of four shows, to be televised in September and October on TV2, Frida and Claes would be the presenters and would also sing, along with other guests. Frida said: 'It's fun to try to do something new. I love working in front of an audience. Unfortunately, I don't do it very often. *Lite Grand i Örat* is a programme straight from the heart. It's a bit rocky but is aimed at the whole family. There'll also be room for improvisations.' Rehearsals and filming for *Lite Grand i Örat* took place during the second two weeks of August at the Grand Hotel.

22 August Norwegian television celebrated the twenty-fifth anniversary of the Eurovision Song Contest on the programme *Momarkedet*. All the winners of the contest had been invited to come and sing their winning song in Oslo. Profits from the show would go to the Norwegian Red Cross. ABBA didn't take part in the evening. Kerstin Sehlin, from Polar Music, announced: 'The group are busy preparing their new album. Nevertheless, they won't be missing from the programme because Norwegian television came to record a message from the four members of ABBA last June.' Since the BBC had refused permission to show the Brighton clip, the Norwegian TV station decided to show ABBA singing 'Waterloo' on *Momarkedet* during the summer of 1975.

27 August Anni-Frid took part in the *Solklart* (Obvious) programme on radio station P3. She was interviewed by journalist Kjell Dabrowski, and was more open than usual in speaking about both her private and professional lives.

2 July The press announced that Frida and Claes af Geijerstam would host a series of four TV shows entitled *Lite Grand i Örat*. Claes explained: 'The idea came up last December but was delayed because of Frida's divorce. She finally accepted as soon as her problems had been sorted out. Frida has a natural charm and the ability to express herself. She is very talented.'

10 July Epic released 'Lay All Your Love On Me' / 'On and On and On' as a 12-inch single in the UK. A week later, it reached No. 7, the first time that a 12-inch single had got to such a high position in the charts. The British press seemed to have a problem accepting ABBA's continuing success. *Melody Maker* wrote: 'Over a Euro-disco backdrop, the two perfect couples weave their anthemic magic. A lovely record for Prince Charles to put on the royal turntable before consummating the wedding of all time. Lady Di should love it.'

In the United States, 'On and On and On' (which has an extra verse which was never released) did not rise any higher than No. 90 in the charts. As for 'Lay All Your Love On Me', a remixed version was a huge hit in the clubs and discotheques. Elsewhere, 'Lay All Your Love On Me' did quite well: No. 9 in France, No. 13 in Belgium and No. 26 in Germany. No videos had been filmed for these tracks; for 'Lay All Your Love On Me' a montage of old clips was created. For 'On and On and On', Anders Hanser used hundreds of photographs he had taken during the 1979 tour to create a film.

1 August Björn and Lena travelled to the Hockenheim racing circuit in Germany to give Swedish driver Tommy Slim Borgudd some encouragement before the Formula 1 Grand Prix. Tommy's car had been sponsored by ABBA.

9 August ABBA were awarded the title of Best Vocal Group of 1981 (the award covered the period 1980–81) by the American Guild of Variety Artists and the show was televised live from Las Vegas on NBC. ABBA appeared at 12.55 a.m. (9.55 a.m. European time), and after the *Show Express* clip of 'On and

29 August Lasse Hallström filmed the promotional video for 'When All Is Said and Done' at the Filmbolaget studios in Solna. The sequences in which Anni-Frid walks on the rocks were filmed in one of the islands of the Stockholm archipelago.

1–9 September ABBA were working in the Polar Music studios. Several new songs were recorded: 'Head Over Heels', 'I Let the Music Speak' and 'Should I Laugh Or Cry'. With 'Head Over Heels', Björn and Benny wanted the song to have a lively rhythm and a hidden meaning in the text. The first results were disappointing. There was a lack of humour and it was a bit heavy. Frida explains: 'Of course, our split-ups left their mark on the atmosphere in the studio. The joy that had always been present in our songs, even if the song itself was downbeat, had disappeared. We were growing apart, and the unity that had been a part of our recordings was gone.' (*The Complete Recording Sessions*, 1994.)

12 September ABBA travelled by private jet to Bournemouth, England, for the CBS sales conference. John Spalding and Judd Lander from Epic were there to welcome the four Swedes and drive them to their hotel. ABBA's attendance at the event, which the managers of CBS had kept secret, was to be the high spot of the evening. After having had some time at the hotel to recover, John, Judd and Carole Broughton (Bocu Music) drove the group to the Carlton Hotel for the cocktail party and dinner. Agnetha and Anni-Frid looked fantastic, and, for once, Björn and Benny were wearing ties. When they walked into the restaurant everyone stood up and applauded. After cocktails had been served and many speeches made, dinner began. The members of the CBS sales team were very touched by the group's presence at their annual conference, as they very rarely had the chance to meet the artists they worked for during the year. ABBA also had the opportunity to meet Jaap Eggermont, the creator of the 'Stars On 45' concept, who had had a big hit that year with his 'ABBA Medley'.

On the same day, Swedish TV screened *Dick Cavett Meets* ABBA. Even if the programme wasn't exceptional, it gave the public the chance to see and hear the group perform live. Despite the fact that everyone had worked very hard, the programme lacked warmth and spontaneity. In *Expressen*, Erik Hörnfeldt didn't mince his words: 'The programme sums up ABBA's current image. Four established, content people without any great enthusiasm who oscillate between indifference and the spirit they have to show for the fans. No one in the ABBA camp wants to admit it, but everyone knows that the group will never tour again. They're quite lazy. Although as soon as the chat is over and ABBA start singing on stage, it's sensational!' Swedish viewers had the opportunity to see the promotional video for the new song 'When All Is Said and Done'. *Dick Cavett Meets* ABBA was bought and screened in numerous other countries.

14 September   Agnetha left for a week's holiday in Mallorca with her sister Mona.

In the middle of September, Olivia Newton-John made a brief visit to Stockholm for the release of her new album *Physical*, which was being distributed by Polar Music. Olivia, Frida and Stig posed for photographs in the producer's villa in Djurgården. During the evening they went for dinner at the Café Opéra.

18 September   Swedish Television screened the first show in the *Lite Grand i Örat* series. Frida and Claes were joined by Björn Skifs, Lena Andersson, Pugh Rogefeldt and Janne Önnerud. The orchestra was led by Anders Eljas. The show was made up of a few interviews and lots of music. In weekly magazine *Hänt i Veckan*, Frida said: 'I agreed to do the project because I've known Claes for many years. We are good friends. Having the chance to present a TV show proved to me that I am able to do other things as well as singing. The audience was great. But, believe me, I've got no intention of abandoning ABBA .'

23 September   Swedish magazine *Vecko-Revyn* published a long interview with Agnetha by Inga-Lill Walfridsson. For the first time, the ABBA singer spoke very openly and sincerely about the past and the present.

'When I started, I wanted glamour and to make some money. I thought that would be what would make me happy, but I knew nothing … It's hard for me to say whether I married too early or not. I was only twenty-one years old and Björn was twenty-six. I was in love. When you're young, you don't imagine it could come to an end. Nowadays I'm very distrustful … Björn doesn't live far away. The children spend as much time with him as with me. We will never be a family again with a mother, father and children. If I meet someone new, it wouldn't be a real family for us. … I don't want to live through another divorce. One day Linda said to me: "Are you going to meet your Prince Charming tonight?" She has a feeling that I'm lonely. I would like to meet someone but would it be me they would love or my money and my fame?

'I'm lucky to have a job which is a hobby. After all these years, I feel more sure of myself. I'm used to working under pressure and to making compromises. … I don't know how long we're going to carry on with ABBA. We no longer need to do tours. Maybe we'll do a musical or a film. That all depends on Björn and Benny. I'd like to try to be in a film but I'd have to have the main role.

'We have to be interested in others and to show more feeling, to be more open and warm to each other. The way that people are so cold right now scares me. It's like it's forbidden to be happy. Let's give more of ourselves, we've got nothing to lose.'

In an interview in *Dagens Nyheter*, Björn confided:

'In the beginning, the lyrics didn't have much meaning for us. They were just a few clichés put back to back to give the girls something to sing. Their voices are a part of our music. But now we've matured and we want the words that Agnetha and Frida use to have a meaning. But nevertheless the music and the voices are the most important thing. … Unhappy love affairs are more interesting and more dramatic. I'm not trying to deliver any message. I hate moralistic lessons. All I want is to create an atmosphere and to give some kind of feeling, whether it be melancholy or happy. … Our musical roots are European – we like French and Italian songs. This is probably why our songs work well in the countries of Latin America. … In the United States, pop music is heavily influenced by the blues, soul and gospel – which isn't in ABBA's heritage.'

30 September *Hänt i Veckan* magazine revealed that Agnetha had a new boyfriend, Torbjörn Brander, a thirty-eight-year-old police inspector. The couple had known each other for almost a year. At the time of their meeting, the group had just received kidnap threats and needed close supervision. Agnetha and Torbjörn had been living together for seven weeks. He told the magazine: 'We've been to the cinema, out to a restaurant and we've had a week's holiday in Majorca. I'm surprised in fact that no one discovered the relationship earlier!'

The ABBA family was about to grow: both Lena Ulvaeus and Mona Nörklit were expecting babies the following January. Björn and Lena had just bought a huge villa in Lidingö which looked out onto the sea.

There was talk that Agnetha might be appearing in the American soap *Dallas* and that one of the producers, Swede Gunnar Hellström, had contacted the singer to offer her a role. In the end, Agnetha confirmed that it was only a rumour.

Polar Music's offices in Baldersgatan had grown too small for the company and its partners. The record company was to move to 11 Hamngatan, in the centre of town. At the time, Görel Hanser explained: 'Our old offices were great but too small. We have no regrets. Polar Music is today one of the biggest companies in Sweden. Thirty-five people work there full-time. We mainly invest in companies. The ABBA members take part in all administrative decisions and they are really interested in this.'

Throughout the whole of October and right up to the middle of November, Björn, Benny, Agnetha and Anni-Frid were in the Polar Music studios to complete the recording of the new album. Discussing the song 'The Visitors', Frida later said: 'Before beginning the recording sessions, I spent more than fifteen days trying to get my voice to sound like a sitar, I love playing around with my voice. That's probably where my talent lies. After that, I did the same thing again for "I Let The Music Speak".' And about 'Like an Angel Passing Through My Room', Frida added: 'This song means a lot to me. Benny and I

press release. Otherwise, it's just like any other Christmas record. It's no better and no worse. However, it has got one positive thing in the fact that the choice of songs is very pleasant. Little Linda sometimes sings out of tune and has trouble in holding notes, but this in fact makes the whole thing more charming.'

11 November At a special reception, Agnetha and Anni-Frid were presented with an award for the Best Album Recorded and Produced in Sweden for *Super Trouper* by the Academy of Swedish Music and magazine *Musikrevy*. Björn and Benny were busy in the studio and unable to attend.

14 November Frida was invited to a party to celebrate her friend Alexandra Charles's thirty-fifth birthday at her nightclub, the Alexandra.

During November, Benny made a flying visit to Doncaster, England, to buy two race horses, Secret Army and Hurtwood Lass.

Agnetha collaborated on a song with Ulf Lundell, entitled 'Snön Faller' (The Snow Is Falling).

23 November Lasse Hallström filmed the main scenes of the 'One of Us' video in his own apartment. This time, he directed Agnetha playing the role of a woman moving to a new flat.

24 November ABBA recorded 'No Hay A Quien Culpar' and 'Se Me Esta Escapando', the Spanish versions of 'When All Is Said and Done' and 'Slipping Through My Fingers'. These two tracks would be featured on the new album in Spanish-speaking countries.

25 November ABBA gave a press conference at Sverigehuset (Sweden House) in Stockholm. About fifty Swedish and foreign journalists were present for the launch of the new album, *The Visitors*. Figures for advance sales were already impressive: 400,000 copies in Scandinavia, 600,000 copies in Germany and 500,000 in the United States. Benny said: 'It's harder

'IT WORKED THIS WAY: THAT EVERY SONG WORTH RECORDING SHOULD BE A POSSIBLE SINGLE. IT WAS NEVER LIKE RECORDING TWENTY AND SEEING WHETHER THERE WERE ONE OR TWO OUT OF THOSE TWENTY. SO, THERE WAS NEVER ANY EXCESS MATERIAL.' BJÖRN

were alone in the studio. Alone with the "tick-tock" of the metronome. I love this kind of song.'

2 November A team from German magazine *Bravo* visited Polar Music, along with photographer Dieter 'Didi' Zill and a young fan called Brigitte Sdun, who had been invited to spend a few hours with her Swedish idols. After visiting the new premises, Brigitte presented ABBA with the silver *Bravo*-Otto 80 award which had been voted for by *Bravo*'s readers. Two members of the group had a new look – Frida had a new, slightly punky, hairstyle (perhaps inspired by her friend, Olivia Newton-John, who had sported a similar style when she had come to Stockholm), and Björn now had a beard, like Benny. Agnetha and Frida invited Brigitte to take part in the filming of a children's TV programme, *Razzamatazz*. The TV crew had come over especially from Britain and filmed in Polar Music's large kitchen. On the programme, the presenter and the two female singers talked about the customs and traditions of Christmas in Sweden and spoke about the group's new album.

6 November Agnetha and Linda's album, *Nu Tändas Tusen Juleljus* (A Thousand Christmas Candles Are Now Being Lit) was released. Jöran Stridbeck wrote in *Expressen*: 'No doubt the name and picture of Agnetha on the sleeve will make this the Christmas album of the year, as it is being described on Polar Music's

and harder with each record. We want to avoid doing what we've already done or what others are doing.' The group concluded the meeting after 45 minutes. Before leaving, Agnetha and Frida recorded a Christmas message for the Russian TV cameras.

26 November Vogue released *The Visitors* album and the 'One of Us' single. The B-side was a surprise unreleased track sung by Frida entitled 'Should I Laugh Or Cry'. In France, 'One of Us' reached No. 1 and stayed on the RTL chart for thirteen weeks. It also reached No. 1 in Belgium.

27 November Lasse Hallström recorded the videos for the two Spanish songs, 'No Hay A Quien Culpar' and 'Se Me Esta Escapando', at the Filmbolaget studios in Solna, a Stockholm suburb. During the session, Lasse also filmed the additional scenes of the 'One of Us' video with all four of the group.

30 November Polar Music released the album *The Visitors* in Scandinavia. This was ABBA's ninth album, counting *Gracias Por La Musica*. The production and arrangements were more sophisticated than on previous albums. The group was constantly evolving, but, while the album was still of exceptional quality, the ABBA magic seemed to have disappeared. The sombre lyrics (about fear, paranoia or separation) gave a heavy and morose feel to the album. There are some surprises though, like 'I Let the Music Speak' (a theatrical song demonstrating Björn and Benny's new musical direction), 'Head Over Heels' (a humorous tango number) and 'Two For the Price of One' (sung by Björn).

The sleeve, which was also very dark, perfectly reflected the atmosphere of the album and the group's mood. There was even talk that it was hard to get the four Swedes together for the photo shoot and that they spoke very little during the event. None of them are looking in the same direction. Was it a sign of what the future would hold? Rune Söderqvist said: 'With each new album, we looked for ideas and locations to use for the sleeve. I knew the painter Julius Kronberg's studio in Skansen very well and immediately thought of this place when I found out that one of the songs was called "Like an Angel Passing Through My Room". He had painted this huge angel, called Eros, which you can see on the sleeve. I love the atmosphere created by photographer Lars Larsson, although I have bad memories of the photo shoot because it was very cold. Benny arrived late, there was no heating and the atmosphere was tense. You know that my role as artistic director included relaxing everyone and making sure that everything went well. But in this particular situation, there was nothing I could do. You could feel that it was the end of the group. When you look, you can see that they are all standing away from each other. The photo shoot was very brief that day because everyone was in a hurry to leave.'

Erik Hörnfeldt wrote in *Expressen* that 'The majority of the songs are quite usual. What ABBA know how to do best is write big pop songs and divorce. The musical arrangements are heavily influenced by classical music. But at the same time the members of ABBA say that their dream is to write a musical. I personally feel that they would like to write an opera. You can't feel ABBA's classical ambitions anywhere better than on the track "I Let the Music Speak". And in *Aftonbladet*, Jan-Olov Andersson wrote: 'On the whole, the record is disappointing. But of course it isn't all negative. "Head Over Heels" has got a great melody, a chorus in true ABBA style and Agnetha's remarkable vocals. "One of Us" and "When All Is Said and Done" have got enough melody and powerful-enough choruses to be able to be added to a long list of ABBA hits."

3 December Benny married Mona Nörklit. The ceremony, which had been kept secret, took place at 5 p.m. at the Gustav Adolf church in Stockholm. The newlyweds then joined their friends at the Operakällaren restaurant.

4 December Epic released the 'One of Us' single in Britain. It entered the charts a week later and finally peaked at No. 3. In other countries, it also did very well: No. 1 in Germany, No. 11 in Holland, No. 1 in Ireland, No. 2 in Sweden and No. 1 in Spain. On the other hand, it didn't do so well in Australia, where it reached No. 48, or in New Zealand, where it peaked at No. 43.

11 December Epic released the album *The Visitors*. A million copies had already been pre-ordered and the album entered the British charts on 19 December and stayed at the No. 1 spot for three weeks.

15 December An important dinner took place. Around the table in a large Stockholm restaurant sat Björn, Benny, Richard Vos, Tim Rice and Stig. Richard Vos was an American musical producer and Tim Rice the co-writer of the musicals *Jesus Christ Superstar* and *Evita*. The two ABBA musicians' dream might become reality at last. Richard Vos said: 'I like ABBA's music and I always thought that the two guys had the talent to write a musical. I was pleasantly surprised when Stig told me that their dream was to write one.' Tim Rice added: 'We are, of course, going to keep in touch. They write excellent music and need a plot and lyrics. That's my job!'

At the end of December, at a reception at Polar Music studios, ABBA received the Ampex Golden Reel award for the *Super Trouper* album.

Gerhard Wick, the European Manager for Ampex, the studio tape supplier, gave each member an award and a monetary gift of $1000 which ABBA forwarded to Svenska Handikapps Förbundet (Swedish Sports Association For Disabled Persons).

☆ ☆ ☆ ☆

The careers of the four members of ABBA had started to take an unexpected turn. Even if they didn't admit to a certain exhaustion within the group, they no longer hid their desire to do other things, as future projects would demonstrate. Björn and Benny would devote their time to the writing of a musical, Agnetha wanted to make a movie and to record a solo album, and Frida announced that her next solo album would be produced by Phil Collins.

It is clear that *The Visitors* was a crisis record. The lyrics dealt with more serious subject matter than before, and the melodies seemed less powerful. Even though sales were still exceptional and the fans remained devoted to their idols, the public were disconcerted by the darkness of this album compared to the previous ones. ABBA's new lack of enthusiasm made the future less predictable than before.

'IF THE NEXT ALBUM IS NO FUN TO MAKE, THEN WE PROBABLY WON'T RELEASE IT AT ALL AND WE'LL SPLIT UP THE GROUP. THAT'S THE SIMPLE PHILOSOPHY WE HAVE. WE'RE NOT GOING TO GO ON IF WE DON'T THINK IT'S FUN ANYMORE.' BJÖRN

Reception at the Belfry Club, London

'THE ABBA PERIOD WAS FUN AND RESTLESS. THE SWEDES WERE ALMOS
THE LAST ONES TO REALIZE HOW BIG WE WERE EVERYWHERE. BUT
SWEDEN IS A BIT LIKE A DUCK-POND. WE'RE NOT USED TO THINKING
BIG AND THAT'S PROBABLY WHY IT TOOK SO LONG FOR US TO GET
ACCEPTED … I THINK THAT THE VERY GOOD THING WE DID FOR THE
POP MARKET IS THAT WE GOT AMERICAN AND BRITISH PEOPLE TO
UNDERSTAND THAT A POP SONG CAN COME FROM ANYWHERE IN
THE WORLD.' STIG

'THE REASON OUR PROFESSIONAL RELATIONSHIP HAS ENDURED IS THAT WE ARE VERY GOOD FRIENDS WHO TRUST EACH OTHER ON EVERY LEVEL. I WAS LIKE THE BROTHER BENNY NEVER HAD, AND I SUPPOSE HE WAS THAT FOR ME TOO.' BJÖRN

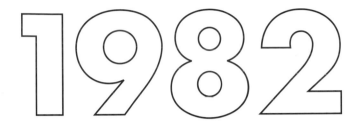

3 January Lena Ulvaeus gave birth to a baby daughter, who was named Emma. The baby was 50 centimetres long and weighed 3.1 kilograms.

10 January It was Benny's turn to become a father again. His wife Mona gave birth to a 2.8-kilogram boy, Ludvig, four weeks before reaching full term.

21 January Lasse Hallström filmed the video for the song 'Head Over Heels' at Svenskfilmindustri film studios in Gröndal, near Stockholm. This is certainly the group's funniest-ever video. Anni-Frid plays the leading role of a woman who rushes through her life, running in and out of stores every day in search of new outfits to wear; her husband, played by Björn, is completely exhausted.

23 January The Swedish press announced that Agnetha would be starring in director Gunnar Hellström's next film.

27 January ABBA recorded a special film clip at the Polar Music Studios, in which Björn addressed a message of solidarity to Poland. The short film would be shown on the American television programme *Let Poland Be Poland* in March.

5 February Epic released 'Head Over Heels' in Britain. The single reached No. 25 in the British charts. It was the first time since 'I Do, I Do, I Do, I Do, I Do' in 1975 that an ABBA single had not reached the Top 10.

During the month of February, a Spanish TV crew travelled to Stockholm to film part of the *Aplauso* show with ABBA. The promotional videos for 'No Hay A Quien Culpar', 'Head Over Heels' and 'One of Us' were shown and the group answered questions. However, the interview wasn't one of their best, and Agnetha, Björn, Benny and Anni-Frid gave the impression that their hearts weren't really in it. They seemed indifferent, had little enthusiasm and looked unhappy. They had never been seen like this before. The *Visitors* album was No. 6 in the Spanish charts at that time and the 'Head Over Heels' single No. 18.

13 February The album *The Visitors* peaked at No. 29 in the American charts. Bill Provick wrote in the *Citizen*: 'This is a really good album with good-quality sound, production and performance. Great to listen to in every way.' In the United States, Atlantic had decided to release 'When All Is Said and Done'/'Should I Laugh Or Cry' as a single. It reached No. 27 on 13 March.

Between 15 February and 31 March, Frida was recording her solo album at the Polar Music studios. The record was produced by Phil Collins. For the duration of the recording, Phil and his musicians stayed at Stockholm's Grand Hotel. The team was made up of Mo Foster on bass, Daryl Stuermer on guitar, Peter Robinson on keyboards and Phil Collins on drums and percussion, as well as Phil's sound engineer Hugh Padgham. Choosing the songs was difficult, and Frida listened to hundreds of tracks written especially for her by numerous well-known and unknown composers.

Frida says: 'I remember the first week; I was pretty nervous because it was the first thing I have done outside ABBA. But I found that it was a group of very nice people. After a week, we really had it together. It was a very relaxed situation, a very nice atmosphere. I really loved to work together with those musicians. I wanted Phil to write a song for me. But he didn't have the time to do it, because he was on tour with his group Genesis. And then, he suggested to me to do this song "You Know What I Mean".' During the month of March, the whole team travelled to London's Air studios to record the harp sections (played by Skaila Kanga) and strings of the Martyn Ford Orchestra, directed by Martyn Ford.

At the end of February, Vogue released a compilation entitled *The Must of ABBA*. This record was only available in France and Belgium.

Björn and Benny were working very little at this time. Their project of writing a musical with Tim Rice hadn't yet been confirmed. As far as their work with ABBA was concerned, the two musicians had intended to make a double album featuring one record of studio songs and another recorded live at a series of concerts in a town somewhere in either Sweden or Europe. But due to a lack of time, energy or creativity, the project was abandoned. Björn and Benny decided to work only on songs for a forthcoming album. Also, since becoming fathers, the two men had reduced their musical activities considerably in order to be able to spend more time at home.

For a while, they had been thinking about writing a song for Frida's album, but eventually put the idea on hold. Björn explained: 'I would say we haven't really analysed exactly what it is that we think Frida would want for this album. But every idea that comes up, we ask ourselves "Is this something? No, I don't think so." And, so far, we haven't come up with anything. It's an experiment, because it's the very first time that a producer takes the song and produces it without us being there.' Benny added: 'We have kept a lot of things, but maybe not suitable for this album. Maybe more suitable for us.'

13 March *Let Poland Be Poland* was screened on American TV, featuring artists and personalities protesting against the Soviet Union's domination of Poland. ABBA's message and the video for 'When All Is Said and Done' were shown. There was an immediate response: the group was banned from then on in the U.S.S.R. ABBA – *The Movie* was withdrawn, their records were taken off the shelves and the four Swedes were heavily criticized in the newspapers.

18 March Vogue released 'Head Over Heels' as a single in France. It reached No. 13 in the RTL chart. In Belgium, where the record had been released slightly earlier, it was already No. 3; in Germany it was at No. 19 and in Holland No. 4. (In Sweden, following the success of 'One of Us', Polar Music decided not to release the new single.) Some fans were disappointed with the choice of 'The Visitors' as the B-side, feeling the song deserved A-side status. It would have been a good opportunity for the group to chart with this unusual song, heralding the 'new' ABBA sound.

29 March Frida, Phil Collins and Stig Anderson held a press conference in the Polar Music studios. The atmosphere was very friendly. Frida said: 'I've been working on this album from the very beginning. I mean, I've chosen the songs, the material, together with Phil, of course. And, since we started to record, I've been in the studio and have followed the process from the very beginning. I think it's very good that he is a singer and drummer as well. Because he has another sense of rhythm that I don't have. So, he can teach me a lot of things, and I appreciate that.' About the album, Frida declared: 'It's beyond what I expected it to be. I could never imagine that it would be so good as it is today!'

'I HAD A DREAM AND IT WAS FULFILLED BY MEETING BENNY, BJÖRN AND AGNETHA. WHAT WE DID DURING THIS PERIOD IS ABSOLUTELY SOMETHING VERY FANTASTIC, ALTHOUGH I THINK THAT BJÖRN AND BENNY ALREADY HAD A KIND OF GOAL. THEY KNEW WHAT THEY WANTED TO DO.' FRIDA

'IF YOU TALK ABOUT INTERNATIONAL ACTS, IT MAKES NO DIFFERENCE IF THEY'RE FROM VANCOUVER, STOCKHOLM OR BERLIN, BECAUSE IF YOU TAKE CARE OF THE MARKETING THE RIGHT WAY, ANYTHING IS POSSIBLE FOR THAT ACT.'
STIG

Frida backstage with the Human League, Stockholm

A British TV crew, directed by Stuart Orme and Peter Mackay, had been in Stockholm to film a 55-minute documentary based on the recording of the album entitled *Something Going On – The Making of a Record Album.*

At the end of the press conference, Frida went to see British group Human League in concert at the Konserthuset in Stockholm. At the end of the show, she went backstage to congratulate the five members of the group. The Human League, who were very popular at that time all over Europe, had never hidden their passion for ABBA and the fact that they had been influenced by the group. Frida then went to the Swedish Television studios to appear on the show *Måndagsbörsen.*

During April, RCA Australia finally decided to release the *Gracias Por La Musica* album, renamed *The Spanish Album.* There seemed to be little motivation from the record company; the album was released with a badly printed sleeve, the words of the songs were missing and little effort was made at promotion. ABBA were no longer hot property in Australia, and *The Visitors* album had only spent twelve weeks in the charts, peaking at No. 22. The single 'When All Is Said and Done'/'Soldiers' had recently only managed to reach No. 81.

Björn and Benny were back in the studio and had resumed recordings for a new ABBA album, although there seemed to be little inspiration following the few months of reduced activity.

At the beginning of July, Frida was in London to film two promotional videos, 'I Know There's Something Going On' and 'I See Red'. The ABBA singer again worked with Stuart Orme, the director of the documentary on the making of her album. A scenario had been written for the first song. It was filmed at the Primrose Hill photographic studios, Stringfellows discotheque, Little Venice and Covent Garden. Frida's apartment and the set for the second film were built in the Fulham Film Studios. At the end of filming, Frida made a private stopover in Paris.

31 July Gunnar Hellström, director and star of the film *Raskenstam,* invited the main actresses (Agnetha Fältskog, Inga Gill, Lena Nyman, Yvonne Lombard and Harriet Andersson) to a costume-fitting session at Mago's designers. They had created a special wardrobe for Agnetha, whose character would be pregnant twice during the film.

At the beginning of August, Björn and Benny resumed recording sessions at the Polar Music studios. The idea of a live album or a completely new ABBA album had been abandoned. The two musicians had decided to release a double compilation album featuring all the group's singles recorded between 1972 and 1982, plus two new songs.

10 August Agnetha's first day of filming. In the film, she plays the part of Lisa Mattsson, a fisherman's daughter, who falls madly in love with Gustav

'SOMETHING'S GOING ON WAS MY FIRST STEP OUTSIDE THE GROUP AND I WANTED TO GIVE EVERYTHING.' FRIDA

10–12 April An ABBA Weekend was held in the United States. Record company Atlantic, in conjunction with several hundred radio stations, had put together a huge promotional campaign around *The Visitors* album. One of the high points of the weekend was a 90-minute radio interview with Bob Hamilton and the transmission of a long remixed version (7 minutes 20 seconds) of the track 'The Visitors'. Unfortunately, despite these efforts, the song rose no higher than No. 63 in the American charts.

Once recording of her album was complete, Frida gave herself a few days off. During April, she was spotted in Cannes on the terrace of the Carlton Hotel, together with her new boyfriend, businessman Bertil Hjert.

From 3 May onwards, Björn and Benny were recording new demos for ABBA. Among the new songs were 'You Owe Me One', 'I Am the City' and 'Just Like That'. The last of these tracks was, without doubt, the most interesting of the three. Unfortunately, after having tried out different versions of the song (at a faster tempo, adding saxophone, and so on), the two musicians decided to leave 'Just Like That' unreleased. In 1985, they reworked the song for the duo Gemini (Anders and Karin Glenmark).

31 May The press announced that Agnetha was to star in a film entitled *Raskenstam,* directed and interpreted by actor Gunnar Hellström. She announced in *Expressen*: 'I've accepted the offer and I think it will be exciting. But please don't write that I'm going to become a "film star". It's just a trial and a challenge for me. This is something I've had in my head for a few years. It will be my first real role. It's quite important and my character appears regularly throughout the film.' *Raskenstam* retraces the true story of Gustav Raskenstam, a Swedish Don Juan who swindled several hundred women in the 1940s by seducing them and promising them marriage. Once he was behind bars, it was discovered that he had had several hundred romances and was engaged to thirty-two women.

Agnetha, who had just finished recording a duet with Tomas Ledin, entitled 'Never Again', announced that she was going to record a solo album the following year. The producer had not yet been chosen.

Raskenstam and has two children by him. Gustav, a confirmed womanizer, carries on cheating on her but ends up marrying her. Filming took place at the Filmhuset studios in Stockholm, as well as at Ljusterö, in the archipelago. Agnetha would get up at 4.30 a.m. and arrive at the studios at 6.45 a.m. Rehearsals began after make-up, hair and wardrobe. For the outside shots, the team began their work early because of the light. A bus would carry the actors to the port of Roslagen. Agnetha said 'I'm trying to play the role with my own personality, which I'm doing because it's more fun that way. This is new to me and I'd like to do my job well. I don't have a great deal of experience in cinema. I'm trying to express the feelings of the fisherman's daughter. She has a child by Raskenstam without being married to him. At that time this was scandalous. She knew that he had hundreds of mistresses but she loved him deeply.'

17 August Frida's single 'I Know There's Something Going On' was released simultaneously throughout Europe. Written by Russ Ballard, the song was an excellent choice to announce the imminent release of the album. The very least you could say about the song was that it was stimulating and powerful. Although dominated by Phil Collins' drums, Frida's powerful vocal performance remains unspoilt. The B-side, 'Threnody', was actually a poem by American writer Dorothy Parker, put to music by Per Gessle, who went on to form Roxette. Susanne Ljung wrote in *Expressen*: 'Lots of noise for nothing. It's very professional, naturally. But it's more like an ambitious cocktail of different types of music. There are more methods here than ideas – and not to say talent.'

20–26 August Agnetha, Björn, Benny and Anni-Frid finished recording three new ABBA songs in the Polar Music studios: 'Cassandra', 'Under Attack' and 'The Day Before You Came'.

1 September In an open letter to *Dagens Nyheter,* Agnetha attacked the lies printed in Swedish weeklies *Hänt i Veckan* and *Svensk Damtidning*; the latter had recently carried the headline: 'Agnetha on her own and pregnant again!' next to a photo taken from the film *Raskenstam.*

Agnetha said: 'I think it's time that the readers realized the huge fraud they are subject to and for which they pay each week. I'm a strong person. But even for me there are limits. I'm fearful for my private life and for the welfare of my children.' In her letter, she wrote: 'Deceit, lies and speculation. A fraud against the readers. I hate seeing myself, week after week, on billboards, magazine covers and in interviews which I have never given. Their methods are unbearable. A journalist from *Hänt i Veckan*, among others, even went to the police station where Torbjörn works and offered him money in exchange for revelations. And for another thing, I am not pregnant. Lisa Mattsson is pregnant. There is a difference. *Svensk Damtidning* have invented a romance between myself and Gunnar Hellström, supported by photos from the filming of the movie. Billboards read: "This year's big romance" or "This is how love has changed Agnetha". There is no romance between Gunnar and myself!' Agnetha decided to send all the libellous articles to the ombudsman of the Swedish press and urged other celebrities to do the same thing.

6 September Frida's long-awaited album *Something's Going On* was released. Instead of a photo on the sleeve, there was a pencil drawing by Yves Poyet, a French friend of the singer. The record was ambitious and very risky, but the outcome of Frida's collaboration with Phil Collins was extremely

13 September A week after its release, *Something's Going On* had already achieved gold-disc status in Sweden, having sold more than 50,000 copies. As for the single, it had sold more than 25,000 copies, earning a silver disc. This was sweet revenge for Frida, who had been heavily criticized by Swedish journalists. She told *Expressen*: 'When you've been part of a group for so long, it's very stressful to do something on your own. But I stand by the work I've done 100 per cent. I really like my album and I like every one of the songs. Anyway, people can say what they want, I don't care.'

She told British journalist Michael Cable from the *News of the World*: 'I've decided to be on my own. I want to be able to live life my way. It's great to be alone, to discover new things and to have new friends. I've never felt this freedom before. I'm happy like this for now. In fact, I'm really making the most of my new life!'

Between 21 and 30 September, Frida took a break in Stockholm, in the middle of her promotional tour. Her records were already selling extremely well in some countries. The *Something's Going On* album was No. 1 in Sweden, No. 2 in Belgium, No. 12 in Germany, No. 18 in Britain, No. 4 in Holland, No. 18 in Italy and No. 40 in Australia. The 'I Know ...' single was No. 3 in

'FOR "THE DAY BEFORE YOU CAME", WE WANTED AGNETHA TO BE ORDINARY AND NOT USE HER SINGING ABILITIES, IN ORDER TO ACT [LIKE] AN ORDINARY WOMAN IN THE SUBURBS. I THINK THAT WAS A MISTAKE, BECAUSE IF YOU WANT TO ACT A ROLE IN A SONG, YOU DON'T NECESSARILY HAVE TO UNDERUSE YOUR ABILITY AS A SINGER.' BENNY

successful. He produced eleven real gems from songs written by Stephen Bishop, Jim Rafferty (Gerry's brother), Tomas Ledin, Giorgio Moroder, Russ Ballard, Per Gessle, Rod Argent, Bryan Ferry and Phil Collins himself. Among the songs that had been recorded, only one was not used: 'Shot Down In Action', by Pat Benatar. The only criticism one can make of Phil Collins's production is that on some tracks he drowned out Frida's voice with the instruments. If one compares it with Benny's expert production and the mixing of *Frida Ensam*, there is a huge difference. Stefan Bokström wrote in *Vecko Revyn* magazine: 'It's a bit disappointing. Frida's new style isn't so different. And it can't be true that these eleven songs are the best among the five hundred which had been written. Of course you can hear that the record has been produced by a drummer. His personal touch gives the record some rhythm.'

Agnetha was to become known in a completely different way when she joined the Riksförbundet Narkotikafritt Samhälle (RNS) – the national association against the use of drugs. She had decided to join the fight against the growing problem after she had learnt that the son of one of her friends had become a drug user. She announced: 'I believe that you have to commit yourself as much as you can. This is something that could hit my family too. I've got children and I want to keep them informed but it's difficult. I want to know more about these problems.'

The release of Frida's album had been meticulously planned. The singer, supported by Görel Hanser, had put together a promotional tour which would take her to about ten countries, including Europe, Canada and the United States. On the trip she would be giving radio and press interviews, doing TV appearances and meeting her fans. Frida always had a lot of time for her fans. She said: 'I always do my best for them. To refuse an autograph can be very frustrating for a fan.'

Sweden, No. 1 in France, No. 1 in Belgium, No. 5 in Germany, No. 43 in Britain, No. 3 in Holland, No. 7 in Italy and No. 5 in Australia.

21 September ABBA filmed a video for the song 'The Day Before You Came'. Björn had called upon two new directors, Kjell-Åke Andersson and Kjell Sundvall. Scenes were shot at Tumba railway station, south of Stockholm, as well as in the car park of Arlanda airport, and the China theatre. The video was like a mini-film starring Agnetha and actor Jonas Bergström, with Frida, Björn and Benny making only a brief appearance at the end.

The 'Never Again' single, sung by Agnetha and Tomas Ledin, was released at the end of September. The duet with the ABBA singer had been Stig's idea. The producer thought that it was an effective way of launching Tomas – and his new album *Human Touch* – in the international market. Unfortunately, despite the video and frequent radio airplay, the record didn't take off, except in Sweden where it reached No. 2 in the charts. It also made it to No. 3 in Norway, No. 9 in Belgium, No. 37 in Germany and No. 24 in Holland.

8 October Epic released 'The Day Before You Came' as a single in Britain. Other countries followed. This new track marked the release of the double compilation album *The Singles – The First Ten Years*. Even if some people found the song disappointing, one could not say that ABBA were afraid to try something new. Björn and Benny had left the verse/chorus/verse formula to one side and had gone for a long repetitive melody to accompany a humdrum day in an ordinary woman's life. Björn's excellent lyrics were accentuated by Agnetha's sad and sorrowful vocal performance. Despite all its qualities, the two musicians still thought that they could have given the song a better treatment. The B-side, 'Cassandra', was strong and melodious in true ABBA style, superbly performed by Frida.

15 October Agnetha and Tomas Ledin performed 'Never Again' on the Swedish programme *Nöjesmaskinen*. Polar Music announced that Agnetha would be recording a solo album the following February and that the producer would be Mike Chapman, composer and producer of Mud, Suzi Quatro, Sweet and Blondie. 'I'm in the middle of looking for songs,' Agnetha told journalist Frank Östergren. 'Three songs have already been chosen and Mike Chapman is going to let me hear some that he's just written. This will be a more up-tempo record than my previous ones, and will feature less ballads.'

18 October Polar Music released 'The Day Before You Came'/'Cassandra' as a single in Scandinavia. Susanne Ljung said of the record in *Expressen*: 'Of the two songs, I prefer the A-side. Agnetha sings like she's giving a lesson in how to pronounce English clearly and distinctly.'

3–7 November ABBA were in London for the release of the double compilation album *The Singles – The First Ten Years*. The four Swedes were given a very warm welcome in Britain. (See the separate section at the end of this chapter.)

5 November Epic released *The Singles – The First Ten Years*. The photo on the sleeve was taken by Lars Larsson, based on an idea by Rune Söderqvist. The mood was far removed from that of *The Visitors*, with the group all smiling again. Rune explains: 'We had great fun that day. They were all on form and were making jokes. I asked the set designer from the Opera House in Stockholm to paint the background canvas. I really like this photo and it gives you the impression that they're going to a big function somewhere.'

Twenty-three songs, including two new ones, were featured on this anniversary double album. Stig and ABBA had chosen the twenty-one songs which had been released in most countries. Even if the choice of songs was contested, it sold considerably well. The general public were pleased to be able to have all the group's hits together on one record for the first time. The compilation did very well in the charts: No. 19 in Sweden, No. 33 in Norway, No. 1 in Belgium, No. 5 in Germany, No. 1 in Britain, No. 4 in Holland, No. 40 in Italy, No. 13 in Spain, No. 62 in the United States and No. 18 in Australia.

8–11 November ABBA were on a promotional trip to Germany. They were guests of honour on TV programme *Show Express*, where they sang their three new songs, 'The Day Before You Came', 'Cassandra' and 'Under Attack'. A journalist from *Bravo* wrote of 'The Day Before You Came': 'I've got nothing against ABBA, honestly I haven't. Their music is a bit too soft for my taste, but I admire the group's capacity to reinvent themselves. This time, there is a deep melancholy in Agnetha's voice.'

16 November Kjell-Åke Andersson and Kjell Sundvall filmed the video for the song 'Under Attack'. Shot in a warehouse at Norra Hammarbyhamnen in Stockholm, with flashing lights and no plot, it is the least successful video ABBA made. The group give the impression that they would rather be somewhere else. The final shot seems almost to suggest the imminent break-up, with Agnetha, Björn, Benny and Anni-Frid leaving the warehouse, each walking towards a new horizon.

17 November *Expressen* revealed that Frida had just sold all her shares in Polar Music for the sum of ten million Swedish kronor.

19 November ABBA took part in the programme *Nöjesmaskinen* on Swedish TV. Stina Lundberg and Sven Melander welcomed the four Swedes onto their show. The atmosphere was relaxed. The programme went out live between 9.30 p.m. and 10.30 p.m. In between video clips, everyone joked and talked about their work, the past and their projects. Frida told how she had lost her wig on stage in 1977 during the mini-musical. Sven asked 'During your career, what was the most stupid question you were asked?'

Filming *Raskenstam* – Agnetha with Gunnar Hellström

A gold disc for Agnetha & Tomas Ledin

Benny replied: 'It was in Cannes, during the MIDEM, when a journalist asked me "Do you like music?" and "How do you make a hit?"'. ABBA closed *Nöjesmaskinen* by singing a verse and the chorus of 'Thank You For the Music', accompanied by piano and guitar, and 'Under Attack', which they performed to playback. After the show, Frida served champagne to the crew.

ABBA had only 30 minutes of airtime to mark their ten years of success; Swedish Television missed the opportunity to do something to mark this anniversary. The Dutch television company Veronica did make an hour-long documentary entitled *The Story of* ABBA. Agnetha, Björn, Benny, Anni-Frid and Stig were interviewed by journalist Annette van Trigt, speaking at length about their careers, before and during ABBA.

20 November Stig Alkhagen wrote in *Expressen*: 'The quartet are, in my opinion, better than ever. Their singing style has evolved considerably. Particularly Agnetha on the song "Thank You For the Music".'

Those who had predicted a commercial flop for 'The Day Before You Came' were proved wrong. The record reached No. 3 in Sweden, No. 5 in Norway, No. 32 in Britain, No. 19 in France, No. 1 in Belgium, No. 3 in Holland, No. 5 in Germany, No. 29 in Spain, No. 19 in Mexico and No. 48 in Australia.

At a private reception on the top floor of Polar Music, Stig had recently handed out a number of awards for record sales in Sweden. Each member of ABBA, as well as Michael B. Tretow, had been given a gold disc for *The Visitors* album. There was also a gold disc for Agnetha and Tomas Ledin for their song 'Never Again'. Finally, Frida was presented with a platinum disc for the *Something's Going On* album and a gold disc for the single 'I Know …'. Overseas, the first reports of sales of her album were promising: 100,000 copies sold in Sweden, 98,000 copies in Germany and 50,000 in Canada. In France and Belgium, Vogue had sold more than 400,000 copies of the single 'I Know …'.

25 November Frida sent a letter to the Swedish daily newspapers to announce her decision to move to London. By writing directly to the newspapers, the ABBA singer hoped to avoid any rumours or speculation which could arise after her departure from Sweden. She wrote: 'I've decided to leave Sweden. It's something that I've wanted to do for the past two years and is now going ahead. I want to protect my integrity as a private person and I also have a need for some anonymity which I can't have in Stockholm or in Sweden. My career as an international solo artist has also influenced my decision. I will be spending a great deal of my time in Britain, so London is therefore an ideal location for my activities. ABBA is not breaking up. We will carry on working together for as long as it is beneficial to us. There is no political or economic reason behind my decision to leave.' Frida had sold her Stockholm flat to Görel and Anders Hanser and had bought herself a pied-à-terre in Mayfair. Her children weren't going with her. Her son Hans, who was nineteen, was working as a sound engineer in Sweden and her daughter, Lise-Lotte, who was fifteen, was studying in the United States.

3 December The single 'Under Attack' was released in the UK, a record very unlike ABBA's others. The B-side was an unreleased track, 'You Owe Me One'. The song was not memorable and it was arguable whether this style really suited the group. One had the impression that through lack of time or inspiration, they had thrown together the vocal arrangement and the production. They had favoured an electronic sound and technique to the detriment of originality.

On the same day, Anni-Frid took part in the programme *Nöjesmagasinet* on Radio P3. She was interviewed by journalist Kjell Dabrowski and talked about leaving Sweden.

Strangely, the 'Under Attack' single wasn't released at the same time everywhere. It was released in January 1983 in France and Australia, while

Polar Music didn't release it in Scandinavia until 21 February. The single's chart positions were mixed: No. 26 in Britain, No. 1 in Belgium, No. 5 in Holland, No. 9 in Germany and No. 96 in Australia (in February 1983). 'Under Attack' didn't chart in Sweden or Norway. It reached No. 19 in France in May 1983.

11 December ABBA appeared on Noel Edmonds' *Late, Late Breakfast Show* in Britain via a live link from a TV studio in Stockholm. They performed 'I Have a Dream', surrounded by children. This was ABBA's final exclusive performance of the year, and afterwards Noel asked them some rather banal questions: 'What's your favourite animal?', 'What was the most boring film you ever saw?' and 'What were your worst holidays?' It's easy to understand why Agnetha, Björn, Benny and Anni-Frid seemed uninspired by this interview. The four Swedes concluded their appearance on the show with 'Under Attack'. After the cameras had stopped rolling, the group were presented with the *Expressen* Spelmannen Prize for Best Musicians of 1982. According to Hans Åstrand, from the Swedish Academy of Music, 'What motivated the jury's choice was ABBA's professionalism more than anything else. It seems that there's no room for improvisation in the ABBA sound.'

With *The Singles – The First Ten Years*, the final chapter in an extraordinary success story was coming to an end. The group's worldwide sales were estimated at 175 million in 1982; no other group since the Beatles has surpassed ABBA's achievement. In Britain alone, ABBA sold more than 18 million records in eight years, a real achievement in a country considered the world leader in pop music, and where it was almost impossible at that time for a foreign artist to break through.

Agnetha, Björn, Benny and Anni-Frid talked about having a long break from ABBA to work on their individual projects. Agnetha was preparing her solo album with producer Mike Chapman. Anni-Frid wanted to record a new album, too, while Björn and Benny were still having discussions with Tim Rice about writing a musical.

But was it a break or a separation? No one could answer that question – not even the four members of ABBA themselves. During their career, they had often said: 'ABBA will carry on as long as we enjoy working together. The day that we are tired of it, we'll stop.' That day had perhaps arrived, but nobody dared admit it. For more than a year, there had been a certain sense of weariness, which manifested itself through a general feeling of gloom. The magic had gone. One should not forget that the strength and the balance within ABBA was, before anything else, derived from the fact that the two couples were together constantly both on stage and off. Benny and Anni-Frid's divorce only escalated the crisis which had begun when Björn and Agnetha had separated in 1979. Despite the tensions, everyone tried to keep the flame alive. But their hearts were no longer in it. The four Swedes were no longer all looking in the same direction.

In her book *As I Am*, Agnetha described the situation very well: 'We had reached a dividing line. We felt pretty tired of ABBA and everything surrounding it. It was time for all of us to go our separate ways, so that we could grow. It was a natural progression. Was it just a temporary break? Would ABBA ever make a new record together? We couldn't answer the questions ourselves, because none of us knew. Whether our paths crossed again depended on how we all developed. Perhaps, in the back of our minds, we thought that if Björn and Benny did any suitable songs we might work together again.'

The group's last official TV appearance took place on 18 January 1986. Agnetha, Björn, Benny and Anni-Frid sang 'Tivedshambo' on a programme paying homage to Stig Anderson, entitled *Här Är Ditt Liv* (This Is Your Life). The clip was filmed during the afternoon of 16 January in Benny's work room, on the top floor of the Polar Music building. Görel Hanser organized everything in secret while Stig was away. Benny played the accordion, Björn

'I CAN'T IMAGINE ANY OTHER GROUP BETTER TO WORK WITH BECAUSE THEY WERE ALL EASY-GOING. THE ONLY THING I CAN COMPLAIN ABOUT IS THAT WE NEVER GOT ANY LUNCH AND I WAS HUNGRY FOR TEN YEARS. WHEN I ALMOST FAINTED AND THERE WERE RED MISTS BEFORE MY EYES, THEN THEY SAID, "OK, LET'S BREAK FOR LUNCH!"' MICHAEL B. TRETOW

was on guitar and Anni-Frid and Agnetha read the lyrics from a huge board held up by Görel. At the end of the filming, which lasted an hour, Anni-Frid went back home to Switzerland. Björn and Benny were present for the live screening of *Här Är Ditt Liv* from the Malmö TV studios.

☆ ☆ ☆ ☆

ABBA'S PROMOTIONAL VISITS TO BRITAIN AND GERMANY

For the release of the double compilation album *The Singles – The First Ten Years*, ABBA had planned two important visits to Britain and Germany.

Wednesday 3 November
Agnetha arrived at Heathrow Airport at 3 p.m. After checking in at the Dorchester Hotel, she went to do some Christmas shopping in town. At 8 p.m. she met up with Carole Broughton from Bocu Music who took her for dinner at the Polynesian restaurant Trader Vic, one of Agnetha's favourite places.

Frida arrived at 11 p.m. from New York by Concorde.

Thursday 4 November
Björn and Benny arrived at the hotel at 6 p.m. Before giving several interviews, Agnetha, Björn, Benny, Frida and their entourage went to a secret location for dinner.

Friday 5 November
ABBA arrived at the Park Lane Hotel at 11.30 a.m. for a photo shoot. It was pandemonium and the dining room was unable to contain the crowd. The atmosphere was hysterical. Order was restored when someone decided to organize two separate photo shoots – one for the weekly press and another for the daily newspapers. It was very hot in the room but, despite the non-stop camera flashes, the group carried on smiling.

At 2 p.m., two limousines drove ABBA to the Belfry Club. A reception for the music industry and the press had been organized by Epic to celebrate the group's ten years together. On their arrival, the police had to help Agnetha, Björn and Benny to get through the crowd and inside the club. Meanwhile, Frida, who had got separated from the rest of the group, spoke with fans and signed autographs on the pavement in front of the building. Maurice Oberstein, the president of CBS, gave a speech and presented ABBA with a huge frame containing twenty-three gold discs. After lunch, a massive cake was brought in, complete with ten candles. Agnetha spent a long time talking to her future producer, Mike Chapman.

At 9.30 p.m., Agnetha, Björn, Benny, Stig, Görel, Anders Hanser, Judd Lander (ex-Epic), John Spalding and Carole Broughton went on to a restaurant on the Fulham Road, September's. Frida did not join them.

Saturday 6 November
At 11.15 a.m., Benny and Agnetha arrived at the BBC studios to record the programme *Saturday Superstore*. The two members of ABBA did not seem very relaxed in front of the cameras. Meanwhile, Björn and Frida were giving more interviews at the Dorchester Hotel and were appearing on the radio show *Junior Choice*.

At 3.30 p.m., ABBA were at rehearsals for the TV programme *The Late, Late Breakfast Show*, presented by Noel Edmonds. Several hundred fans were in the studio audience.

The programme was screened live at 6.45 p.m. The group's appearance on the show began with the promotional video for 'The Day Before You Came'. Noel then asked the group questions in between clips from the group's different promotional videos. At the end of the show, Agnetha and Frida sang 'Thank You For the Music', accompanied by Benny on piano and Björn on guitar.

At 10 p.m., the group dined at La Nassa, an Italian restaurant in Chelsea. Tim Rice and his wife joined them there, as well as Helen, Benny's daughter.

Sunday 7 November
ABBA left London for Germany. The group stayed at the Kongress Hotel in Sarrebrück. During their stay, the group gave many interviews, including one for *Tommy's Pop Show*, and did some photo shoots. Polydor held an important reception in their honour.

Monday 8 November
Agnetha and Tomas Ledin travelled to Bremen for the recording of the television show *Musikladen*.

Wednesday 10 November
Dress rehearsal for the TV programme *Show Express* at the Saarlandhalle in Sarrebrück, at 7.30 p.m. Numerous French fans had travelled from Paris to be in the audience.

Thursday 11 November
At 7.30 p.m., *Show Express* was transmitted live, with a studio audience of 2000. Amid fierce applause, presenter Michael Schanze introduced ABBA. Encircled by smoke and standing alone in front of a huge ABBA logo, Agnetha began singing 'The Day Before You Came'. The set began to revolve, revealing the rest of the group, with Frida sitting on a white piano. The atmosphere was electric. After 'Cassandra', ABBA performed 'Under Attack'. The show finished with the crowd going wild and fans storming the stage.

☆ ☆ ☆ ☆

' "THE DAY BEFORE YOU CAME" WAS VERY EMOTIONAL, BECAUSE THAT WAS THE LAST ABBA SONG WE EVER DID, AND IT SORT OF FELT LIKE "NOW IT'S OVER".'
MICHAEL B. TRETOW

'ABBA NEVER OFFICIALLY BROKE UP. IN 1982, WE JUST SAID WE WERE GOING TO HAVE A REST AND THAT WAS IT.' **BJÖRN**

'BJÖRN AND I WANTED TO WORK TOGETHER ON A MUSICAL PROJECT. THIS WAS ACTUALLY WHY WE TOOK A BREAK FROM ABBA. WE NEVER REALLY SAID WE WOULD QUIT, BUT THAT IS WHAT HAPPENED, AND I THINK IT WAS THE RIGHT THING TO DO.' **BENNY**

'THEY WERE THE ONLY GROUP THAT SET MY SPINE TINGLING. THEY MADE GREAT POP TUNES THAT HAVE STOOD THE TEST OF TIME.'
ANDY BELL ERASURE

WHERE ARE THEY NOW?

Agnetha Fältskog

After three solo albums, *Wrap Your Arms Around Me* (1983), *Eyes of a Woman* (1985) and *I Stand Alone* (1987), and an album with her son Christian, *Kom Följ Med i Vår Karusell*, Agnetha withdrew completely from showbusiness.

In 1990, she married surgeon Tomas Sonnenfeld, but they divorced two years later. Today, far from the public gaze in her big house in Ekerö, near Stockholm, she has been called 'the new Greta Garbo'.

In 1996, with the help of her journalist friend Brita Åhman, she published a memoir, *Som Jag Är*. Translated into English under the title *As I Am – ABBA Before & Beyond*, the book was mainly interesting for the photographs it contained. The publication of this semi-autobiography and the simultaneous release of a compilation of Agnetha's songs, entitled *My Love, My Life*, suggested that Agnetha was on the brink of making a comeback. But this was not to be the case.

To the great disappointment of her fans, she has declined all interviews and even refused an invitation to take part in a press conference organized by her Swedish publisher.

Agnetha has been treated badly by journalists for a long time, and one can understand why, for reasons of self-protection, she has severed all contact with the media. It is a great pity that she has not been able to write new songs during these years of peace and tranquillity.

Recently, it has again been rumoured that Agnetha may be planning to make a comeback. In *As I Am*, she said: 'People can get the idea that you have closed all the doors behind you and are no longer interested in anything. But I haven't closed any doors, not to myself, ideas, film opportunities or my songs.'

'WE HAD A GREAT TIME AND WE ARE ALL VERY PLEASED AND PROUD OF WHAT WE HAVE ACHIEVED, BUT EVERYTHING HAS AN END.'
AGNETHA

'I THINK IT'S SO PATHETIC WHEN OLD BANDS WHO HAVE BROKEN UP GO ON THE ROAD AGAIN. I THINK IF WE DID, IT WOULD BE A DISAPPOINTMENT TO EVERYONE. IT WOULD TAKE AWAY THE CHARISMA.' BJÖRN

Björn Ulvaeus

Björn spent part of the 1980s in Henley, England, with his wife Lena and their daughters, Emma and Anna. They have now returned to live in Sweden and currently live in Danderyd, north of Stockholm. Björn spends a great deal of his time writing and being with his family.

Since 1966, his collaboration with Benny Andersson has been almost constant. In 1984, the two musicians wrote the musical *Chess* with Tim Rice. The show ran for several years in London but did not achieve the same success on Broadway. Having worked with numerous Swedish artists (including Gemini and Josefin Nilsson), Björn and Benny began working on a new musical project based on the book U*tvandrarna* (The Emigrants) by Vilhelm Moberg, an epic saga of the Swedes who emigrated to the United States during the nineteenth century. The day after the premiere of the show, entitled K*ristina Från Duvemåla*, journalists were unanimous in declaring it a masterpiece. Björn and Benny's second musical has been an unparalleled triumph in Sweden. They are working on an English version.

In 1999, Björn was back in the spotlight, thanks to his close collaboration on the smash-hit musical *Mamma Mia*.

Benny Andersson

One could say that Benny is a happy man. When he is not involved with his race horses, of which he owns several, he writes new songs, produces new talent on his Mono Music label, or joins folk musicians on stage. He has been passionate about this kind of music ever since his childhood, and has released two instrumental albums (K*linga Mina Klockor* and N*ovember* 1989) and given numerous concerts in Sweden.

His third passion is going to auctions with his wife Mona, sometimes buying works of art and paintings by old masters.

Today, he divides his time between Djurgården, in Stockholm, and his other house in the province of Skåne, in the south of Sweden. The success of K*ristina Från Duvemåla* surpassed all expectations and it has made him one of the most respected composers in Sweden.

At the end of 1997, he was chosen to serve on the committee in charge of the Stockholm Royal Opera.

'TALK OF A REVIVAL IS SILLY IN A SENSE BECAUSE ABBA HAVE REACHED THAT STAGE WHERE THEIR SONGS ARE CLASSICS. JUST AS THE BEATLES HAVE LIVED FOR YEARS, EQUALLY ABBA ARE STILL GOING TO GO ON AND ON AND ON.' STEVE REDMOND EDITOR, *MUSIC WEEK*

'ABBA HAS MEANT VERY MUCH TO ME, AND STILL DOES BECAUSE IT'S
NOT SOMETHING YOU JUST HANG UP LIKE A COAT. ABBA IS A VERY
BIG PART OF MY LIFE, ESPECIALLY SINCE THERE'S BEEN THIS REVIVAL.'
FRIDA

Anni-Frid Lyngstad

At the beginning of the 1980s, Anni-Frid moved to London, then to Paris. Having taken part in a French musical entitled *Abbacadabra*, she recorded a second solo album, *Shine*, in 1984, and took part in several musical projects (with Adam Ant and the Swedish duo Ratata).

Anni-Frid then chose to retire from the music scene in order to devote all her time to her new passion: the environment. In order to raise funds for her Artister För Miljö – Det Naturliga Steget association, she returned to the stage again in 1992 for a one-off concert at the Royal Palace of Stockholm, together with other artists. She didn't feel at all out of place in this setting – she has been a great friend of Queen Silvia's for many years and had herself married Prince Ruzzo Reuss von Plauen, a childhood friend of King Carl Gustaf XVI.

In 1996, Frida made a dazzling return to the music scene with the excellent Swedish-language album *Djupa Andetag*. It was an enormous success, reaching No. 1 in the Swedish charts, but the album's release was limited to Scandinavia. The hectic pace of the ABBA years no longer suits Frida; she wishes to retain the balance and harmony she has managed to achieve in her life over the past few years.

However, in recent years, life has been difficult for Frida. In 1998, her daughter Lise-Lotte was killed in a car accident, and Prince Ruzzo died the next year after a long illness.

Stig Anderson

At the beginning of the 1980s, Stig was one of the richest men in Sweden. However, he was to lose a great deal of money through bad investments. His relations with the members of ABBA became distant, with the exception of Frida, to whom he remained close. In 1989, he sold Polar Music and Sweden Music Publishing to Polygram. Several years later, he created the Polar Music Prize, the musicians' equivalent of the Nobel Prize.

Stig died of a heart attack on 12 September 1997. Björn said in his tribute: 'Stig Anderson meant a lot to me both as a human being and as a mentor.' Stig had written more than 3000 songs.

'I'M VERY HAPPY BECAUSE THE ABBA REVIVAL SHOWS THAT OUR MUSIC
IS STILL OUTSTANDING. AND THIS HAD TO BE PROVED, BECAUSE WE
HAD SO MANY CRITICAL VOICES DURING THE TIME THAT WE WERE
WORKING ACTIVELY. SO THIS IS A KIND OF STATEMENT THAT WE
REALLY MADE IT.' FRIDA

1973 (March)

RING RING

Ring Ring (Swedish version), Another Town Another Train, Disillusion, People Need Love, I Saw It In the Mirror, Nina Pretty Ballerina, Love Isn't Easy (But It Sure Is Hard Enough), Me and Bobby and Bobby's Brother, He Is Your Brother, Ring Ring (English version), I Am Just a Girl, Rock 'n' Roll Band

Remastered CD (1997)
+ She's My Kind of Girl instead of Ring Ring (Swedish version)

1974 (March)

WATERLOO

Waterloo (Swedish version), Sitting In the Palmtree, King Kong Song, Hasta Mañana, My Mama Said, Dance (While the Music Still Goes On), Honey Honey, Watch Out, What About Livingstone, Gonna Sing You My Lovesong, Suzy-Hang-Around, Waterloo (English Version)

Remastered CD (1997)
Same track listing but without Waterloo (Swedish version)

1975 (April)

ABBA

Mamma Mia, Hey Hey Helen, Tropical Loveland, S.O.S., Man in the Middle, Bang-a-Boomerang, I Do I Do I Do I Do I Do, Rock Me, Intermezzo No.1, I've Been Waiting For You, So Long

Remastered CD (1997)
5 tracks added: Waterloo, Hasta Mañana, Honey Honey, Ring Ring, Nina Pretty Ballerina + 2 bonus tracks: Crazy World, Medley: Pick a Bale of Cotton/On Top of Old Smokey/Midnight Special

1975 (November)

GREATEST HITS

S.O.S., He Is Your Brother, Ring Ring, Hasta Mañana, Nina Pretty Ballerina, Honey Honey, So Long, I Do I Do I Do I Do I Do, People Need Love, Bang-a-Boomerang, Another Town Another Train, Mamma Mia, Dance (While the Music Still Goes On), Waterloo

N.B.

Fernando was included on later pressings

1976 (October)

ARRIVAL

When I Kissed the Teacher, Dancing Queen, My Love My Life, Dum Dum Diddle, Knowing Me Knowing You, Money Money Money, That's Me, Why Did It Have to Be Me, Tiger, Arrival

Remastered CD (1997)
+ Fernando

1977 (December)

ABBA – THE ALBUM

Eagle, Take a Chance On Me, One Man One Woman, The Name of the Game, Move On, Hole In Your Soul, The Girl With the Golden Hair: Thank You For the Music/I Wonder (Departure)/I'm a Marionette

Remastered CD (1997)
No bonus tracks

1979 (April)

VOULEZ-VOUS

As Good As New, Voulez-Vous, I Have a Dream, Angeleyes, The King Has Lost His Crown, Does Your Mother Know, If It Wasn't For the Nights, Lovers (Live a Little Longer), Kisses of Fire

Remastered CD (1997)
+ Summer Night City, Lovelight

1979 (October)

GREATEST HITS VOLUME 2

Gimme! Gimme! Gimme! (A Man After Midnight), Knowing Me Knowing You, Take a Chance On Me, Money Money Money, Rock Me, Eagle, Angeleyes, Dancing Queen, Does Your Mother Know, Chiquitita, Summer Night City, I Wonder (Departure), The Name of the Game, Thank You For the Music

CD version (1983)
No bonus tracks

1980 (June)

GRACIAS POR LA MUSICA

Gracias Por La Musica, Reina Danzante, Al Andar, Dame! Dame! Dame!, Fernando, Estoy Soñando, Mamma Mia, Hasta Mañana, Conociéndome Conociéndote, Chiquitita

CD version: ABBA Oro (1993)

Fernando, Chiquitita, Gracias Por La Musica, La Reina Del Baile (new title for Reina Danzante), Al Andar, Dame! Dame! Dame!, Estoy Soñando, Mamma Mia, Hasta Mañana, Conociéndome Conociéndote

1980 (November)

SUPER TROUPER

Super Trouper, The Winner Takes It All, On and On and On, Andante Andante, Me and I, Happy New Year, Our Last Summer, The Piper, Lay All Your Love On Me, The Way Old Friends Do

Remastered CD (1997)

+ Gimme! Gimme! Gimme! (A Man After Midnight), Elaine, Put On Your White Sombrero

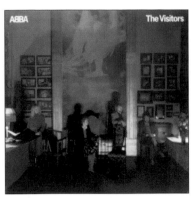

1981 (November)

THE VISITORS

The Visitors, Head Over Heels, When All Is Said and Done, Soldiers, I Let the Music Speak, One of Us, Two For the Price of One, Slipping Through My Fingers, Like an Angel Passing Through My Room

Remastered CD (1997)

+ Should I Laugh Or Cry, The Day Before You Came, Under Attack, You Owe Me One

1982 (November)

THE SINGLES–THE FIRST TEN YEARS

Ring Ring, Waterloo, So Long, I Do I Do I Do I Do I Do, S.O.S., Mamma Mia, Fernando, Dancing Queen, Money Money Money, Knowing Me Knowing You, The Name of the Game, Take a Chance On Me, Summer Night City, Chiquitita, Does Your Mother Know, Voulez-Vous, Gimme! Gimme! Gimme! (A Man After Midnight), I Have a Dream, The Winner Takes It All, Super Trouper, One of Us, The Day Before You Came, Under Attack

CD version (1983)

No bonus tracks

1986 (August)

ABBA LIVE

Dancing Queen, Take a Chance On Me, I Have a Dream, Does Your Mother Know, Chiquitita, Thank You For the Music, Two For the Price of One, Fernando, Gimme! Gimme! Gimme! (A Man After Midnight), Super Trouper, Waterloo

CD version

+ Money Money Money, The Name of the Game/Eagle, On and On and On

Remastered CD (1997)

No bonus tracks

1992 (September)

ABBA GOLD

Dancing Queen, Knowing Me Knowing You, Take a Chance On Me, Mamma Mia, Lay All Your Love On Me, Super Trouper, I Have a Dream, The Winner Takes It All, Money Money Money, S.O.S., Chiquitita, Fernando, Voulez-Vous, Gimme! Gimme! Gimme! (A Man After Midnight), Does Your Mother Know, One of Us, The Name of the Game, Thank You For the Music, Waterloo

1993 (June)

MORE ABBA GOLD

Summer Night City, Angeleyes, The Day Before You Came, Eagle, I Do I Do I Do I Do I Do, So Long, Honey Honey, The Visitors, Our Last Summer, On and On and On, Ring Ring, I Wonder (Departure), Lovelight, Head Over Heels, When I Kissed the Teacher, I Am the City, Cassandra, Under Attack, When All Is Said and Done, The Way Old Friends Do

Agnetha, Björn, Benny, Frida Fan Club
P.O. Box 3079, 4700 AB Roosendaal
The Netherlands
e-mail: abba@concepts.nl
website: www.abba.muziek.net

ABBA News Service
P.O. Box 21, Avonmouth
Bristol BS11 9AZ
United Kingdom
Send sae (UK) or 2 IRCs for a reply
ABBA information line:
0906 702 7022 (50p per minute)
e-mail: abbanews@netgates.co.uk
website: www.abbanews.com

'ABBA'S HITS ARE SO MUCH BETTER THAN ANYONE THOUGHT AT THE TIME. MANY OF THEM STAND UP AS WELL AS THE BEATLES.' **TIM RICE**

'ABBA WERE POP MUSIC IN ITS PUREST FORM. MOST AMERICANS HAD NO IDEA THEY WERE SWEDISH, EVEN WHEN THEY WENT TO No.1! MY FAVOURITE TRACK HAS TO BE "DANCING QUEEN" – IT WAS BACK THEN AND IT STILL IS TODAY.' **TINA TURNER**

'IT WAS VERY UNFASHIONABLE TO LIKE ABBA AT THAT TIME. THEIR SONGS ARE BEAUTIFULLY CRAFTED AND THE PRODUCTION WAS ALWAYS IMMACULATE, EVERYTHING BEAUTIFULLY TUNED IN TIME, AND THE GIRLS' VOICES WERE FABULOUS.' **BRIAN MAY**

'ABBA'S RECORDS REMAIN MASTERPIECES. EVEN AFTER ALL THESE YEARS, THEY'RE AS FRESH AS EVER. THEIR SONGWRITING AND PRODUCTION ARE IN A CLASS BY THEMSELVES. I HAVE HAD THE PLEASURE OF MEETING ABBA SEVERAL TIMES, AND I WILL ALWAYS CHERISH THE MEMORIES.' **NEIL SEDAKA**

'ABBA SAVED MY LIFE, IT'S UNDENIABLE. *ARRIVAL* IS A HAPPY RECORD. "DANCING QUEEN" IS THE BIGGEST SONG IN POP-MUSIC HISTORY, PURE ECSTASY, IT MAKES YOU WANT TO FLY.' **BJÖRK**

'ABBA HAVE WRITTEN THE BEST POP MUSIC OF ALL TIME.' **THE EDGE** U2

'BJÖRN AND BENNY WERE MASTERS OF MELODIES AND LYRICS. THEY REPRESENT THE OLD SCHOOL OF COMPOSERS. THEY MADE PURE, SIMPLE AND INCOMPARABLE POP SONGS.' **SHARLEEN SPITERI** TEXAS

'THEY WERE THE ONLY GROUP THAT SET MY SPINE TINGLING. THEY MADE GREAT POP TUNES THAT HAVE STOOD THE TEST OF TIME.' **ANDY BELL** ERASURE

ACKNOWLEDGEMENTS

I dedicate this book to my mother, Oscarine, and my grandmother, Augustine.

My heartfelt thanks go to Thierry Lecuyer for his support throughout this project.

I particularly want to thank the following: Philippe Elan for his invaluable help, his optimism and support at times of doubt and discouragement, and for his friendship; Rod Campbell for his advice and for supervising the translation; Görel Hanser for being so helpful and for giving me access to ABBA's photographic archive; Ingemar Bergman of Polar Music; Rune Söderqvist; and Colin Collier.

Thank you to Aurum Press for having believed in this project, particularly Karen Ings and Graham Eames, whose enthusiasm and professionalism made *Abba: The Book* a reality. It has been a pleasure working with you. Thanks also to Graham Peake and the team at Two:Design for their excellent work on the design of the book.

I would also like to thank all those who assisted me in my research and gave up their time so freely: Lillemor Andersson (Pressens Bild), Géraldine Atlani, Eddy Becker, Åsa Bergold (Polar Music), Alain Boublil, Torbjörn Calvero, Kathryn Courtney-O'Neill, Philippe Denis, Annette Falck (IMS Bildbyrå), Lars Falck, Gunilla Gunnerheim (Folkparkerna), Johan Hellekant, Catherine Hinard, Johan Hjertberg, Bo Jensen, Helga van de Kar, Anita Notenboom and René Nieuwlaat (Agnetha, Benny, Björn, Frida Fan Club), Marc Krantz, Ola Lager, Patrick Largeteau, Michael Leckebusch, David Legrand, Sandrine Martin (RTL), Jean-Claude Misse, Alex Mizrahi, Bob Navez (Vogue Belgium), Thomas Nordin, Jokke Norling, Tomas Nyh (EMA-Telstar), Jean Pajot, Carl Magnus Palm, Sven Åke Peterson (EMI Svenska AB), Phillip (PM ART), Jean-Michel Poncelet, Olle Rönnbäck (Polar Music), Marie-Laure Sanchez, Ivan Sandell, Hervé Tete, Vogue France.

Last, but not least, thank you to Agnetha, Björn, Benny and Anni-Frid for their remarkable talent and the pleasure their music has given me since 6 April 1974.

SOURCES
Books
Från Abba till Mamma Mia!, Carl Magnus Palm and Anders Hanser (Premium Publishing, 1999)
Abba Människorna och Musiken, Carl Magnus Palm (Tiden, 1996)
Som Jag Är, Agnetha Fältskog with Brita Åhman (Norstedts, 1996; translated into English as *As I Am*, Virgin, 1997)
Abba: The Complete Recording Sessions, Carl Magnus Palm (Century 22, 1994)
Abba: The Music Still Goes On, Paul Snaith (Castle Communications, 1994)
Abba Gold: The Complete Story, John Tobler (Century 22, 1993)
Stikkan: Den Börsnoterade Refrängsångaren, Oscar Hedlund (Sweden Music Förlag, 1983)
Abba In Their Own Words, Rosemary York (Omnibus Press, 1982)
Abba For the Record, John Tobler (Stafford Pemberton, 1980)
Succé På Världs-scenen, Leif Schulman and Charles Hammarsten (Allerbok, 1979)
Abba, Harry Edgington and Peter Himmelstrand (Magnum Books, 1979)
Bogen Om Abba, Rud Kofoed (Chr. Erichsens Forlag, 1977)
Abba By Abba, Christer Borg (Stafford Pemberton, 1977)

Newspapers and magazines
Abba Infos (Guy Bodescot), *Abba/International Magazine*, *Abba 5 Years*, *Aftonbladet*, *Allers*, *Arbetet*, *Bravo*, *Bild*, *Dagens Nyheter*, *Das Freizeit*, *Expressen*, *France-Soir*, *Hemmets*, *Juke Box*, *La Dernière Heure*, *Le Soir*, *Podium*, *Poster*, *Record Mirror*, *Salut*, *Saxons*, *Se*, *Svensk Damtidning*, *Télérama*, *Vecko Revyn*.

Television and films
Abba-Dabba-Dooo!!, *Abba In Australia*, *Abba – The Movie*, *Aplauso*, *Dick Cavett Meets Abba*, *Gå På Vattnet Om Du Kan*, *Gäst Hos Hagge*, *Hylands Hörna*, *Made In Sweden For Export*, *Nöjesmaskinen*, *Raskenstam*, *Senoras y Senores*, *Stikkan Om Stikkan*, *Studio 2 – Abba In Poland*, *Thank You Abba*, *The Best of Abba – Musikladen*, *300 Millones*, *Words and Music*.

PICTURE CREDITS

Pressens Bild: pages 41 (left), 51, 52, 64, 66, 67, 72, 83, 85, 96, 98 (top and bottom), 100, 108 (centre), 139, 161 (bottom), 179, 195, 215, 224, 225, 240, 245 (top), 252, 255, 256
Kjell Johansson: pages 2, 44, 113 (top)
Stig Anderson collection: pages 8, 22, 23, 26, 36, 37, 38, 43, 60, 69, 87, 132, 134, 150, 153, 161 (left), 200, 206, 207, 209, 211
IMS Bildbyrå: pages 12, 14, 17, 18, 20, 24, 45, 47, 48, 49, 55, 58, 59, 65, 68, 71, 74, 75, 104, 109 (right), 131, 133, 198, 199, 231, 238, 245 (bottom)
Lars Larsson (IMS Bildbyrå): pages 223, 227, 235, 250
Jean-Marie Potiez collection: pages 15, 16, 34, 46, 50, 170, 171, 174, 182, 184, 205, 208
EMI Svenska: pages 29, 30 (top left), 30 (right), 40, 41 (right), 54
Polar Music: pages 32, 140, 142, 144, 147, 148, 151, 156, 158, 159, 162 (bottom), 163, 164, 166, 167, 168, 169, 175 (top), 186, 188, 190, 200, 212, 217
Jean Pajot: page 56
Premium Publishing: pages 78 (Bengt H. Malmqvist), 95, 129, 191 (Ola Lager), 178 (Torbjörn Calvero)
Bill Thomas: page 202
Vogue Records: pages 86, 91, 110, 111, 113 (bottom), 116, 118, 123, 172, 183, 201, 218, 219, 232, 236, 243, 247
Camera Press: pages 89, 90, 106, 108 (left), 115, 175 (bottom)
Guido Marcon: pages 92, 112 (top and bottom)
Michael Leckebusch: pages 126 (top), 127, 128, 192
Phillipe Elan collection: pages 10, 30 (centre left), 62, 76, 77, 99, 102, 124, 137, 149, 187, 230
Ragnvi Gylder: page 81
PM Art Australia: pages 126 (centre and bottom), 130, 145
RCA: pages 154, 161 (right), 162 (top and centre)
Discomate: pages 180, 181, 213, 214